The History
of
the Parish of Ruabon

* * * * * * * *

The Town, Fields, and Folk of Wrexham
in the Time of James the First

* * * * * * * *

Offa's and Wat's Dyke

* * * * * * * *

The Welsh Settlements, East of Offa's Dyke

* * * * * * * *

Notes on Ancient Welsh Measures of Land

* * * * * * * *

Ancient Welsh Measures of Capacity

A.N.Palmer (1847-1915)

Alfred Neobard Palmer was born in the Norfolk market town of Thetford on 10 July 1847, the son of Alfred Palmer, a prosperous local coach builder. He was educated at the local Grammar School and at a private academy run by Morgan Lloyd, an Independent minister, who fostered the boy's interest in science. On leaving school, he was employed for six months as a pupil teacher at Soham in Cambridgeshire before returning to Thetford where he worked with his father. The prospect of spending his life in the manufacture of horse drawn vehicles did not appeal to him and he was apprenticed shortly afterwards to a druggist in Bury St Edmunds and went on to pass both the Minor and Major examinations of the Pharmaceutical Society which awarded him the Jacob Bell Scholarship giving him one year's free tuition at the Society's London headquarters, as well as a grant of £25. After completing his studies, he was employed as an analytical chemist in Bury St Edmunds and London before moving to Manchester in 1874. There he met, and married, Esther, the daughter of John Francis the city surveyor and a leading figure in the city's Welsh community. By 1880, he had returned to Thetford to recover from an illness and, while there, was prompted to apply for the position of chemist at the newly founded Zoedone Works in Pentrefelin, Wrexham. His application was successful and he moved to the town and took up residence at 3 Ar-y-Bryn Terrace, Earle Street.

Throughout his adult life Palmer complained of ill health although there is no evidence to confirm that he suffered from any chronic illness. His belief that he was not a well man was to have a profound effect upon his professional life and opened up the field of local history to him. Less than twelve months after his arrival in Wrexham, he had left his position at the Zoedone Works (because of his health) and had set up his own practice at his home in Earle Street. The following year (1882) he was appointed industrial chemist at the Brymbo Steel Works and from 1891 until 1904, he was the consultant analytical chemist at the Cambrian Leather Works, although two small legacies in 1892 and 1894 allowed him to devote much of his time to historical research which had, by this time, become his driving passion; by 1894, he was stating his occupation as "historical writer" . A basically private man, Palmer's only involvement in public life appears to have been as a member of the Wrexham Library Committee and one of the founders of the town museum which was housed in the library building. Palmer had been keenly interested in archaeology since childhood but his need to earn a living had prevented him pursuing his passion for history until he was middle aged. Undoubtedly, his father-in-law's involvement with the Welsh literary and cultural groups in Manchester had influenced him and, shortly after arriving in Wrexham, he set out to master written Welsh. The fact that his wife was a fluent Welsh speaker must certainly have aided him in his task and her role in his life's work has not been recognised.

An interest in history coupled with analytical and methodical scientific training made Palmer the perfect individual to set about recording the uncharted wilderness that was then the local history of the Wrexham area. He read through all the parish registers for the district and indexed the names he found; he tabulated the data on land occupation shown in the church-rate assessment books, the churchwarden's accounts and the tithe schedules; he recorded all the field names that he came across on a 6":1 mile Ordnance Survey map; he made notes from deeds and from interviews. He then began to write up his findings.

"Ever since I was a lad I have had to work for my living, and I have always been more or less an invalid. So I have had little leisure and my books have not received the revision which ought to have been accorded them. I wanted to get the results I had accumulated committed to paper, and I have written against time. Many of the obvious slips and errors that deform my work had their origin in these facts".

That he was a local historian of great talent is beyond question but his skills as a writer of prose do leave something to be desired, a fact which is nowhere more evident than in *Owen Tanat,* his only attempt at a novel. This is, however, of little consequence when one considers his achievements in the field of history. Many people have criticised his books on Wrexham, stating that they are too difficult to read and do not fit in with the modern concept of a history of a town or parish. They are, of course, mistaken in their understanding of the term history and take it to mean a flowing story giving an overall picture of the past events of a particular place or person. In Palmer's case this was not what he set out to achieve. His was an attempt to record together in one place a multitude of historical facts which had previously been scattered amongst numerous public and private archives. This is perhaps best illustrated by the chapter dealing with High Street in his *History of the Town of Wrexham* where he gives a detailed house by house description of the ownership of the properties in the street which provides the basis for a fascinating study of the commercial growth of the town and the demography of the area. Palmer's books cannot be regarded as light reading but they are an essential source for any study of the history of the Wrexham area. As early as 1894, Sir O. M. Edwards was writing in his magazine *Wales*:

"Young men who are investigating the history of other places should carefully peruse his [Palmer's] volumes, in order to see with what conscientious care history should be written ... Wrexham is fortunate among the towns of Wales in possessing a historian whose splendid work will be a delight to the readers of many an age."

More recently, in 1965, the late Professor A. H. Dodd, himself a Wrexham man and one of the most outstanding Welsh historians of any age, wrote that Palmer was:

"...a man of rare fineness and integrity of character, who came to Wrexham at the age of thirty [sic] and made it his home for the rest of his sixty-seven years ... having crammed into those thirty-seven years more than a lifetime of service to his adopted town. He first introduced us to our history; it would hardly be too much to say that he first made us aware that we *had* a history. His stature as a historian was recognised far outside the borough. His authority in his own field was accepted by scholars like Frederic Seebohm and Sir John Rhys ... [and] scholars are still working on the foundations he laid. Palmer ... introduced me to the craft of the historian. It was a rare piece of luck for a young beginner."

Palmer's first historical publication was *The Town, Fields, and Folk of Wrexham in the time of James the First* which appeared in 1883. Two years later he published *A History of Ancient Tenures of Land in the Marches of North Wales* which was republished twenty five years later as a much enhanced volume produced in conjunction with Edward Owen.

In 1886 his first case bound volume *The History of the Parish Church of Wrexham* appeared followed two years later by *The History of the Older Nonconformity of Wrexham and Its Neighbourhood.* This latter work, although one of his most fascinating books and an invaluable source for the genealogy of the area and an account of Wrexham during the Civil War, has not received the attention which it deserves in our own time, perhaps its title misleads potential readers into thinking that it is a theological study of the various nonconformist groups in the district. Today, his most popular work is *The History of the Town of Wrexham, its Houses, Streets, Fields and Old Families* which first appeared in 1893 and provides a record of the town before, as Professor Dodd wrote, "railway development had involved much wanton destruction of the older part of the town". There was then a gap of ten years before his next volume on the history of the parish of Wrexham appeared in the form of *The History of the Thirteen Country Townships of the Old Parish of Wrexham* being, in the main, a study of land ownership and genealogy. There then followed a series of articles published in the learned journals of the Honorable Society of Cymmrodorion and in *Archæologia Cambrensis* between 1903 and 1909 covering the histories of Gresford and Holt. In addition to these, he published *John Wilkinson and the Old Bersham Ironworks, The Broughtons of Marchwiel, Notes on the Early History of Bangor is y Coed, Offa's and Wat's Dykes, Welsh Settlements, East of Offa's Dyke, during the Eleventh Century*, as well as numerous other short articles in these same journals and in *Wales* and *Bye Gones.*

In 1904, Palmer was granted a small pension from the Civil List in recognition of his contribution to the history of North East Wales and, the following year he was responsible for the discovery of the Roman origins of the town of Holt. In 1910, he was given the post of Assistant Inspecting Officer to the Royal Commission on Ancient Monuments in Wales and Monmouthshire.

In 1894, Palmer was called upon to give expert evidence to the Royal Commission on Land in Wales. During the course of the Commissions enquiry a dispute arose regarding the common rights in the parishes of Ruabon and Esclusham, at the heart of which was the sale in 1857 of Crown land to Sir Watkin Willimas Wynn. Palmer's evidence was not to the liking of Wales' premier landowner and, as a consequence, the baronet denied Palmer any access to the Wynnstay estate papers in the future. This had its greatest effect when work commenced upon the history of the Parish of Ruabon causing him to leave out a large part of the parish and, as a consequence, he decided not to publish his findings. This was, to say the least, unfortunate for what he had pieced together was worthy of being made available to the public, as Professor Dodd wrote:

> "Baulked of the Wynnstay papers, Palmer did the best he could with what was available, and he completed in manuscript ten chapters, with the usual pedigrees, dealing successively with the townships included in the parish. Incomplete as it is, it has the genuine Palmer touch, and remains of lasting value."

Fortunately, the Ruabon manuscript survived and passed into the hands of Mr Edward Hughes of Glyndwr, Bersham Road, Wrexham whose widow allowed the manuscript to be copied by the University College of North Wales and typescript copies were deposited in the College library and in Wrexham Public Library. On the death of Mr Hughes' daughters, the original manuscript passed into the care of the Clwyd Record Office at Ruthin and it is through that office's generosity that *The History of the Parish of Ruabon* makes its first appearance in print in this volume.

During the latter years of his life, Palmer found it increasingly difficult to either conduct any new research or to put on paper any more of his earlier findings. Living at Inglenook, Bersham Road, he was a leading figure in that small group of early local historians of Wrexham and his diaries record many discussions (often lasting into the early hours) with Edward Hughes who lived nearby. He died at his home on 6 March 1915 and was buried in the Ruabon Road Cemetery. The Borough of Wrexham paid for a bronze bas relief plaque to be placed in the library in memory of Alfred Neobard Palmer, 'Wrexham's Historian' which was later moved to the new Library and Arts Centre. Being a very private man Palmer may not have wanted any recognition for the legacy which he left his adopted home but it does seem rather sad that his name is not placed more prominently in the town of Wrexham that owes him such a debt.

W.A.W.

A HISTORY

of the

Parish of Ruabon

by

ALFRED NEOBARD PALMER, F.C.S.

WREXHAM:

BRIDGE BOOKS

This edition is of 300 numbered copies
of which this copy is number

8
....

First published in Great Britain by
BRIDGE BOOKS
61 Park Avenue
Wrexham, Clwyd
LL12   7AW

1992

© Clwyd Record Office, W Alister Williams
& Bridge Books

ISBN 1 872424 25 2

Printed in Great Britain by
Longdunn Press
Bristol

CONTENTS

PREFACE		13
INTRODUCTION		15
CHAPTER I:	The Township of Ruabon	
	(a) Hamlet of Hafod	17
	(b) Hamlet of Belan	26
	(c) Hamlet of Rhuddallt	29
	(d) Hamlet of Bodylltyn	33
CHAPTER II:	Township of Dininlle Issa	50
CHAPTER III:	Township of Dininlle Ucha *alias* Cristionydd Fechan	56
CHPATER IV:	Township of Coed Cristionydd	60
CHAPTER V:	Township of Cristionydd Kenrick	61
	Appendix: The Morton Family	66
CHAPTER VI:	Township of Morton Wallicorum	67
CHAPTER VII:	Township of Morton Is y Clawdd, *alias* Morton Below	76
CHAPTER VIII:	Morton Anglicorum	79
CHAPTER IX:	Ruabon Mountain	84
CHAPTER X:	Ruabon Church	89
APPENDIX I:	Inscriptions in Ruabon Church	101
APPENDIX II:	Memorials in Ruabon Churchyard	103
APPENDIX III:	Ruabon Charities	106

MAPS AND PEDIGREES	*Facing page*
Map of the Township of Ruabon	18
Pedigree Eytons of Ruabon	20
Pedigree Wynns of Gwydr and Wynnstay	21
Pedigree Lloyds of Pentreclawdd, Ruabon	22
Pedigree Lloyds of Plas Madoc, Ruabon (Part I)	36
Pedigree Lloyds of Plas Madoc, Ruabon (Part II)	37
Map of the Township of Dininlle Issa	52
Pedigree of Lloyds of Pen y lan, Dininlle Issa	54
Map of the Township of Cristionydd Kenrick	62
Pedigree of Jones' of Llanerchrugog	68
Pedigree of Sontleys	70
Pedigree of Lloyds of Morton Wallicorum	728

PREFACE

That one should attempt to write a history of Ruabon parish without having been able to consult the archives of Wynnstay, the owner whereof possesses so much of the land of the parish, may seem presumption. But the deeds of many other proprietors within the parish have been seen by me, together with deeds of lands which in later years have been absorbed in the Wynnstay estate. I have also taken notes from the Ruabon parish registers, examined and carefully compared the great surveys of 1546, 1562 and 1620, and consulted many of the minister's accounts of the mediaeval period. In short, I have something to say which, although incomplete, is important enough to be recorded.

INTRODUCTION

According to Archdeacon Thomas' *History of the Diocese of St. Asaph* (p.834, 1st edition), the townships in the old parish of Ruabon, were "Belan, Bodylltyn, Christionydd Kenrick, Coed Christionydd, Dynhinlle ucha, Dynhinlle isa, Hafod, Moreton Anglicorum, Moreton Below (Offa's Dyke) and Rhyddallt". But this statement required correction as the Archdeacon has left out of his list the important and extensive township of Moreton Wallicorum or Moreton Above and is also mistaken in that Belan, Bodylltyn, Hafod, and Rhuddalt never were separate townships, but hamlets only in the township of Ruabon - which is not named at all in the Archdeacon's list. It is however true that the tithe map preface designates these four hamlets as being "townships", but that document gives the name township, using the term very loosely, to any small area wherein the tithes had a distinct assignment. As a consequence of this, we find mention, in the preface to the tithe map schedule, the townships of "Tre Robert Lloyd" (*Robert Lloyd's township*) and "Tre pwll glo" (*Coal pit township*), the last named being described in the body of the schedule as in Moreton Above, and Tre Robert Lloyd as in Moreton Below.

The hearth tax assessment, first imposed in 1662, jumbled together Morton Above and Morton Below under the name of Morton Wallicorum, although for centuries before 1662 the two townships were distinct, and are distinct now. The subject will not be pursued further at this point, but as the account of the parish which follows is arranged under its several townships, a later opportunity will be afforded of discussing the matter more minutely and fully.

And we begin with the township after which the parish takes its name.

CHAPTER I

The Township of Ruabon

This township contains the four hamlets of Hafod, Belan, Rhuddallt and Bodylltyn, and must be distinguished not merely from the parish but from the manor of the same name. The *manor* of Ruabon comprised the township of Ruabon with its four hamlets, the township of Marchwiel in the parish of Marchwiel, and the township of Ruyton (now Royton) in the parish of Bangor is y coed. The only township in the parish of Ruabon which belongs to the manor of the same name is Ruabon, the parish and manor here as elsewhere in Bromfield not coinciding.

The hamlets composing the township of Ruabon will be treated, as far as may be, separately starting with -

(a) *The Hamlet of Hafod.*

This hamlet is called in a deed dated on Monday before Michaelmas day in the 8th year of Henry IV, "havot y gallo" for Hafod y gallor and was still so designated in 1620. It is true we should expect the form "Hafod y callor" rather than "Hafod y gallor", but I have elsewhere seen "callor" treated as a feminine noun and it is so treated in the name of this hamlet, which means *Summer dwelling of the cauldron.*

In Hafod hamlet stands Wynnstay, formerly 'Watstay' but it would be superfluous and absurd in a treatise of this character to give a long and detailed pedigree of the two families successively possessed of this famous seat. Still, abbreviated sketch pedigrees are absolutely necessary for the reader, who, without them, would be bewildered and without a guide when he finds certain persons more or less connected with one or other of the two families mentioned. All that will be further attempted here is to give a brief notice of the devolution of the Wynnstay estate and to present some ordered notes, not elsewhere accessible in a printed form.

It is essential to say that the idea of the Eytons (the predecessors of the Evanses and of the present family, the Williams-Wynns') possessing, during the mediaeval epoch, a large compact landed estate in Ruabon, is one that must be dismissed from the mind.   Such an idea is incompatible with the evidence of those early deeds and surveys which have been preserved.   In the survey of the 23rd year of Henry VII, John Eyton was merely a portioner with many others in three gafaels or tribal holdings in Ruabon, namely in Gafael Sanddef, Gafael Meilir ap Elidur, and in Gafael Madoc Warwyn, and in the two gafaels last named he had land which was formerly held by David Lloyd ap Madoc and by Ieuan ap Madoc ap Llewelyn.   However, John Eyton was a portioner in gafaels elsewhere in Bromfield and also paid 7s. yearly for seven acres of land then late of the sons of David ap Madoc, and 7s. more for seven other acres there, late of the sons of Iorwerth ap Madoc and of Einion ap Llewelyn. He also had a fulling mill.

Those holding in gafaels, one of the chief features of which was gavelkind (sharing according to certain definite rules) exercised already by 1508 a sort of severalty within the gafael. It is impossible now to say what proportion of the several gafaels, which John Eyton was a portioner in, was held by a particular freeholder but, whatever proportion he did hold lay scattered, and intermixed with the lands of the other portioners.   However, in the 27th year of Henry VIII gavelkind was abolished, and most of the portioners then began to exchange portions or to purchase the portions of others, so as to have their land adjoining and in one place. Soon after that date, the estate that adopted the name Watstay began to appear distinct from other land holdings and Wat's Dyke (Clawdd Wad), which ran in front of the house, was at this time or afterwards by Sir John Wynn, cleared away[1].

Despite the fact that the Watstay estate had not yet emerged, John Eyton, better known as "John ap Elis Eyton" was a very important freeholder of Ruabon. He fought at Bosworth, and a fine monument of himself and his wife still stands in Ruabon church. (See *Royal Commission's Report of Denbighshire* p.177). The main property of the Eytons was in Eyton and Ruyton where they had a compact estate, which would be regarded as small according to modern notions.

By the time of Tidderley's Survey (made about the year 1546) William Eyton esq. (son of John Eyton and grandson of John ap Ellis Eyton) had a free capital messuage, a tenement and lands - the crown

1. It must have been once here for it formed the boundary at this point between the hamlets of Hafod and Belan. A line drawn southwards from the point outside Wynnstay Park where the dyke *stays* or stops represents the course of that dyke within the park and is still a recognised boundary.

rent of which (35s. 2d yearly) was larger than that of any other person there - held "to him and his heirs in fee".

In 1562, William Eyton esq. had in Ruabon the tenement in which he lived with 150 acres adjacent to the same; 20 acres of land called 'Sounde'; one tenement formerly in the tenure of David Lloyd (containing 50 acres); 10 acres formerly the property of Richard ap Llewelyn Gethin; and one tenement called Tythen y gove (Tyddyn y gof - *Farmstead of the smith*), containing 10 acres, by estimation 240 (customary or about 570 1/2 statute) acres in all. He also had four closes, the acreage of which is not given, one called "Kay Gwas myhangell" (*Field of the servant of Michael the Angel*) and another "Maes y groes (*Field of the cross*) together with 8 (customary or nearly 17 statute) acres more, late in the tenure of David ap Edward ap Howel, all free.

In addition to the above, there also belonged to William Eyton esqr. in 1562, three tenements in Ruabon with appurtenant free lands amounting to 400 (customary or 846 statute) acres which were attached to the manor of Isycoed.

In 1620, the estate of Mr Edward Eyton, son of the above-named William Eyton, consisted of a capital messuage called 'Wattstay', containing about 180 customary acres; a tenement called 'Tir Swnd' of 20 acres; a tenement formerly of David Lloyd, containing 50 acres; 10 acres lately of Richard ap Llewelyn Gethin; another tenement called 'Tyddyn y gou' of 10 acres and two water grain mills on the river above the township of Ruabon containing in all 270 customary, or 571 statute, acres. He also held two messuages and 30 acres of land pertaining thereto, and various parcels of land of 8 customary acres late in the tenure of David ap Howel (of David ap Edward ap Howel according to the 1562 survey), making altogether about 651 1/2 statute acres. Then there were 340 (customary or 719 statute) acres in Ruabon and Dininlle, belonging in 1620 to Mr. Edward Eyton, part of the manor of Isycoed. Mr. Eyton's grandson and heir presumptive, Mr. Thomas Evans (son of Richard Evans by Dorothy, sole surviving daughter of the said Mr. Edward Eyton) had at the same time various tenements and lands in Ruabon containing 40 (customary or 84 1/2 statute) acres. All this, together with 'The Lower Mill', came into the Watstay estate when Mr. Thomas Evans succeeded to it . Eyton Evans, the son of Thomas Evans just named, married in 1623/4 his kinswoman, Elizabeth, daughter of Gerard (afterwards Sir Gerard) Eyton, of Eyton. One of Mr. Eyton Evans' daughters, Jane, to whom Watstay was assigned, married Sir John Wynn, baronet (son of Henry Wynn esq., of the Gwydir family), whose

wife left him the Ruabon property to be disposed of according to his
will. Sir John Wynn, who had no legitimate children, changed the name
'Watstay' to 'Wynnstay', surrounded the house with a walled park, and
planted many trees and an avenue. In 1670, Wynnstay was already a
big house, rated for eleven hearths, and Sir John was estimated in 1715
to have an income of £5000 a year. He was buried at Ruabon 22 January
1718/9 aged 91, his baronetcy dying with him. He left Wynnstay to
Watkin Williams esqr., son of his cousin Jane (Thelwall), wife of the
second Sir William Williams, bart., of Llanforda. This Mr. Watkin
Williams took the additional name of Wynn, and became, on the death
of his father in 1740, the first Sir Watkin Williams-Wynn of Wynnstay,
baronet. Since that time, Wynnstay Park has been gradually enlarged
so as to take in large portions of all the four hamlets composing the
township of Ruabon.

The next most important holding in Hafod after Wynnstay was and
is Pentreclawdd (*Dyke hamlet or dwelling*), the head of an old estate on
Watt's Dyke. In speaking of this holding I shall say nothing more than
I have actually seen in contemporary deeds and surveys. Most of the
details will be relegated to a pedigree as the history of an old Welsh
family, duly authenticated, is not without interest from the social as well
as from the genealogical standpoint.

On 8 November, 1492, three several persons were bound to Ieuan
and David, sons of John ap David ap Ieuan ap Griffith, in the sum of
£100, and on the 1 February 1508/9, Howel ap Madoc ap Howel and
Madoc ap Griffith ap Bady granted all their lands within the lordship of
Bromfield, lately belonging to Edward ap David ap Griffith ap Howel,
to David ap John ap Ieuan ap Griffith. This David ap John was one of
the two brothers mentioned above, whose name appears as second in the
Pentreclawdd pedigree hereto annexed.

In Tidderley's Survey, made at the end of the reign of Henry VIII
(about 1546), John David ap John is returned as holding freely a
messuage and two closes in Ruabon. The lands which David ap John
purchased in February 1508/9 had probably been held in gavelkind and
scattered in various fields, but his son, John ap David, had a distinct
although small estate which was afterwards extended and became known
as Pentreclawdd. The aforesaid David ap John ap David of Ruabon,
gent., was still living in 1553. In the first year of the 16th century he
had a dispute with John ap Edward ap Madoc[2], of the parish of Ruabon,

---

2. John ap Edward ap Madoc Puleston, of Plas Ucha, in Cristionydd Kenrick.

SKETCH ABBREVIATED PEDIGREE OF EYTONS OF RUABON

John Eyton Hen of Eyton =
Steward of Bromfield 1477
son of James Eyton ap Ieuan
ap Madoc ap Llewelyn

Elis Eyton of Ruabon = (1) Elizabeth, daughter of = (2) Angharad, daughter of   William Eyton of Eyton =
                  Griffith Hanmer of Hanmer,   Madoc Puleston of Bers   died 1479
                  o.s.p.

John ap Elis Eyton = Elizabeth, daughter of Sir Hugh Calveley,   David Eyton   Elis Eyton   Edward Eyton
died 28 Sept. 1526.   died 11 June 1524   a priest.

...n Eyton Fychan of Ruabon =(1) Emma, daughter of = (2) Annest, daughter of Elisse   Margaret = Robert ap Iorwerth
...ied Holt Castle in 1534 for   Sir Roger Kynaston   ap Griffith ap Enion of   died 1528   of Llwyn on.
slaying William Hanmer   of Hordley   Gwyddelwern

...iam Eyton of = (1) Gwenhwyfar vz Richard ap Rhys =(2) Agnes, vz William ap William   Owen Eyton of Eglwysegle
...atstay, living   ap Griffith of Cochwillan   living 20 May 1589
...0 May 1589

       Elizabeth = Martin Bromfield   5 daughters   Roger Eyton o.s.p.   Richard Eyton of Belan
                                                                         Serjeant at arms living
                                                                    20 May 1589.

...vard Eyton of Watstay = [1]Catherine dau. of John   [2] Elizabeth, dau. of Kenrick   William Eyton   John Eyton   Roger
...25 Nov.1623;   Wynn Puleston of Plas   ap Robert of Marchwiel   of Plas Newydd   of Belan   o.s.p.
...g 20 May 1589.   Issa in Cristionydd.   relict of Rev. Dr Dd Powell   in Rhuddallt   bur. 5 Aug.
                                        of Ruabon.

                                                            Mary = Edward Eyton of Eyton

...Dorothy = Richard Evans of Treflach.   Mary
                                    died young.

       Thomas Evans of Watstay   = Anne dau. of Rev. Dr. David Powell
       bapt. at Ruabon 27 Apl. 1591   of Ruabon   bur. 6 May 1654 at Chirk
       buried there 22 March 1641-2   W.M.M.

                 Eyton Evans of Watstay   = Elizabeth dau. of Sir Gerard Eyton of Eyton
                 bapt. 20 Dec. 1609:   bapt. 29 Sept. 1608:
                 died 13 Oct. 1655,   married 3 Jan. 1623-4.
                 bur. at Ruabon.

Jane Evans   =   Sir John Wynn, bart.   Elizabeth   Sarah   Mary
died 18 Feb. 1675-6   died 11 Jan. 1718, aged 91.
aged 43. o.s.p.   changed the name of house
                    from Watstay to Wynnstay
                    which he left by will to
                    Watkin Williams esq., son
                    of Sir William Williams of
                    Llanforda, 2nd baronet.

ABBREVIATED SKETCH PEDIGREE OF THE WYNNS OF GWYDR AND OF THE WILLIAMS WYNNS OF WYNNSTAY

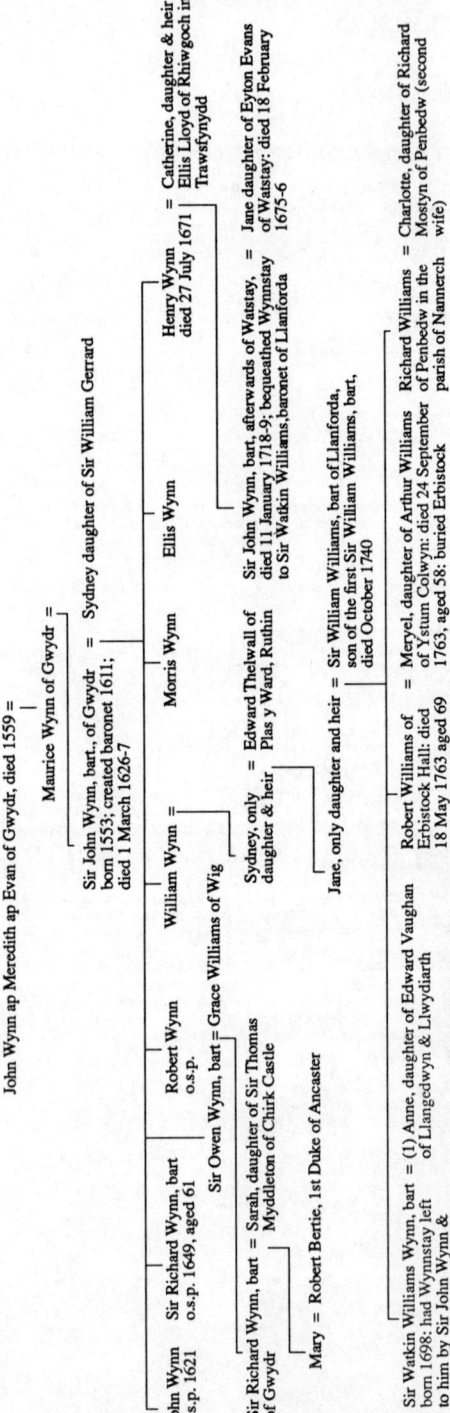

concerning a sitting or standing place, as well as concerning the order
of sitting therein in Ruabon church, Sir John Elys being then the vicar
of the parish. Whereupon Robert Puleston, who, as vicar general of the
bishop of St. Asaph, was called in to settle the dispute, summoned a
jury of twelve men of riper age of the parish, who testified that the
parents of the said David ap John occupied the seat which the said David
and his wife had used for forty years or more, the seat being called "the
seat (sedilis) of Jenkyn ap Atha". Nevertheless, the twelve sworn men
adjudged that David ap John ap David should allow, for kindness sake,
while she lived, Angharad verch David ap Griffith ap Howel to use the
said seat. And this decision was to be solemnly announced between
mass (*inter missar'*), and all parishioners were to be interdicted from
molesting David ap John ap David in the occupation of the said seat
under penalty of the greater excommunication and of the sum of ten
pounds to the fabric of the cathedral of St. Asaph. The award was dated
2 April 1500. The seat in the Latin of the document is called
indifferently "sedilis", "stabellum", and "stannum" or "stannus". The
probablity is that Angharad, although a tenant to John ap Edward ap
Madoc, conceived herself to have some heritable right in the disputed
sitting. David ap John, besides Pentreclawdd, had a messuage formerly
of David ap Madoc ap Ieuan, which had belonged to David ap Jenkyn
ap Adda, a fact which explains why the seat was called that of Jenkyn
ap Adda, from one of whose family, it is likely, Angharad's ancestor had
obtained permission to use the seat. I have tried to trace back the history
of this seat, but can only find that the Jenkyn ap Adda named in the
award, otherwise called Jenkyn ap Adda ap Madoc Llewelyn, granted
on the feast of the ascension in the 25th year of Henry VI, 1447, all his
lands in the township of Ruabon to his bastard son, David ap Jenkyn ap
Adda, and the son of this son, on the 15th January, 20th year of Edward
IV, 1480/81, granted the same lands to David ap Madoc ap Ieuan, from
whom they passed to one of the owners of Pentreclawdd. It may be
added that Angharad's brother, Edward ap Madoc ap Griffith ap Howel,
was living at Ruabon on 1 August 1492.

On 20 October 1593, John ap Robert of Pentreclawdd, calling himself
"yeoman", agreed with his son David Lloyd ap John that he would assure
and convey to the said David, in the usual terms, all that capital messuage
with appurtenances in the township of Ruabon commonly called
'Pentreclawdd' and all other his messuages, lands etc., in the county of
Denbigh, and in default of legal issue to David Lloyd, then in succession
to the use of the younger sons of John ap Robert ap David, who was to

enjoy the same during his life, the premises to be conveyed "by the names of fower messuages, two cottages, sixe orchardes, sixe gardens, fower hundred acres of lande, threescore acres of meadowe, two hundred acres of pasture and thirty acres of wood". These figures would add up to 710 acres (more than twice that amount if we regard them as customary acres), but we must not treat fines to be levied with too great strictness in this respect.

In 1620, David Lloyd, gent., held in Ruabon the messuage (Pentre-clawdd) in which he lived and two other tenements, late of Robert ap David ap John (his grandfather), containing, by estimation, 30 (customary or 63½ statute) acres. And this statement of the acreage of his estate must be taken as approximately accurate at that time, although doubtless he had sold some of his lands and his property was then reduced in extent. He was the first of his stock to adopt a surname, but as there was more than one David Lloyd in the parish, he was generally known as 'David Lloyd ap John Robert'. He had an elder[3] son, Owen Lloyd, and a daughter, Judith, married to John Erthig of Erddig. Lumley Williams, gent., was trustee for Barbara, Owen Lloyd's wife, who according to *Powys Fadog* was daughter of Henry Williams of Cochwillan, by his wife, Jane Salusbury.

Mr. David Lloyd ap John Robert and Mr. Owen Lloyd, his son, sold, on 30 August 1630, for £1300[4] to Kenrick Edisbury, esq., formerly of Bedwell, their ancestral estate of Pentreclawdd, and on 12 September 1631, Mr. Edisbury, in consideration of £40 paid to him, leased to Mr. David Lloyd that messuage in Ruabon wherein the said David Lloyd then lived, with the appurtenances and "the purparts" of Kenrick Edisbury in those classes called Meusydd y llan (*village fields*) and Maes Howell (*Howel's field*), Kae Howell ap llen (*Field of Howel ap Llewelyn*) and Bryn y wiwer (*Squirrel's Hill*) and those two crofts called Vron Goch (*Red brow*) and Erw Grach (*Scabby field*) for 80 years, if the said David Lloyd, Katherine his wife, and Ann verch Edward, mother of the said Katherine, should so long live. This is the last mention I have found of Mr. David Lloyd, thus reduced from the position of a Welsh gentleman to that of a tenant farmer, holding by lease for lives.

Powys Fadog (Vol. III, pp. 59 and 60) suggests that Owen Lloyd, David Lloyd's son, was the owner of Plas Drain. This, however, was

---

3. I think he had a younger son, John David Lloyd, who is mentioned in 1620 as though he were then dead.

4. Of this sum, £300 were to be paid to Lumley Williams esq., for the maintenance of Mrs Barbara Lloyd, and the rest used for the discharge of the debts of Mr. David Lloyd and Mr. Owen Lloyd.

PEDIGREE OF THE LLOYD FAMILY OF PENTRECLAWDD, RUABON

John ap David ap John ap Ieuan ap Griffith
Last will made 24 January, proved 28 February 1569/70
=
Katherine verch John
mentioned 24 January 1569/70

David ap John of Pentreclawdd =
living 8 November 1492, still
living in 1553

John ap John
mentioned in 1569/70

Robert ap David ap John of Pentreclawdd =
last will dated 2 October 1580, proved 10 July 1589

John ap Robert ap David of Pentreclawdd = Gwenhwyfar, daughter of Hugh ap John
mentioned in the will of his grandfather, ap Ieuan, gent. of Rhosllanerchrugog, pre-nuptial
still living in 20 October 1594 settlement dated 16 November 1556

William ap Robert*   David ap Robert*   Owen ap Robert*   Richard ap Robert*

David Lloyd ap John Robert of Pentreclawdd   =   Katherine verch Howel ap Edward
mentioned 24 June 1569: sold his estate 30 August   of Cefn y Fedw in Cristionydd Kenrick [*PF*]
1630 to mr Kenrick Edisbury: still living 12 September 1631

Edward†   Richard†   Martin†   John†   Robert†

Katherine
mentioned 24 January 1569/70

Judith   1627   John Erthig of Erddig,
buried at Wrexham,   =   coroner
30 July 1681

Owen Lloyd, tenant of Plas Drain   =   Barbara
buried at Ruabon, 17 July 1671

*   All living on 2 October 1580
†   All mentioned as residuary heirs on 20 October 1594

not the case. Owen Lloyd at Plas Drain in Morton Wallicorum, a farm-house situate in a wild, desolate, wind-swept upland, was the tenant of Mr. Kenrick Edisbury. One of Mr. David Lloyd's brothers, Robert ap John Robert, was living in Ruabon in April 1614 when he was described as "yeoman".

Mr. Kenrick Edisbury himself lived at Pentreclawdd for some time after he had purchased it, and bought lands adjoining. His son, Mr. John Edisbury, also lived at this house until about the year 1660, when he transferred his abode to 'Erddig House', now Erddig Hall. In 1670, Pentreclawdd was rated to hearth tax for nine hearths, and in 1715 the farm was returned as containing over 282 acres, as being rented at £150 a year, and having on it two fields called 'Vron Durras' (for 'Vron Ddyrys' - *Brambly Brow*), two meadows called 'Tir Sound' (*Tir Swnd),* a field known by the same name, and other fields with names less interesting. We shall meet with this name again and some fifty years ago it was applied to a field a little east of Ruabon Cemetery. The following is a description of Pentreclawdd in 1715: "House, 9 bays, 1 story high; Wooden Barn, of 9 bays; 3 bays of Cowhouse; 2 bays of Daiary house and Corn Room; a small bay of swinestie; 5 bays of Brick barn".

The other tenements worthy of note in Hafod hamlet are the Cinders, Cae Cyriog and Llwyn Howel.

The Cinders farms, for there were three so called in Ruabon, as well as in 1620 a 'Syndre ucha' in another township near (probably in Morton is y clawdd) represent old holdings to which the name 'Cinder' or 'Synder' was attached, but except that last named, they do not appear to be specifically mentioned in any of the three great surveys. The two Cinders Farms near the Crimble belong to the Wynnstay estate, but there was another 'Sinder Tenement' part of the Erddig estate in 1715, but later leased under the name of 'Caia Clapiog' together with Yr Afon goch: it was, according to an old map, located on the east side of the road leading from Crabtree Green to Oswestry.

Cae Cyriog was until about thirty years ago a small farm, with some 30 acres attached, famous as the home of the Griffithses, one of whom compiled the well-known Cae Cyriog book of pedigrees. As the site of this house is likely now soon to be forgotten it may be well to indicate its exact locality. Passing along the road from Ruabon Church to Overton Bridge, with the park wall on the right, there is a lane on the left a little past Ruabon vicarage. In a meadow on the left hand side at the further end of this lane stood Cae Cyriog. Griffith ap John ap David (ap) Ieuan is mentioned in the survey of 1620 as one of the leasehold tenants of Ruabon and as holding 'Kae Kiriog', and he is named in the same survey as claiming a messuage and free lands in Ruabon then in the actual possession of Thomas ap David (his great uncle) formerly of John David ap Ieuan ap Llewelyn (his father). Griffith ap John above named had a son, John Griffith of Cae Cyriog, the father of John Griffith, the genealogist and of two younger sons, Roger Griffith and Peter Griffith. John, the eldest of these sons, was baptized on 29 April 1654, Roger on 14 February, 1656, and Peter on 24 August 1658. According to the first of two deeds which I once saw and roughly summarized, dated 17 February 1684/85, John Griffith of Ruabon, gent., conveyed to Edward Owen of the Woodhouse, county Salop, gent., and to William Wynne of Ruabon, gent., as trustees for his younger sons, Roger and Peter, a messuage in Bersham, with six parcels of land thereto annexed (formerly in one) which the said John Griffith had lately purchased from Martha Roberts, widow (of Roger Roberts, of Wrexham, gent., second son of John Roberts, esq., of Hafod y bwch, fawr). It is noted that the six parcels were called 'Cae brwynog' (*Rushy field*), a name by which the house was, and still is, also known. In the second deed, dated 23 December 1780, Thomas Symond, of Llanerch gron, in the parish of Clocaenog and Thomas Symond, the younger, also of Llanerch gron, are mentioned. It states that Roger Griffith died without issue and intestate, and that Peter Griffith's daughter, Margaret, married Hugh Jones, whose daughter, Elizabeth, married the aforesaid Thomas Symond, the elder, and had Cae brwynog, which was sold in 1809 to William Abraham. For this holding in the poor assessment book for 1737, "Widow Griffith" was charged 2s 4d.

The house of Cae Cyriog contained in 1670 two hearths only. Let us now return to John Griffith, the genealogist, who is said to have died in 1698 and was succeeded by his son of the same name, who married Rebecca[5], one of the daughters of Thomas Hughes of Pen y nant, in Belan, which estate he thus acquired. John and Rebecca Griffith had two sons, (1) the Rev. John Griffith, vicar of Nannerch, who died without issue, 17 September 1774, aged 62, and (2) Thomas Griffith of Cae Cyriog and Pen y nant, who died 26 April, 1808, aged 97. The son of this Thomas, also named Thomas Griffith, was a surgeon in Wrexham, of whom I have given an account of on p. 53 of my *History of the Town*

---

5. A "Rebecca Griffiths of Pen y nant", probably John Griffiths' wife, was buried at Ruabon, 7 May 1724.

of Wrexham. One of his eleven children, Thomas Taylor Griffith, baptized 2 January 1796, became a notable and skilful surgeon, living at Chester Street House, Wrexham (see *History of the Town of Wrexham*, p. 98). He married at Llangollen, 17 April 1827, Miss Mary Anne Robertson, who was a clever sketcher and possessed a mild poetic gift. She published a ballad, beginning with the words "Trickle, trickle", which was set to music by the late Mr. John Hughes, of York Street, Wrexham ('Hughes the Music' as he was commonly called). Mr. Griffith died on 6th July 1876, leaving two sons and one daughter. The elder of these two sons (baptized at Wrexham, 29 April 1828) was the late Rev. Thomas Llewelyn Griffith, M.A., who, although rector of Deal for 42 years, lived at Pen y nant on and off during that period and was responsible for pulling down Cae Cyriog and rebuilding Pen y nant. His eldest son, a sub-lieutenant in the 24th Regiment of Foot, was killed in the Zulu war. The Rev. Griffith died on 10 December 1904, and his children or executors sold Pen y nant and Cae Cyriog to the present Sir Watkin Williams Wynn, and Parkside, Allington, to Alfred Ashworth, esq., of Horsley Hall. Nearly all, if not all, the land in Wrexham, formerly of Mr. Thomas Taylor Griffith, has also been sold.

In 1844 there was a house near Cae Cyriog called Little Cae Cyriog, but attached to Llwyn Howel and belonging to Wynnstay.

Llwyn Howel in Hafod is mainly interesting because, according to *Powys Fadog*, Vol. IV, it was part of the portion of Elizabeth, sixth daughter of Mathew Trevor, esq., of Trevor. This Elizabeth married (firstly) Captain David Maurice, a Parliamentary officer in the civil war. All this is no doubt true, but Captain Maurice did not live at Llwyn Howel. Mr. W. M. Myddelton tells me that Captain Maurice, son of Thomas Maurice of Llangedwyn, served under Sir Thomas Myddleton, and in 1648 had a lease from the knight of a good house called The Court (now in ruins) in Halton in the parish of Chirk where he lived until his death in 1653. In his will, dated 25 April, proved 29 July 1653, by his second wife Ellen Maurice and his father, Thomas Maurice, he bequeathed his lands in Ruabon and Cristionydd Kenrick to his daughter Sara who also shared with her stepmother in the testator's debentures in the Lordship of Bromfield and Yale and elsewhere. His other daughter, Mrs Dorothy Bell of Wrexham, by his first wife, and his son of his second, must have died before 1653. The overseers of his will were Morgan Lloyd and Daniel Lloyd, both of Wrexham, Watkin Kyffin of Glascoed, and the testator's brother Hugh and mother Jane Trevor.

The Afon Goch farm in Hafod, which belonged to the Erddig estate in 1715, lay south of the river (*Afon Goch*) from which it took its name, and contained about 36½ acres of land. On it were then two fields called 'Tir Sound mawr' and 'Tir Sound vechan', which had been leased by Mr. John Edisbury in 1652, apparently as part of Pentreclawdd, when we find these fields mentioned under the names of 'Tir y Swnd Ucha', 'fflash tir y swnd', and other lands called 'Tir y swnd'. In 1620, as we have seen, the tenement called 'Tir Swnd' belonged to Edward Eyton, esq. That it afterwards was part of Pentreclawdd was due doubtless to the process of exchange, with a view to consolidation, which went rapidly on in the 17th century.

Richard Mathew had in this hamlet a free estate called 'Havod y gallor' containing 24 (customary or nearly 51 statute) acres.

(b) Hamlet of Belan.

'Belan' means some sort of mound, although it is difficult now to designate the especial features which distinguished a 'belan' from a mound of another kind which has been differently made.

The vicarage house of Ruabon, located in Belan hamlet, contained eight hearths in 1670. It was much enlarged by the Rev. B. M. M. Bonnor, and has annexed to it about 36 acres of glebe. In a deed of 1586, hereafter to be summarised, this house is designated as 'Plas y vicar' (*The vicar's hall*), and as late as the date of the tithe map (1844) a field on the glebe, just to the east of the vicarage house, was still known as 'Cae pen plas y vicar'.

The deed just indicated is perhaps worthy of more attention. Thereby, Robert ap David ap John, of Pentreclawdd, sold to David Lloyd ap Edward ap Ieuan ap Owen, among other lands, a close in Ruabon called 'y koed kae uwghben plas y vicar' - Coed gae uwchben plas y vicar - (*Woodfield above the vicar's hall*). The same field is also mentioned in a deed of 7th February 1564/5, wherein David ap Matthew, of Trevor ucha, gent., conveys to the same Robert ap David ap John "all those syxe p'cells of land ... beinge all and whole parte and porcon [portion] of the said dd ap matthew of and in those foure fyldes or clausures of land comonlye cald kae hoell ap llen, maes y llan issaf, *Coed kae'r vickar*, and y kae crwn", the said parcels lying within well-known meres and limits within the said four fields. This summary is interesting because it shows that the portion which was sold did not consist of the whole of the four fields, but of quillets lying separately within them, and that the process of consolidation, whereby the whole of each field became the property of single persons, was a later operation.

This operation is revealed to us as going on in an earlier deed, dated 20 May 1569, whereby Richard Eyton and William Eyton[6], of Ruabon, esq., were bound to Robert ap David ap John ap David (of Pentreclawdd) and to John ap Robert ap David, his son and heir, on condition that the said Robert ap David and John ap Robert should hold "for ever the whole parte or porcon of the above bounden Richard Eyton esquier off and those thre clausures or p'cells of land with th'app'tennces whereof the first ys cald y bryn uchaff, [the second], kae david laas, and the thyrd y bronnyth. As Also All those two p'cells of land, with th'appurten'nees whereof thone [the one] ys cald Erw kae David laas & thother garth y tyg Ar y clawdd" etc.. Here, as I interpret the deed, Richard Eyton, with the consent of his brothers and nephew, convey to Robert ap David and to John ap Robert the whole of two closes, and all his quillets lying seperately intermixed with those of others in three other closes. And we see how, by exchange or purchase, consolidation of the quillets was gradually effected. We have to picture to ourselves the fact that many of the fields in Ruabon and elsewhere at this time, although small, were broken up into seperately owned quillets which were only by separate processes brought together and made one field or more fields in single ownership.

The other chief houses in Belan are Pen y nant, Maes y llan, Pentre issa, and Belan Place.

Pen y nant (*Top of the dingle*) is the name of the house which in *Powys Fadog* (Vol. II, p.181) is called 'Pennant y belan', a designation unknown outside books and certain genealogies, or one which, if ever used, never 'caught on' so as to become permanent. Thomas Hughes, said to have been one of the two sons (Griffith Hughes being the other) of John ap Hugh ap Edward, lived at Pen y nant which after his death passed with Pentre issa into the possession of one of his sons-in-law, John Griffith of Cae Cyriog, and the Griffiths lived here until their removal to Wrexham and elsewhere. It was a small house, having only two hearths in 1670, but probably better in many respects than Cae Cyriog, which was also charged for two hearths in the same year. The late Rev. Thomas Llewelyn Griffith rebuilt it on a scale quite disproportionate to the area of the land connected with the holding, and in 1906 his heirs or executors sold it to Sir H. Ll. Watkin Williams-Wynn, the present baronet.

6. William Eyton was of Watstay. Richard Eyton of Rhuddallt and Owen Eyton of Eglwysegle were his brothers, and Edward Eyton was his son.

Pen y nant is most romantically and beautifully situated, overlooking the gorge, covered with solemn woods, through which the Afon Eitha runs down to the Dee.

The farmhouse of Pentre issa, with about 60 acres of land, belonged to Pen y nant, the whole estate of which in Belan hamlet did not contain much over 125 acres.

We have already seen that in 1564/5 David Mathew, of Trevor ucha, esq., sold, among other lands, all his purpart and portion in Maes y llan issa to Robert ap David ap John, of Pentreclawdd. When Mr. Kenrick Edisbury purchased Pentreclawdd this portion passed with it. But another portion, including the house, did not so pass. The holding lay dispersed, and it was some time before all the land around the 'Tyddyn', or farmstead, called *Maes y llan*, (a name which should here probably be translated as *village field*) was bought up, and formed into a single compact farm. On 23 September 1636, Mr. Kenrick Edisbury and Mr. John Edisbury, his son, in order to hasten this process, purchased for £85, from Sir Thomas Myddelton of Chirk Castle, knight[7], "all those severall pieces or parcells contayninge therein thirty and two butts of arable butts with th'app'tennces lyeing dispersed within the closures called maes y llan ucha and maes y llan issa, and nowe or late in the sev'all tenures or occupation of Richard Lloyd, Doctor in Divinity and William ap John ap Edward or their underten'nts And also all that other piece or parcell contayninge therein by estimacon two acres of Landes more or lease w'th th'app'tennces in Maes y llan issa" in occupation of said Dr. Richard Lloyd, and that messuage in the tenure of the said William ap John ap Edward wherein Edward Lloyd now dwells, and the parcell of land whereon the said messuage; those two clausures called yr Erw and yr Erw hir, his late part of the said Maes y llan issa; that piece containing by estimation one acre lying in a field called kae howell ap llên; that other piece containing two butts of land in the closure called Y Clwtt (*the patch*); and "those Tenne peaces or Cuttings and Ends of butts lying Likewise w'thin the said closure called Y Clwtt", which messuage and lands last mentioned were in the tenure of the said William ap John and situate in the township of Ruabon.

As late as 1715, when the area of Maes y llan farm was over 50 acres, and the rent £24, the vicar of Ruabon had many quillets and whole closes within its ambit, containing in all 5 acres, 1 rood, 1 perch, the

---

7. The late Chevalier Lloyd in *Powys Fadog* asserts that Maes y llan in Ruabon township had formerly belonged to Sir Edward Broughton, but he was thinking of the farm having the same name in Marchwiel which did really belong to Sir Edward.

house being described as of two bays, the barn of three bays, and cowhouses and stable of three bays.

Belan Place is a large stone built house with nearly 83 acres of land in Belan hamlet and there pertained to it in 1844 Gardd y pentre farm of about 49 acres in Dininlle Issa. At that time Belan Place belonged to Richard Jones esq., of the family of Jones of Mossfield, Whitchurch, Salop, who was high sheriff for county Denbigh in 1806. He occupied this house during the greater part of his life, and died 5 Sept. 1862, aged 78. John Eyton of Belan was buried at Ruabon 5 August 1627. He was the son of William Eyton and a younger brother of Edward Eyton esq., of Watstay.

The tower, or mausoleum, of Nant y belan is nobly perched, overlooking the voluptuous windings of the river Dee, surrounded by beautiful scenery, and commanding most wonderful distant views. It was erected by the third Sir Watkin Williams-Wynn to commemorate the officers of the Welsh regiment, commonly called 'The Ancient Britons', which helped to surpress the Irish rebellion of 1798.

In 1562 Martin Bromfield held four customary acres of the queen's waste in Nant y belan, which had been leased for 21 years on the 30 November, 6 Edward VI (1552), and in the preamble to the survey of Ruabon manor in 1620, the jury stated that "there is a rough and rockye common within the townshippe of Ruabon, called Nant y belan, and belongeth to his highness' tennaunts" who paid 16d yearly to the baliff of the manor. "And sayen further that there is another common called Nant y Glyn Ddu being moorishe and rough, overgrowne with brambles and shrubbes w'ch belongeth to the freeholders of the townshippe of Ruabon as appurtenaunt to their freehold landes".

(c) Hamlet of Rhuddallt.

The hamlet of Rhuddallt (*Red Cliff*) belongs now almost entirely to Wynnstay, and a great portion of it is within the park, while Plas Newydd, which is not in the park, is the property of Sir Watkin. But there were formerly at least two distinct estates, not annexed to Wynnstay, and called respectively 'Rhuddallt Issa' and 'Rhuddallt Ucha'. They cannot at present be identified with any certainty, although Plas Newydd seems to be neither of the two, but a quite distinct free holding.

Powys Fadog (Vol. II p.352) suggests that Rhuddallt Issa belonged to a family surnamed "Davies", and is correct in so doing. The first to bear this surname here was Richard Davies, gent., son of David ap Edward of Trevor by his wife, Catherine, who called herself 'Catherine

Edwards', one of the daughters and heiresses of Edward ap Randle ap
John, of Rhuddallt, ap John ap Madog. This Edward ap Randle, gent.,
is described in the survey of 1620 as having a messuage and twelve
parcels of land containing 40 (customary or nearly 85 statute) acres, one
of these parcels being known as 'Bryn y Bygelese', and another, an
entire croft, as 'Erew y nant'. The grandfather of Edward ap Randle
ap John, who was John ap John ap Madoc, was living as a freeholder
in the year 1562.

Catherine Edwards, daughter of Edward ap Randle[8], and wife of
David ap Edward of Trevor, bought up all the rights of her sisters in
Rhuddallt, and handed them on to her son, Mr. Richard Davies. In 1663,
Catherine Edwards of Trevor was 'presented' as a Quaker by the grand
jury of county Denbigh, and her son maintained 'a meeting' at his house
in Rhuddallt. I feel sure that she was connected, by kin or marriage,
with the famous 'friend' and Quaker missionary, John ap John of Plas
Ifan, Trevor Issa, but cannot gather up all the relevant clues. That
Catherine, wife of John ap John, died at Rhuddallt (9 January 1694) is
one of the least significant of these clues.

Mr. Richard Davies of Rhuddallt and Trevor must be distinguished
from Richard Davies of Cloddiau cochion (near Welshpool). He
bequeathed his principles to his three sons. Of these, the two younger,
John Davies and David Davies, just before their emigration to
Pennsylvania[9], received from the Nantwich (Cheshire) monthly meeting
a letter dated 20th of 1st month (March) 1712/3, which they presented
on the 3rd of the 5th month (July) 1713, at the Philadelphia monthly
meeting, when they were described as sons of Richard and Ann Davies
"of Rhieddallt in ye parish of Ruabon and county of Denby in Wales
(who are a family of good repute among friends and others)". I believe
it was the late Mr. Edward W. Lloyd, of Philadelphia, who sent me the
interesting extract last quoted.

Mr. Edward Davies, the eldest son of Mr. Richard Davies, remained
at Rhuddallt, continued a Quaker, being a trustee for the Friend's
meeting-house at Wrexham, and was still living on 5 April 1723. After
his death, the estate of Rhuddallt Issa seems to have been sold, and to
have come into the possession of a family surnamed 'Lewis'. The few
Quakers of the neighbourhood then built themselves a meeting-house at

8. Edward ap Randle and Catherine vz Dd (?) were married at Llangollen, 17 June, 1590.
These were probably the parents of Catherine Edwards.

9. I learn from Mr. Thomas Allen Glenn's *Meirion in the Welsh Tract* (1896) that Mr. Richard
Davies purchased 5000 acres in Pennsylvania from the proprietary. This represents probably the
provision, or part of it, which Mr. Davies made for his two younger sons.

Cefn bychan in Coed Cristionydd, adjoining the hamlet of Bodylltyn in
the township of Ruabon. This house still stands but has been converted
to other uses.

On the 4 January 1754, Lewis Lewis, gent., executed a settlement
previous to his marriage with Bennette, youngest daughter of Edward
Lloyd. esq., of Plas Madoc in Bodylltyn, Ruabon. In this settlement Mr.
Lewis names the messuage called 'Ty'n y Ryddallt' or 'Rhyddallt Issa',
with the lands appertaining thereto in his occupation, other messuages
in Wrexham Regis, and the freehold farm called 'the Parkie' in the
(township of Pickhill and) parish of Bangor is y coed, belonging to him.
The marriage portion of Miss Bennette Lewis was £400. They were
married at Ruabon on the 8 January 1754, and their eldest son Edward,
of whom hereafter, was baptised there, 18 January 1760. Mr. Lewis
Lewis died intestate on 7 January 1777. On the 8 March 1792, Mr.
Edward Lewis, the eldest son of Mr. Lewis Lewis paid £800 to his
younger brothers and sisters to bar all claims. These younger children
of Mr. Lewis Lewis were:- Ann Rogers, wife of John Rogers; Bennette
Lewis[10]; Ruth Lewis; Roger Lewis; Lewis Lewis; and Robert Lewis,
another son, Godfrey Lewis, having lately died. The eldest son. Edward,
transferred himself to London, where he flourished; married (3 July
1788) Augusta Beauvais (by whom he had a son, Edward Lewis, junior,
afterwards of Hertingfordbury, Herts) at Chiswick, and was buried in
November 1827 at Pentonville Chapel in the parish of St. James,
Clerkenwell. He sold his Pickhill property to Sir Robert Henry Cunliffe,
of Acton, county Denbigh, and Rhuddallt either directly to Sir Watkin
Williams-Wynn or to his brother-in-law, John Rogers, from whom Sir
Watkin obtained it.

It seems very likely that the above-named Mr. Lewis Lewis of
Rhuddallt was son of Mr. Roger Lewis of Ruabon by Ruth, his wife.
Mr. Roger Lewis died before 2 January 1749, when his widow, Mrs Ruth
Lewis, was still alive.

In the crown rent-book for 1794, Roger Lewis (one of the sons of
Mr. Lewis Lewis?) is charged under Faborum Manor, but a note is

10. Mrs Newling, of Rockferry, told me in 1904 that Bennette, one of the daughters of John
and Anne Rogers of Rhudallt, married at Chirk, 13 February 1810, Thomas Evans of Ruabon,
whose daughter Ruth Evans married, at Ruabon 29 June 1853, the Rev. John Jones, curate of
Ruabon, afterwards vicar of Nevern, and that she (Mrs Newling) was one of the four daughters
of this Rev. John Jones and Ruth his wife. Various inscriptions in Ruabon churchyard which I
have copied and give later in my account of the church, throw a good deal of light on the history
of the families of Lewis, Rogers, and Evans of Rhuddallt. There is now no *house* called
'Rhuddallt' in the parish of Ruabon.

annexed as to whether the entry did not apply to Rhuddallt "*exchanged with Sr Watkin*".

Rhuddallt Issa or *Lower Rhuddallt* presupposes a Rhuddallt Ucha or *Upper Rhuddallt*, but I have not yet found the name of the hamlet expressly so designated.

In the survey of 1620 Roger Griffith ap David ap John ap Ieuan Goch is described as holding a free tenement in Rhuddallt called 'Y wern', with appurtenant lands containing 15 (customary or 31¾ statute) acres, and he had two other tenements with 30 customary acres elsewhere in Ruabon. His grandfather, David ap John ap Ieuan Goch, had been in possession of the Wern in 1562. What became of the Griffiths of Rhuddallt is a matter which remains unexplained. *Powys Fadog* says that their lands passed into the possession of Mr. Kenrick Eyton of Eyton.

Powys Fadog (Vol. II, p. 344) asserts that John Rogers, second cousin of the above-named Roger Griffith, was living at Rhuddallt in 1620, but the survey of that year does not bear out this statement. A John Roger, however, was then possessed of a small freehold estate in Ruyton which belonged to the *manor*, but not to the township of Ruabon.

In 1620, George Salusbury of Erbistock, esq., is mentioned as having in Rhuddallt a messuage in the occupation of William Lloyd and seven parcels of land called 'Cae rhwng y ddau dy' (*Field between the two houses*), 'Cae Cadwgan' (*Cadwgan's field*), 'Dwy dryllie cochion' (*Two red patches*), 'Cae Bedw', 'yr erw wair', and 'y berllan'.

Daniel Powell, eldest son of Dr. David Powell, vicar of Ruabon, had also within this hamlet a "gavel of free land" containing 6 (customary or about 12 statute) acres, which he derived from his father. This 'gavel' was possibly the nucleus of the estate of the Powells of Rhuddallt, whose name afterwards so often occurs.

The following notices relating to the children of Mr. Daniel Powell are found in the Ruabon registers:- Katherine (bapt. 10 Sept. 1615); John (bapt. 13 May 1617), and Anne (or Annie, buried 30 July 1625).

John Powell, the son of Mr. Daniel Powell, succeeded his father at Rhuddallt. I believe the John Powell, who was buried at Ruabon 20 January 1640/1, to have been his uncle, youngest son of Dr. David Powell. In that case, Mr. John Powell, of Rhuddallt, was he who, on 14 August 1653, was appointed civil registrar for the parish of Ruabon. His wife was Catherine daughter of Edward Lloyd, M.A., of Plas Madoc, by whom he had a son, John Powell, junior, whom he survived, dying in January 1726/7[11]. His son was buried at Ruabon 23 June 1692 and his son's widow, Mrs Judith Powell of Rhuddallt on 22 January 1723/4.

John and Judith Powell had a daughter named Mary who was baptised at Ruabon on 21 August 1687. In 1794 some property in Bodylltyn, then belonging to Sir Watkin Williams-Wynn is described as being "late [of] Judith Powell"[11].

There were other free proprietors in this little hamlet, but there is no need to mention them here.

Plas Newydd in Rhuddallt has, for more than two centuries, belonged to the Wynnstay estate. William Eyton, brother of Edward Eyton, esq., occupied it at the beginning of the 17th century.

In 1844 there was a tannery in Rhuddallt quite close to Plas Newydd, carried on by Mr. Edward Edwards, and in 1794, John Williams, tanner, of Ruabon is mentioned.

In the ringild's account for Ruabon manor from Michaelmas eve 1479 to Michaelmas eve 1480 is a very interesting entry relating to Rhuddallt ferry and bridge which may be thus translated:- "And half of the profits accruing from the boat or passage of ferry of and upon the water (river) of Ruralth, this year not rendered because no such boat or passage now exists, and because there has been built a new bridge there of and upon the water aforesaid in the aforesaid year". In the accounts of the receiver of Bromfield and Yale from Michaelmas eve 1388 to Michaelmas eve 1389, 15d. appears for a piece of iron bought for making a chain for Rhuthalth boat. The bridge built in 1479 was, of course, over Afon Eitha, and probably quite near to the site of the present Ruabon bridge, which was erected in 1819 and widened in 1894.

The parish church of Ruabon is situated in Rhuddallt township, but it must be treated by itself in a seperate chapter. However, it may be noted that Edward II in 1318 enquired of the bishop on what day and place Griffin, son and heir of Madoc "de Glyndowerdwy" married Elizabeth daughter of John le Strange and the reply was "apud Rhyddalt in 15° Johannis Baptiste, 1304 (Arch. Camb. 1868, p. 331).

(d) Hamlet of Bodylltyn.

'Bodylltyn', sometimes formerly written 'Bodyllyng', can only mean the dwelling of Ylltyn, of Gylltyn, or Illyn, or the like.

This hamlet contains many important estates, but one of them was always specifically and simply known as 'Bodylltyn', and is probably

11. In Oswestry Church is a tombstone containing the following inscription:- "Here lieth the body of Judith Powell, spinster of Rudallt, in the parish of Ruabon, county of Denbigh, interred Jan. 5, 1755. Here lieth likewise ye body of Mary ye wife of Nathanial Jones of this town, butcher, and nece to ye above Judith Powell, interred June 27, 1755, aged 37".

the very stone house, much modernised, called 'Bodylltyn farm' standing
in Wynnstay Park in 1911.   Roger Eyton, one of the illegitimate sons
of John ap Elis Eyton, married the heiress of Bodylltyn (Gwenllian
daughter of Edward ap Madoc ap David, according to *Powys Fadog*)
and lived there.   His son Edward, named 'Edward Eyton' in the
pedigrees, the famous poet and genealogist, called himself and was
almost invariably known in his lifetime as 'Edward ap Roger'.   He is
described in 1562 as holding in free tenure a tenement in Ruabon which
he inhabited and 100 acres of land, and two other tenements there each
with 30 acres, all probably customary acres, and in copyhold tenure a
piece of waste in Ruabon called 'vron dan y vynnwent' (Fron dan y
fynwent - *brow below the graveyard*), a close called 'Gwern y newadd'
(Gwern y neuadd - *Alder-marsh of the hall*) containing eight acres,
parcels of waste called 'gwas y brawde' and 'y gwerne gerwyn' alias
'gwern y kraw' etc..   He is undoubtedly, by all these tokens, to be
identified with the Edward ap Roger of Ruabon named in Tiddersley's
Survey taken in 1546.   He died on 15 May 1587 and is said to have
had nine sons and five daughters, being succeeded at Bodylltyn by his
second and eldest surviving son, John Eyton, who was buried at Ruabon
in June 1606, and leaving by his wife Jane, a son of the same name
whom we may here call 'John Eyton junior'. In the survey of 1620, the
last named, under the style of 'John Eyton gent.', is described as holding
a messuage, in which he dwelt, and 160 (customary or 382½ statute)
acres of free land, formerly it is noted belonging to Edward ap Roger,
his grandfather, confirming thus the account of his descent above given.
Two of the names of fields included in the 160 acres are interesting
enough to be quoted - 'Erw y garnedd' (*Acre of the tumulus*)[12]   and
'Maes y Neuath' (*Hall field*). John Eyton junior had also in 1620 another
tenement of six customary acres in Ruabon, late of Sir John Salusbury,
knight, and afterwards of George Salusbury esqr..   He sold Bodylltyn to
John Wills, silk mercer of London, whose daughter, Jane, married John
Powell, citizen and mercer of London. This John Powell was a younger
brother of the first Sir Thomas Powell *baronet*, and, it is said, died at
Bodylltyn in 1629.   John Powell had three daughters, co-heiresses. [See
before, under Rhuddallt].   It is not known what became of John Eyton,
junior, of Bodylltyn.   He was not the 'John Eyton Vychan', buried at
Ruabon on 28 October 1628, this person being one of his uncles, a son
of John Eyton ap Edwrd ap Roger of Bodylltyn.

12. This carnedd has been destroyed, but its site can still be recognized.

The Lloyds of Plas Madoc in Bodylltyn were for centuries resident at the house so named. Their history is set out in full in the 2nd volume of *Powys Fadog*, which has been found accurate wherever tested, so that only a few supplementary notes will here be given, together with an abbreviated sketch pedigree, necessary for purposes of reference. The first of this family to adopt the surname of 'Lloyd' was John Lloyd ap Randle ap John, who is mentioned in the surveys of 1546 and 1562, and heads the annexed pedigreee. In both cases John Lloyd ap Randle is described as holding twelve closes and a meadow, late of Llewelyn ap Ednyfed (his ancestor), no house being named. John Lloyd ap Randle was one of the two constables for the township of Ruabon in 1555.

In 1620, Edward Lloyd, grandson of the John above-mentioned, is returned as possessing in Ruabon not merely his tenement or messuage with 60 customary acres attached, but also two other tenements there, containing in all 110 (customary or over 232½ statute) acres. In 1670 Mr. Lloyd's house (Plas Madoc) was rated for seven hearths.

I have seen the draft of a mortgage dated 2 February 1727/8 between Edward Lloyd esqr., great great grandson of the Edward Lloyd of 1620 and Miss Mary Myddelton of Croes Newydd in which certain parts of his property are enumerated, namely, Plas Madoc in the township of Ruabon with its appurtenances, all the tithes of corn in the township of Cristionydd Kenrick[13], a water corn mill in Trevor issa called 'Melin y coed', a messuage and lands in Cristionydd Kenrick in the tenure of Hugh ap Reginald, and those five closes in the same township called y coed mawr, y coed bychan, erw sheet, y kae glas, and y ddol, containing 46 acres; that other messuage in Cristionydd aforesaid with two parcels of land called Tir clack, otherwise Tir calch, and cae vedwen, in the tenure of James Betton, gent[14]; three several closes in Ruabon called 'Gwerglodd y Sanney', kae ucha, and kae James issa, in the tenure of the said James Betton; that messuage and land in Cristionydd Kenrick in the tenure of Edward Kyffin; those several closes in Ruabon and Cristionydd Kenrick called 'Henvaes issa', 'y werglodd vawr', 'y Derlwyn'[15], 'Erw Sheat'[16], 'Kae brywyn', 'Tir y gath', 'yr henvaes ucha',

13. These tithes, together with those of the hamlet of Bodylltyn, were bought by the first Edward Lloyd of Plas Madoc, from Edward, Lord Wotton of Marley.

14. Described as "James Betton of Halton in the county of Denbigh, gent".

15. The 'Derlwyn' (*Oakgrove*) containing 4 customary acres, had in 1562 been held by copyhold tenure, as had 24 like acres called y wern vawr, also in Ruabon, which had been forfeited by Ieuan & Howel, sons of David Lloyd ap Madock and granted by copy 26 July 1455 to Madoc ap Llewelyn ap Ednyfed, his heirs and assigns for ever.

16. 'Erw sheat' means *Escheat land*.

'y kae hir', 'y kae bychan', 'y kae crwn', 'Gwerglodd y coed', and 'Maes y ddarwen'; those several parcels in Ruabon called 'wern ucha', 'Tir y bryn', and 'yr ...'; that house in which Rubelo Jones dwelt; that messuage in Ruabon called 'Plas Ithel'; two pieces of land there called 'Gwerglodd tan y bryn' and 'Gwern ganol', and all other messuages and lands (of the said Edward Lloyd) saving such as were excepted in an indenture of the 28 September preceding. This mortgage was doubtless executed for on 23 July 1729 Mr. Lloyd entered into a further bond of £200 with Miss Myddelton.

It is generally believed that the Plas Madoc property was mortgaged to the late Mr. George Hammond Whalley, who foreclosed in 1858. No doubt there was a mortgage, but questions arose under the will of Mr. Thomas Watkin Youde, which were submitted to the Court of Chancery, and in 1844 the property stood in the names of the trustees of Mr. J. W. Youde's will and of Mr. Whalley, *as receiver appointed by the Court*. The Plas Madoc estate was sold, Mr. Whalley offering the best price and paying off all incumbrances, so that the receiver became, about 1858, the owner and thereafter lived at Plas Madoc until his death on 8 October 1878. Mr. Whalley was an able, but narrow-minded and erratic man, best remembered as M.P. for Peterborough and as a supporter of the Tichborne claimant in whose cause he must have squandered vast sums. His own expenditure and the impecuniosities of his son, the late Captain G. H. Whalley, rendered necessary the sale after his death of the Plas Madoc property, which was purchased by the late Sir Watkin Williams-Wynn. The representatives of the ancient possessors, the Lloyd-Verneys, retain, however, the good estate of Clochfaen in Llangurig parish, Montgomeryshire. The present Plas Madoc is a large red brick house dating from about the end of the 18th century.

We now give as good an account of Plas Bennion in Bodylltyn as the imperfect original manuscripts accessible to us will allow.

The Lloyds of Plas Bennion are believed to have descended from John Lloyd ap Richard ap Llewelyn who in 1620 was a freeholder in Sutton and Cristionydd Kenrick, a leaseholder in Coed Cristionydd, and a tenant at will in Cacca Dutton, but does not appear to have owned the land on which Plas Bennion afterwards stood. Two sons of his are named, John ap John ap Richard, also calling himself 'John Lloyd' and Edward ap John ap Richard. I first find the name of the house mentioned on 28 December 1698, when "Edward Lloyd of Plas Benion, gent" was buried at Ruabon, then or shortly after in the occupation of Mr. William Lloyd, who was buried at Ruabon on 25 September 1707. A John Lloyd,

ABBREVIATED PEDIGREE OF THE LLOYDS OF PLAS MADOC, RUABON (PART I)

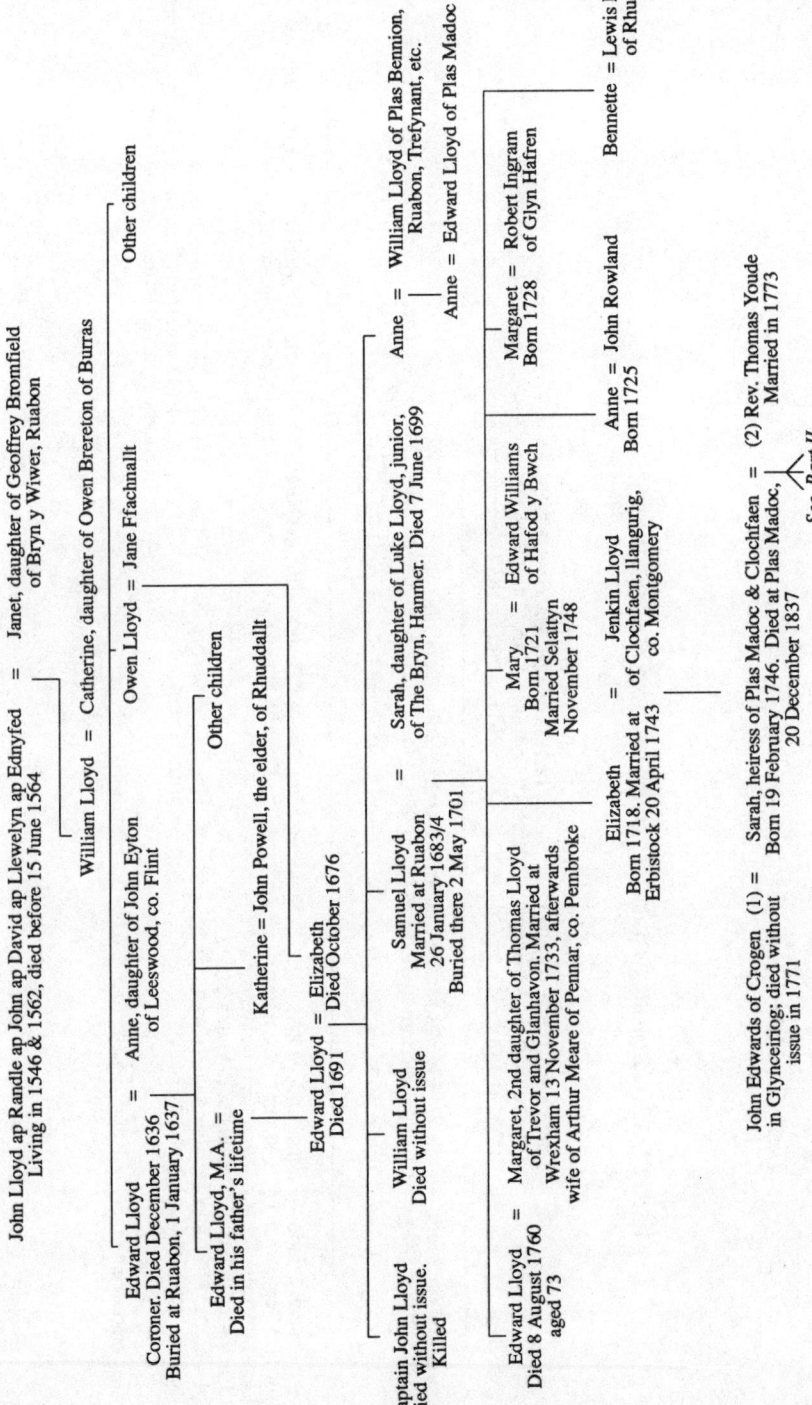

ABBREVIATED PEDIGREE OF THE LLOYDS OF PLAS MADOC, RUABON
(PART II)

John Edwards of Crogen (1) = Sarah, heiress of Plas Madoc & Clochfaen = (2) Rev. Thomas Youde
in Glynceiriog: died without   Born 19 February 1746. Died Plas Madoc,   Married in 1773
issue in 1771   20 December 1837

Thomas Watkin Youde
died unmarried 1821

Charles Madoc Youde
died unmarried 1797

Edward Youde = Mary Greenaway

Harriet
eventual sole heiress
Born 30 March 1787.
Died 24 October 1856

Sarah*   Julia Elizabeth*

Captain Jacob William Hinde
Died 1 July 1868. Lost Plas Madoc
in 1858

Jacob Youde William Hinde, M.A.
Born 20 September 1816, assumed the name of
Lloyd instead of that of Hinde and was known
as Chevalier Lloyd of Clochfaen: died unmarried
14 October 1887 leaving his estate to his niece
Mrs G. Hope Verney

Major General Charles Thomas Edward Hinde = Harriet Georgina,   other children
Died 15 May 1870   daughter of Captain Souter

Harriet Julia Morforwyn = Colonel George Hope Verney, 2nd son of Sir Harry Verney
Born 6 September 1844   of Claydon, Bucks., assumed the name of Lloyd-Verney of
Clochfaen in 1888: died 14 June 1896, aged 54

*died unmarried

also evidently of this family, married at Ruabon on 29 July 1680, Elizabeth, daughter of Edward Dymock gent. of Sontley, two of whose children, Elizabeth Lloyd and John Lloyd, are named in the will of Mr. Dymock made on 10 July 1686. These particulars are mentioned to show that the pedigree of these Lloyds given on page 13, Vol. III of *Powys Fadog* is accurate, although imperfect, and may be trusted to eke out the imperfections of our own knowledge. Who was the Edward Lloyd of Plas Bennion, dying there in 1698, is not made quite clear. But the Mr. Williams Lloyd above-named is declared to be the second son of Joseph Lloyd of Ireland (Castle Lyons, county Cork) who was the second son of John Lloyd ap Richard above named, while Edward Lloyd ap John Richard was father of the John Lloyd of Coed Cristionydd who married Elizabeth Dymock.

We now return to the Mr. William Lloyd, already mentioned, who according to the pedigree rebuilt Plas Bennion in 1685. He married Anne daughter of the Mr. Edward Lloyd of Plas Madoc who died in 1691. By his wife Anne, Mr. William Lloyd of Plas Bennion had, besides a son Edward (perhaps the Edward Lloyd whose death is recorded in 1698), two daughters, Mary (born 6 April 1687) and Anne. Mary married George Meare of Pennar, Pembrokeshire[17], and had, if not Plas Bennion itself, her share of the Plas Bennion lands, which, however, came ultimately to her younger sister Anne, who married the Mr. Edward Lloyd of Plas Madoc who died in 1760, and one of her daughters, also named Anne Lloyd, married John Rowland esq., who had purchased lands in Ruabon parish, and established the family of Rowland of Plas Bennion, Bryn, Acrefair, Delph, etc.. This Mr. John Rowland died 20 March 1803, aged 87, his wife having died on 17 December 1796 and built in her lifetime four almshouses at Nant y gwaliau. Mr. Edward Rowland, of Gardden Lodge, high sheriff for Denbighshire in 1815, who died on 6 March 1815 aged 63, was the son of Mr. John Rowland by Anne his wife.

The Plas Bennion estate turned out to be very rich in iron and coal, and the house became unfit for the abode of persons accustomed to the amenities of life, and was allowed to become ruinous. Therefore, Mr. Edward Rowland lived at Gardden Lodge. He had at least two sons, John Rowland, esq., who died on 27 May 1815, aged 28, and Edward

17. I remember noticing two or three, or perhaps more, notices relating to the Meare family in the Ruabon registers of which the following is the only relevant one copied: "Jeffrey Meare [buried] 11 November 1677".

Lloyd Rowland, esq., of the the Bryn, Ruabon, who died on 28 July 1828, aged 39, together with a daughter, Miss Anne Rowland, who endowed her grandmother's almshouses with £400, and died in 1859.

On 14 April 1825 a sale took place of Mr. Edward Lloyd Rowland's estate, made by assignees under his commission, the whole property offered in 34 lots, the description of some, taken from the catalogue, may here be summarized:-

Lot I   The freehold estate called 'Acrefair' (in Cristionydd Kenrick), containing 49A 1R 38P, with coal, ironstone, fire-clay, clerk's office and house, four stables, and sundry dwellings for workmen, a small part of the land being let on a building lease to Thomas Roberts for 48 years at 12s. a year. The Ruabon, or Acrefair, Iron Works stood on this estate, and had an easy communication by railroad with the Ellesmere and Chester canal, which was within 100 yards of Trefynant. Also the said Trefynant estate (in Cristionydd Kenrick), adjoining Acrefair, containing 103A 3R 22P, with coal, ironstone, and fire-clay, farm-house with outbuildings, detached house with garden, 1½ acres of land with lime kilns thereon, nine workmen's dwellings, two tenements with gardens and two pews in Ruabon, the land tax on both Acrefair and Trefynant being redeemed. A colliery, open on this lot, had been partially worked for supplying the iron-works, and nearly thirty pits sunk. The Acrefair iron-works comprised two blast furnaces, 43 feet high; a large double casting-house; a blast steam engine on Boulton and Watt's principle (45 horse-power, 24 inch cylinder), rolling mill steam engine (45 horse-power, 36 inch cylinder); turning lathe, etc., 16 puddling furnaces, warehouse, machinery, etc..

Lot II   The freehold estate of Plas Bennion in Bodylltyn, Ruabon, containing 71A 3R 24P, with coal, ironstone, clay, etc., the old mansion being in ruins, but there were stables (which are still used), outhouses, and some small houses yielding in rent £15 2s. 0d. yearly, and the farm was held by three yearly tenants who paid £136 yearly. Many pit shafts had been sunk, but the coal had been only partially worked, and it was estimated there was sufficient coal and iron-stone to supply two furnaces making 3750 tons of bar-iron for 30 years, and yet leave vast supplies of coal for sale, as well as iron-stone. This lot included engine and pump, railroads, and machinery.

Lot III   consisted of an engine-house in Horse block field on Plas Bennion estate and new winding and pumping engine (24 inch cylinder).

Lot IV   comprised the unexpired term of years of the iron-stone ungot under the tenement and lands called 'The Delph', adjoining the Acrefair estate, containing 52A 2R 1P, at a royalty of 25s. per dozen of 42 cwt.

Lot V contained the unexpired term of years of all seams of coal, kennel, and slack ungot under the same land called 'The Delph', a a royalty of one-sixth thereof raised, or of the value of the same, and of the further rent of ten tons of coal to be used by the lessors at a particular mansion-house. Also the right and title of Mr. Edward Lloyd Rowland in one undiverted part of all the mines, beds, and seams of coal, kennel, and slack under the lands called 'The Cheshire Tenement' (in Cristionydd Kenrick) at Plas Kynaston adjoining the Delph lands and Trefynant, containing 7A 2R 16P, held in common with two other persons under a lease, at a royalty of one sixth on coal and slack raised.

Lot VI was the term of years of all the beds and seams of iron-stone under a tenement and lands containing 23 acres in Morton Above (not named, but probably the Pant) adjoining the Delph lands under a lease of which 13 years were unexpired on 23 June 1824 at a royalty of 2s. per dozen of 42 cwt. The iron-stone was entirely ungot, but there were four coal pits open.

Lot VII was the unexpired term of years of all the coal, kennel and slack called 'The Lower Yard Coal' and all other coal there, except "the red coal and two yard coal", under the land of Mr. David Jones of ..ron (Vron?) surrounded by the Acrefair and Trefynant estates; also the unexpired term of years of the iron-stone there ungot, held under a lease of which 14 years were to run from 1 January 1825.

Lot VIII was the term of years of the iron-stone under the lands containing 33A 0R 3P of Mr. Thomas Jarvis of Cristionydd Kenrick adjoining the Acrefair, Trefynant, and Delph lands (perhaps Penbedw), whereof 85 years were unexpired on 11 March 1825.

The freehold Lots IV to VIII inclusive did not belong to the Rowlands', but we find recorded the area of the Plas Bennion estate proper (71A 3R 24P), as well as that of Acrefair and Trefynant, the portion of Anne, third daughter of Edward Lloyd of Plas Madoc, and wife of the Mr. John Rowland, who died in 1803, these three estates containing in all 225A 1R 4P.

We now resume our summary of the remaining lots of the auction catalogue of 1825, it being not quite certain which of these lots represented estates acquired by the Lloyds of Plas Madoc, by the Lloyds of Plas Bennion, or by the Rowlands themselves.

Lot IX comprised three freehold closes of arable land, containing 9A 0R 4P in Cristionydd Kenrick, surrounded by the lands of John Jones esq. (of Pen y bryn Hall) and Edward Lloyd Lloyd esq. (of Pen y lan) held by Richard Jones, whose lease expired at Lady Day, 1832.

Lot X was Pen y bryn mawr itself, a freehold estate in Cristionydd Kenrick containing a farm-house, outbuildings, and seven fields, containing 22A 2R 11P in the occupation of Richard Jones, and a pew in Ruabon church.

Lot XI was Pen y bryn bychan[18], a freehold estate in Cristionydd Kenrick, consisting of farm-house and garden, and five pieces of land containing 5A 1R 18P.

Lot XII comprised the Nant (?ucha) farm in Cristionydd Kenrick, consisting of farm-house, buildings, twelve fields, and plantations containing 37A 3R 0P, with "a valuable common right over the adjoining mountains".

Lot XIII was Tyddyn ucha farm, also in Cristionydd Kenrick with 90A 2R 4P, with "very extensive common rights belonging" thereto. The common and sheep walk adjoining the lands of Tyddyn ucha on the west are called in the map appended to the catalogue 'Nant y Croggrin'. We should read for this 'Nant y Crogfryn', especially as in 1620 there was a field in Dininlle called 'Y crogfryn nessa'r mynydd', *the crogfryn next to the mountain*.

Lot XIV was "a handsome modern stone mansion called 'Garthen' (Gardden Lodge) with 70A 0R 9P, and a pew in Ruabon church, purchased with the timber at the sale for £8121 3s. 10d.

Lot XV comprised Afon Goch house, a well built stone dwelling in Bodylltyn (but really just outside Bodylltyn, and on the border of Hafod hamlet and Morton is y clawdd township, see p. **ZZZ**) let at £20 a year, and a small house, blacksmiths shop and garden, the lot containing about an acre of land.

Lot XVI included two fields of 12A 2R 1P and two small houses and gardens in Bodylltyn, being "a detached of Garthen estate", and "a fine quarry of excellent stone" thereon, sold at the auction, with the timber, for £1311 18s. 5d.

Lot XVII was 'Morton farm in Morton below' in a ring fence, containing 93A 2R 9P, in the occupation of Mr. Richard Griffiths, sold at the auction to the third Sir Watkin Williams-Wynn for £4309 5s. 8d. [As there are three

---

18. It is to be noted that Pen y bryn mawr and Pen y bryn bychan are here to be distinguished from Pen y bryn Hall which in 1825 belonged to the Joneses of that place, who, however, may have sold already these two holdings.

'Morton' farms in Morton below Ditch of about this area, it is not quite certain which one was sold in 1825 to Sir Watkin, but I imagine it to be that generally called 'Morton Below', just north of the Cock farm, which is another of the farms just designated, and the property of Wynnstay, the third (Morton Inn) belonging to Lord Kenyon].

Lot XVIII to XXIX consisted of various houses and cottages at Ruabon, Rhos y medre, and Street Issa, and Lot XXX was the Glascoed farm (that is, the Upper Glascoed, now Glascoed Hall) in Brymbo, containing 83A 1R 19P.

Lot XXXII was a freehold estate of 7A 2R 22P called 'The Green' within a quarter of a mile of Ruabon village and close to Wynnstay Park on the right of the turnpike road to Oswestry (at the point where the road from Llangollen enters it), containing three fields of pasture and nine dwelling houses. It was in Rhuddallt, just south of Tir y fron, and is still called 'The Green'.

Lot XXXIII was a family mansion called Bryn (in Bodylltyn) on the right of the turnpike road from Wrexham to Llangollen and Oswestry containing four acres, with two pews annexed in Ruabon church. The Chevalier Lloyd habitually called this house 'Bryn y wiwair' (*Squirrel's hill*), but it is not on a hill but an absolutely flat area. However, the name 'Bryn' persists, and we must suppose that an older house on the estate actually occupied a higher position, or that a mound or tumulus was on the land. The Bryn is now being hemmed in with streets of small houses. While excavations were being carried on in connection with the sewerage here at the end of June 1900 a 'cistvaen' was discovered wherein was a red earthenware *urn* (belonging to the Bronze period) containing unburnt bones, pebbles, etc., now at the Grammar School, Ruabon. (See *Royal Commission's Report on Denbighshire*, p. 178).

Lot XXXIV was a piece of pasture called 'Cae Revel' (Cae'r efail - *smithy field*) part of the Bryn estate.

Lot XXXV was Afon Goch field containing 12A 1R 8P, part of the Gardden Lodge estate, on which there were two dwelling houses.

The information supplied by the catalogue of 1825 is important not merely because it supplies details unattainable from any other source, but because it shows that at the date named the centre of gravity of the Plas Bennion estate had shifted from the hamlet of Bodylltyn to the township of Cristionydd Kenrick and that by 1825 Mr. Edward Lloyd's freehold estate within the parish of Ruabon contained more than 600 statute acres of land. Gardden Lodge, Morton farm, the Bryn, and other outlying portions were sold at the auction and Plas Bennion, Acrefair, Trefynant, and most of the iron and coal-yielding parts passed into the possession of the British Iron Company, afterwards the *New* British Iron Company, which only ceased operations about twenty-eight years ago. Miss Anne Rowland was occupying the Nant farm in 1844 as owner.

Wynne Hall, in Bodylltyn, is the next house in this hamlet to be dealt with. Mr. William Wynn was living there in 1670 when the house was rated for three hearths. This was Captain William Wynne, one of the commissioners named in the Act for Propagating the Gospel in Wales, 22 February 1649/50, who had served on the side of the Parliament during the great civil war, and died 6 October 1692, being buried in the Dissenters' Graveyard, Rhosddu, near Wrexham, where his tombstone may still be seen. I have been quite unable to prove his paternity, but he is said to have been descended from the Wynnes of Efenechtyd, but it ought to be remembered that there is not merely *the parish* of Efenechtyd in Dyffryn Clwyd, but a farmhouse so called in the township of Cymo and parish of Llantysilio yn Yale. His daughter, Sarah Wynne, married (24 March 1694/5) the Rev. Archibald Hamilton, parish minister of Corstorphine, near Edinburgh, and, after her husband's death (30 April 1709), returned to this country with her daughter, Sarah Hamilton, the eventual heiress. Miss Sarah Hamilton married, firstly, John Taylor, gent., (who died at Wynne Hall 14 January 1720/1, and was buried at Ruabon), and, secondly (14 February 1722/3) the Rev. John Kenrick, minister of Chester Street Presbyterian Chapel, Wrexham, and so founded the family of Kenrick of Wynne Hall. It looks as though the marriages of Sarah, grand-daughter of Captain William Wynne, were arranged for her, but the second marriage, at any rate, as her note-book testifies, was a most happy one. The Rev. John Kenrick[19] died 28 January 1744/5, aged 61. His widow survived him by many years, dying at Wynne Hall in October 1775, in the 80th year of her age, "an excellent Christian", and was buried with her grandfather, mother, and husband in the Dissenters' Graveyard, Rhosddu, Wrexham. Captain Wynne had a brother, John Wynne, gent., a barrister of Wrexham and London, commonly called 'Councillor Wynne', and one of the first trustees (23 March 1697/8) of the Presbyterian Chapel, Chester Street, Wrexham. He

---

19. He was a son of Samuel Kenrick of Wrexham and Bersham.

married Mrs Elizabeth Douglas, widow, daughter and heiress apparently of Mr. Thomas Juxon, of East Sheen, and was buried at Ruabon 7 March 1714/5, leaving no children. In his will he bequeaths to his wife all his estate in the county of Suffolk and that legacy of £1000 given by Mr. Juxon after Mrs Juxon's death. He also had lands in Acton, Glyn Ceiriog, Trevor, and Trevechan, all in the county Denbigh. He speaks of his niece Hamilton, and her daughter Sarah, and of his cousin, John Kenrick - not he who afterwards married the said Sarah, but John, one of the sons of Richard Kenrick, of Woore, Salop, by Rebecca (Gethin) his wife, and one of the brothers of Andrew Kenrick, of Chester, barrister, a trustee for Matthew Henry's Chapel, Chester. Wynne Hall is a most interesting old house of which a sketch is given in my *History of the Older Nonconformity of Wrexham*, to which the reader is referred for further particulars. The Wynne Hall lands in Bodylltyn amounted in 1844 to 79 acres, and Mr. Llewelyn Kenrick, the county coroner, still lives there.

Before we discuss the various houses and estates called 'Gardden', the Gardden (Y gaer-ddin, *The camp fort*) itself, from which they all derive their names, must be described. It occupies the crown of the hill, and contains 4A 1R 4P. The camp is enclosed by a dry stone wall, of excellent workmanship for the most part, the inferior portions being due to modern repairs. On the southern side, adjoining the house of Pen y gardden, it is defended by two banks and three ditches still in fine preservation: on the eastern side the defences also are still very good, but on the western and part of the northern sides are lanes which evidently occupy the sites of the former ditches, the outer banks having being cleared away. Inside the area, which I have heard called by the prosaic name of 'Cae crwn' (*Round field*), against the southern wall, can be seen in dry weather what looks astonishingly like the remains of hut circles. A few hundred yards to the east of the camp and below it, as well as below Pen y gardden and Gardden Lodge, is Offa's Dyke. No systematic excavation of the Gardden camp, which probably belongs to the Bronze Age, has ever been attempted, but a traveller, supposed to be Sampson Erdeswicke (see Harl. MS. British Museum, 473, fol. 24) mentions it in the year 1574 as "one old moniment on a hill called the Garden, dubble trenched which might seeme to have byn a strong castell and is in Bromfeld". Pennant, in the first edition of his *Tours in Wales* (Vol. 1, p. 291, printed in 1778) says: "On my return to Rhiwabon I passed through the turnpike towards Wrexham. On the road I digressed a little to the left to visit a great *Caer* in this parish called the *Garthen* i.e. *Caer-ddin*, seated on the summit of a hill commanding a most extensive view around ... This *Caer* contains about four acres[20] of ground, is protected in some parts by one, in others with two very strong dikes and deep ditches. The inner dike is made of loose stones with the wall of vast thickness on the top. Within the area are many vestiges of buildings, the habitations of the former possessors. It lies between Offa's and Wat's dike". This account is valuable, because, among other things, it contains a reference to the "vestiges of buildings" within the camp.

A great battle is said to have been fought near the Gardden in 1167 by Owen Cyfeiliog, who composed a poem called 'Hirlas Eucin' concerning it. This battle may have been fought somewhere in Maelor about the year specified, and Gardden is actually named in the poem under the form 'Garthan', but the reference is so obscure as to be void of any historical significance.

At least four houses have taken their name from this camp, namely, Pen y gardden and Gardden Lodge, both close thereto, and Gardden Hall, somewhat remote, near the northern boundary of the hamlet and adjoining the southern hem of Morton Wallicorum. In 1784, the farm now called 'Tatham', properly 'Tatham's' on the line of Offa's Dyke, close to the camp was also called 'the Gardden' by Richard Tatham, the tenant from which it takes its present name. Moreover, the old Ruabon Foundry, a little west of the Gaer, on the other side of Afon Eitha, was sometimes described as being in the Gardden, or even as the Gardden furnace.

In the survey of 1620 "John ap John *senior* de Garthen" is mentioned as holding two tenements in Ruabon containing 20 (customary or 42$\frac{1}{2}$ statute) acres. 'John ap John senior' postulates the existence of a 'John ap John junior', that is, of a John ap John ap John, and neither his name nor that of his father appears in the pedigree printed on page 339 of Vol. II of *Powys Fadog*, where we find John ap Edward ap Ieuan ap David Goch of Gaerddin, to whose father's name is appended the date 1620, by which year Edward ap Ieuan was dead, although living in 1562, and holding then a messuage and 40 (customary) acres of land in Ruabon, which his father, Ieuan ap David Goch, had possessed in 1546. But whether it was any of the estates known as Gardden that was owned by these men is not stated although, since John ap John held the Gardden in 1620, it is quite likely that his immediate predecessors did so also.

20. This estimated area is nearly correct, but the statement that the camp lies between Offa's and Wat's Dykes is inaccurate since it stands west of both and was subsequently corrected by Pennant himself.

Let us come to facts. In the parish registers of Ruabon it is recorded that "John ap John de garethan" was buried on the 21 March 1621/2, and Elizabeth verch Thomas, his wife on the same day. It is plain therefore that the pedigree mentioned is imperfect. We can understand, however, that John ap John *junior*, died without issue, and that the Gardden estate came thus to his brother, Thomas ap John, whose son, John Thomas, died in 1690. A "Mary Thomas of Garthin in the parish of Ruabon" was married about May 1657 to John Hughes, corviser of Oswestry. The Chevalier Lloyd, who had access to the Cae Cyriog MSS. asserted that John ap John himself sold the Gardden to Griffith ap John (of Cae Cyriog) from whom it was purchased by Sir Thomas Myddleton, of Chirk Castle, knt., and in this case the Gardden which John ap John sold was that afterwards known as 'Tatham's Farm' which in 1840 still belonged to the Hon. Frederick West in right of his wife Maria, one of the three sisters and coheiresses of the Richard Myddleton, of Chirk Castle, esq., who died in 1796. But we have seen above that John ap John had in 1620 *two* tenements, one of which was probably the farm once called 'Gardden', but afterwards Tatham's, and the other, on or near the site of Gardden Hall, which his grandson, John Thomas, sold to Ellis Lloyd of Pen y lan, esqr. It is certain that Gardden Hall still belonged to the Pen y lan estate in 1844. An "Ellis Lloyd de Gardden" was buried at Ruabon 15 February 1700/1, and a "Mrs Mary Lloyd of Garthen" on 6 November 1703. It is uncertain how these two were related to Mr. Ellis Lloyd of Pen y lan, perhaps they were children of his who, having predeceased him, are otherwise unrecorded. It is however clear that some of the Lloyds did actually live at one of the houses called 'Gardden', at Gardden Hall probably, which, as we have seen, still belonged to Pen y lan in 1844. The estate contained over 81 acres, and the house previously rebuilt has recently been converted into cottages, and the land, as well as Gardden Lodge, is the property of Mr. Reuben Haigh of Pen y gardden, whose father purchased it from Sir Henry Robertson of Palé.

Gardden Lodge, which is just below the south east corner of Gardden camp, belonged to Edward Rowland, esqr., in 1814, who in that year was high sheriff of Denbighshire, and was sold along with the rest of the estate in 1825 by his son, Mr. Edward Lloyd Rowland. In 1844, Mr. Richard Briscoe (formerly of Wrexham, father of, amongst other children, the late Chancellor Briscoe) occupied and owned it and 89 acres of land that pertained thereto.

Pen y gardden, in the lands of which is the Gardden camp, belonged in the early part of the 19th century to David Parry, esqr., who was buried at Wrexham, aged 68, on 19 February 1814. He was succeeded there by Mr. John Parry, one of whose two wives was Catherine, a daughter of Mr. Edward Meredith[21], the once famous baritone singer. And Mary Parry still owned Pen y gardden in 1844, when the property contained about 60 acres.

Various mills are mentioned at different times as being in Ruabon. Thus in 1562 Richard Langford, esqr., of Allington, had a messuage there *with mill* and two gardens. In the same year, Mr. Martin Bromfield also had the site of a mill on his own lands with licence to use the waters of Dee and of Afon Cristionydd (which is the older name for the river now known as 'Afon Eitha') for serving the said mill, by copy. His son, Mr. Edward Bromfield, enjoyed the same licence. I suspect all the mills were on Afon Cristionydd, and when the water of Dee was employed it was by means of a leat. One of these, called in 1620 'ye lower mill', belonged then to Edward Eyton esq., of Watstay. The site of this as well as that of the other grain mills owned by him is probably to be sought in Wynnstay Park. But where was the uppermost mill in Ruabon, which was the property of Mr. Richard Langford in 1562? Its exact location is unrecorded but the approximate site is indicated by the name 'Mill Cottage' near Pont Adam and by the weir just below.

William Eyton, esq., had in 1562 'by copy' from the crown "le quarrell lapid" (*quarry of stones*) upon and beneath "Glasvryn and Keven y Karnedd or elsewhere within the parish of Ruaybon", and Edward Eyton, esqr., his son, had a similar licence for digging stones within the same limits, the first named copyhold grant being dated 30 August, 35 Henry VIII (1543). 'Glasfre' (*Green hill*) is the old name for what is now known as 'Ruabon Mountain' and Cefn y Garnedd was near what was afterwards known as 'Plas Kynaston', at the south western extremity of the parish on the border of that of Llangollen. By the words "elsewhere within the parish of Ruaybon" we must understand on all wastes there not owned by free tenants, or not demised to other persons.

Then in respect of iron mines, I have seen a much earlier lease of such mines from the lords of Bromfield to Robert ap Griffith ap Howell and Ieuan ap Deicws ap Deio, dated 16 June, 12 Edward IV (1472) for eight years, the lessees being granted the liberty of taking iron from upon as as well as under the land from the ditch called "Claughwad (that is 'Clawddwad' or Wat's Dyke) to the mountain of Glasffrey (Glasfre) in the parish of Ruyabon" at a yearly rent of 3s. 4d. Clawdd Wad and

21. Mr. Edward Meredith was buried at Marchwiel, 26 December 1809.

Glasfre represent practically and severally the eastern and western boundaries of the parish. The terms of the lease are most absolute, but here again we must make the same reservations as before, reservations which were quite understood at the time, that the lease related to such waste lands as were at the disposal of the lord. The free tenants certainly enjoyed the minerals under and upon their own lands, and it is doubtful whether the tenants at will, still less the copyholders, would be disturbed, under a short lease, or under any lease, while the mines on the waste remained unexhausted. My chief interest in the lease is that Wat's Dyke is mentioned therein as a well-recognized boundary, better than the eastern limit of the parish, with which it did not exactly coincide.

We have mentioned Mr. Martin Bromfield, undoubtedly a Welsh gentleman of standing, the baptism of many of whose children is recorded in the Ruabon registers, but not the baptism of his eldest son and successor, Mr. Edward Bromfield, because those registers begin too

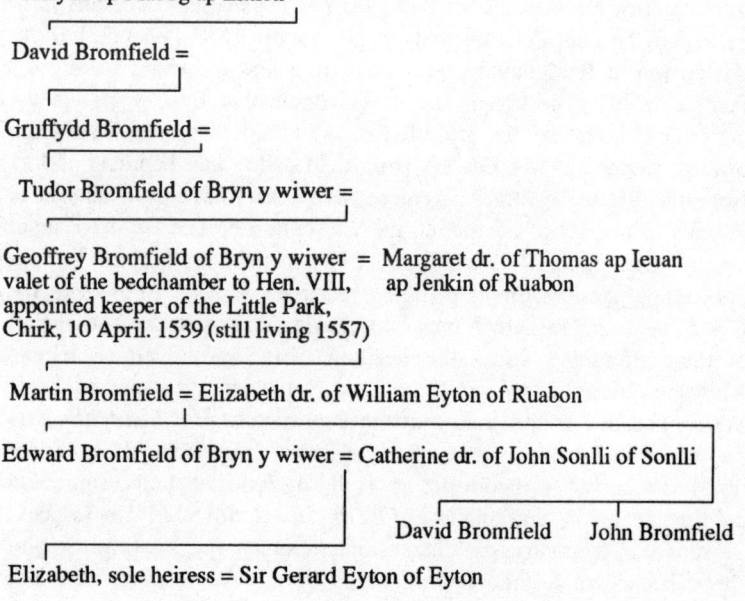

Gruffydd ap Madog ap Einion =

David Bromfield =

Gruffydd Bromfield =

Tudor Bromfield of Bryn y wiwer =

Geoffrey Bromfield of Bryn y wiwer = Margaret dr. of Thomas ap Ieuan
valet of the bedchamber to Hen. VIII, ap Jenkin of Ruabon
appointed keeper of the Little Park,
Chirk, 10 April. 1539 (still living 1557)

Martin Bromfield = Elizabeth dr. of William Eyton of Ruabon

Edward Bromfield of Bryn y wiwer = Catherine dr. of John Sonlli of Sonlli

David Bromfield   John Bromfield

Elizabeth, sole heiress = Sir Gerard Eyton of Eyton

late for such an entry. However, in two deeds seen by me this Edward Bromfield speaks of his father, Martin Bromfield, and of his wife Catherine. Mr. Edward Bromfield was buried at Ruabon 23 February 1640/1 his wife 'Mrs Katherine Bromfield' having been there buried on the 9 January preceeding. It was this Edward Bromfield apparently who acquired Bryn y wiwer (The Bryn) in Bodylltyn, Ruabon, for in 1614 he is described as of Morton Wallicorum, and never, as we shall see presently, Ruabon township. In *Powys Fadog* (Vol. II, p. 328) nevertheless, the Bromfields are described as having been long settled at Bryn y wiwer, according to the abbreviated pedigree above.

Now, as a matter of fact, Martin Bromfield did not hold any free lands in Ruabon in 1562, and was not therefore in possession of The Bryn. His son, Edward Bromfield, did not own much more than a statute acre of free land in the township in 1620, and this land did not include the Bryn. But he did then possess, as a freeholder, a capital messuage and 50 (customary or 105³/4 statute) acres in the township of Morton Wallecorum, not owned by his father in 1562; a messuage in Eyton, county Denbigh, and six parcels there containing 40 (customary or over 84¹/2 statute) acres, a messuage in Cristionydd Kenrick of nearly 40 statute acres, and various scattered leasehold pieces. To all this has to be added the consideration that on 30 August 1630 (see p.22) Bryn y wiwer was a field having quillets in it, some of which belonged to Pentreclawdd. The conclusion is inevitable that Bryn y wiwer, as a house and home of the Bromfields, could not have been built until towards the end of Mr. Edward Bromfield's life (died February 1640/1). Nevertheless, the pedigree is correct as far as I have been able to test it, save in respect of antedating the possession of The Bryn by anyone bearing the name of 'Bromfield'. The same remark must be made concerning the Bromfield pedigree as given in *Llyfr Silin* (see *Arch. Camb.* 1889, p.240) which began to be compiled in 1645. The pedigree is there presented under the heading "Bryn y Wiwair; Maelor yn Rhiwabon", so that we must conclude that by the year named Bryn y Wiwer had become the home of the Bromfields. But *Llyfr Silin* raises another point in the section which begins: "*John Bromffild* ap Edward ap Martin ap Sieffre Bromffild ap Tudor ap Gruffydd" etc.. I have such confidence in the compilation of *Llyfr Silin*, particularly in respect of persons contemporary, or almost contemporary, that we must suppose the existence of a John Bromfield of Bryn y Wiwer, son of Edward Bromfield; if we can trust the *Powys Fadog* pedigree, which states that his sister Elizabeth, Lady Eyton (who died in 1642) was her father's heir, it is necessary to imagine that John Bromfield died without issue. It is also important to distinguish between two or three persons bearing the same name. A "John Bromfield of Cristionydd Kenrick, gent.," for example, was living on 17 February 1656/7, and a Mr. John Bromfield was one of the two head constables for the hundred of Bromfield in 1671.

While speaking of this family it may be added that Martin Bromfield had, in 1562, "half a gavel of land" called 'Tyre hova ap Eignion' as a copyhold tenant of Ruabon.

I have left to the last the discussion of the township-name - 'Ruabon'. It is generally derived from 'Rhiw Fabon', *The slope of Mabon,* 'Mabon' being the old Welsh Apollo and also a personal name.   And this derivation strikes one as very probable, and has as evidence in its favour that in the valor of 1291, *as printed,* the parish appears under the denomination 'Rywnabon', where the first 'n' is almost certainly to be read 'u', that is 'v', now generally represented in Welsh spelling by 'f', which is pronounced exactly like the English 'v'.   But one is bound to add that elsewhere, in the earlier surveys, ministers' accounts, and deeds examined by me, the township is almost always called 'Ruabon' or 'Ruaybon'.   The form 'Rhuabon' occurs in 1340 and 'Ruavon' in the *Valor Ecclesiasticus* of Henry VIII (1535), as well as 'Ruabon'.

CHAPTER II

𝕯𝖎𝖓𝖎𝖓𝖑𝖑𝖊 𝕴𝖘𝖘𝖆

It is necessary to preface our formal account of this township by some preliminary remarks. First, as to the name. All the earliest forms of it, except one (to be noted hereafter) are 'Dynulle', 'Dynille', and 'Dynuthley', the first two whereof are found again and again in deeds, surveys, etc., of the 14th and 15th centuries, and even sporadically in documents as late as the 16th and 17th centuries. In its unextended form, it was often written 'Dynlle', without any mark or abbreviation, or 'Dynull', but occasionally the notes of abbreviation are given so that we get 'Dynlle' or 'Dynull'. There seems but little doubt, therefore, as to what the mediaeval pronunciation was. But as early as the 16th[1] century the name had taken to itself a second 'n', giving rise to such spellings as 'Dyninlley', 'Denynlley', or even on one occasion 'Dunningley'. But, towards the beginning of the 17th century the form 'Dinhinlle'[2] (with an intrusive 'h') arose, which gradually established itself, and is now the common spelling, meaning, when written 'Dinhunlle', *Fort of nightmare*. For my part I refuse to bow down to the pseudo-etymologists and prefer to say 'Dininlle', which, it must be understood, is a word of three syllables. The meaning of 'Dininlle' or of 'Dinille', is difficult to explain, but, perhaps, some personal name is involved.

There was for many centuries, a *manor* of Dininlle, which took its name from the township now under consideration, there being then no township called 'Dininlle Ucha'. This manor included the greater part of Dininlle, the greater part of Cristionydd Fechan (now known as 'Dinhinlle ucha') with detached areas elsewhere. Many areas of Dininlle township did not belong to the manor bearing the same name, but formed

---

1. There is one instance, so early as 1397, of the spelling 'denynthley', but it stands alone, and did not 'catch on' for more than two hundred years.

2. The oldest example I have yet met with of 'Dininlle' spelt with this objectionable 'h' is in the will of William ap John David (dated 26 May 1637) who describes himself as of "Dinhinley", while Roger Meeson in his will (proved 3 June 1689) speaks of his lands "in Dinynlley", where he lived, using practically the oldest form of the name, which was then evidently not forgotten.

part of the manors of Iscoed, Fabrorum, Morton, Ruabon, etc.. Keeping this fact in mind, let us try to visualize the topography of Dininlle township as it was in the beginning of the 16th century. In the midst, between the road leading from Ruabon to Erbistock down to the Dee, southwards, was Dininlle Park. The greater part of the western strip of the township was occupied by the village or 'pentre', still so called, with its fields in severalty, while in the strip to the east of Dininlle Park lay the land held in gafaels or in semi-tribal holding.

It seems necessary to re-iterate the statement that whenever, in early deeds or surveys, 'Dininlle', or any form of that name, is spoken of, we are to understand what is now known as 'Dinhinlle Issa' (*Lower Dinhinlle*), and that no *Upper* township in the parish of Ruabon or lordship of Bromfield, was called 'Dinhinlle Ucha'. The truth is that the greater portion of Cristionydd Fechan being annexed to the *Manor* of Dininlle, the whole township gradually, after the beginning of the 17th century, lost its old name, and came to be called 'Dininlle Ucha', although separated from the head of the manor by the whole width of the large township of Ruabon.

Whatever the true form of the name 'Dininlle', it contains the component 'din' or *fort*. According to the reasoning just set forth, we must seek for it in Dininlle Issa. No trace, however, of any such *din* has yet been found, and certainly the two adjoining fields called 'Cae ty castle' and 'Lower Castle field' do not supply any clue for they formerly belonged to and took their name from Chirk Castle.

Let us now proceed to deal with Parc Dininlle or Dininlle Park, doubtless one of the princely 'reserves' of the Princes of Powys Fadog. The earliest year, however, in which I have found it mentioned is in 1388-9 (Minister's Accounts, Bromfield and Yale 1234/5) when 137 perches of paling were fixed around the park of 'dynunhle', and measured by the chief forester. On 31 December 1397, Thomas del Green was appointed park keeper of "denynthley in Bromfield" for life. In 1472 and 1473 the *villata* or community of the township held the park of 'Dynull' at farm by yearly rent of 18s and still so held it in 1479 and 1480. In the 21st year of Henry VII, Thomas Whitwode was custodian of the park under the crown, and in 1518 Morgan Davy, at a yearly salary of £3 0s. 10d. In Tidderley's survey of Bromfield, taken about the year 1546, we get the following quaint, but vauable, description of this ancient enclosure:-

"The prke of Dynulle ys a seu'all Wodedy grownde beyng two

miles Abowte & di [3], & Encloseyd withe hedge and diche on the one side and the great Ryvor of ... on the oder side the same beying a courte [covert] grownde When yn ys miche ffaire & great Tymber the moste p'te of olde okes to be prscruyd for the mayntence of the kyngs castelle yn those p'tes. The Tymber & Wode theryn lytell worthe to be solde for that the same Stondythe ffer from onye Towne in a Woddye cuntrey & the Ways Ile [ill] to cary the same. The said Grownde withe the arbage [herbage] thereof lett by copye of Courte roll to one [blank] for XXI yeres for the yerely rent xxiiis iiiid."

In 1562, Martin Bromfield and Madoc ap David had the herbage and pannage of the same park, with all rights, profits, and commodities, so to them leased for 21 years by letters patent dated 29 June, 6 Elizabeth (1564) at 30s. a year rent. The park was therefore then intact. It was afterwards leased by the crown to Sir Nicholas Fortescue, knight, who apparently disparked it. His lease was still enduring in 1620, when it contained by estimation 272 (customary or 575$\frac{1}{4}$ statute) acres, divided into fields or closes, some whereof bore such names as 'Y Ferne', 'y lawnt', 'Gwastad y parke', 'y ddole Rydy Kyrw' (Dol Rhyd y Ceirw - *Meadow of the hart's ford*), 'pke John ap Edw' (*Park of John ap Edward*) and the like. And we can today almost trace the boundaries of the old park by existing field-names - 'Lawnt', 'Lower back park', 'Park gwair', 'Park', 'Lower Park', 'Upper Park', and so on. Then there is the Park farm, but the various holdings called 'Coed-leoedd' (*Wood places* or *wood houses*) were not within the park although adjacent to it.

The four gafaels of native land in Dininlle manor mentioned in the survey of 23 Henry VII, all, or most, lay, I believe, within the limits of the township now being described. Their names were 'Gafael Asser', 'Gafael Meilir ap Trahaiarn', 'Gafael Seisyllt', and 'Gafael Rhiwallon'. Two of them were held in several portions, but none had left any trace by the time the survey of 4th Elizabeth, 1562, unless we find it in the place name of 'y wythfed' (*the eighth*, in the sense of *the eighth part*), a name which still persists. "John Wynne o'r Wyddfyd" was buried at Ruabon, 31 March 1631/2.

One of the customs of servile origin to which the tenants of Dininlle manor were subject in 1472 is thus described in *Ministers' Accounts* 1235, 11 under "pannage of pigs": each bondsman having three pigs or

---

3. That is 'dimidium' - *half*, two and a half miles in circuit.

more, the lords should take the better pig, and if having less than three, the tenant should give the lord 2d for every pig. Yet, during this very year the villata rented Dininlle park, so that only 5d. was then due to the lords for pannage.

The pentref, or village, of Dininlle (Issa) is of old date. Gardd y pentre, a farm now existing therein, being mentioned under that name in 1562.

In the same year a copy was quoted of a licence granted, 21 March 1553/4, to John Wynne ap Sir Mathew, to build a water mill on 'Erew dadyr' with freedom to make a water course of the Dee or of any other river there to serve the said mill. In 1620, the jurors reported that this mill was "decayed and fallen downe", and that Mr. Cornelius Manley was then the holder of the copy or lease.

The name 'Pen y lan', and the designation of a large estate in Dininlle Issa does not occur in any of the great surveys. But a holding afterwards absorbed in the Pen y lan estate is duly named in 1620. It contained 18 (customary or 38 statute) acres, and was then copyhold of William David ap Ieuan Lloyd and of Edward (Williams) his son, which 'Edward ap William ap dd ap Ieuan Lloyd' was buried at Ruabon 4 November 1620. He was survived by a son, William Williams, gent., of Hafod House in Esclusham, who married Mary Lloyd the heiress of Pen y lan, according to the pedigree hereto annexed. Ellis Lloyd, esqr., brother of Eubule Lloyd, and of William Lloyd, bishop of Norwich, was in possession of Pen y lan in 1670, when the house was rated to hearth tax for four hearths. He is said[4] to have come into possession of it through his wife, Elizabeth, daughter of Edward ap William ap John ap David, and was buried at Ruabon 10 July, 1712, leaving no issue and being a benefactor to the parishes of Ruabon and Erbistock.

I have seen the will of Mr. Ellis Lloyd's brother, Eubule Lloyd, made on 28 November 1689, proved on 27 April 1703, wherein he describes himself as of "Eglwys Eagle" county Denbigh, speaks of his son John Lloyd, and of his daughters Mary, Julian and Susan Lloyd. The Mary Lloyd, daughter of Eubule Lloyd just mentioned, became owner of Pen y lan on the death of her uncle Ellis Lloyd in 1712, married William

---

4. *Powys Fadog*, Vol II, pp.391 & 394. But, according to the will of this William ap John David (made 26 May 1637, proved 4 January 1637/8) had many children and a married son, Edward ap William. William ap John David had a tenement and land in 'Dinhinley' purchased by him, called Bron i Pursse (Bron y pwrs) together with four parcels of land in Erowe i gwr Lloidd (Erw'r gwr Lloyd) which he left to his daughter Jane vz William, until his son Edward should pay her £40, and, after such payment, to the said Edward. His daughter, Elizabeth, was wife of Edward ap Thomas, and had children.

Williams, gent., of Hafod House, Esclusham, and had at least two sons, Eubule (who was baptized at Wrexham 18 March 1697/8) and Edward. Mr. Eubule Williams, alias Lloyd, married and had children, who left no issue. In 1758, on the death of Miss Margaret Lloyd, the estate passed to her uncle, Edward Williams, who also took the surname of Lloyd, and left a daughter Mary, who married Mr. Roger Kenyon. When Mrs Roger Kenyon died in 1781, her eldest son, Mr. Edward Lloyd Kenyon, became owner of Pen y lan. He died on 9 July 1843, aged 28, and the estate (which included Gardden Hall in Bodylltyn, see p.45), at the time of the 1844 tithe survey, contained in Dininlle, as well as the extensive park belonging to Pen y lan, the Home farm, The Graig, Lower farm, Tyddyn ucha, Bryn Llewenydd and other holdings comprising in Dininlle Issa alone nearly 900 acres. It is believed that Mr. Ellis Lloyd purchased freely, and in 1715, his successor, Mr. Eubule Lloyd, then under age, was estimated to have an income of £700 a year.

In 1844, all the Pen y lan estate was held by the Rev. Henry William Marker of Aylesbeare, county Devon, trustee under the will of the late Edward Lloyd Kenyon esqr., for the benefit of Miss Kenyon, and the greater part of the estate was sold to the late Mr. Edward Hardcastle esqr., M.P. from whom, or from whose executors or heirs, it was purchased by Peter Ormerod esqr., the present owner.

Bryn Llewenydd is the name of a farmhouse within the area in Dininlle Issa, now called simply 'The Bryn', which requires some special name to distinguish it from the other area in Ruabon township (hamlet of Bodylltyn) also now known simply as 'The Bryn', the full name of which is said to have been formerly 'Bryn y wiwer'.

There was in 1620 a moor or 'greene' in this township called 'Rhos John ap Madoc', which name as designating the farmhouse and enclosed fields that occupied its site, still survived in 1767, when Roger Meeson occupied the excellent tenement there. To this family of Meeson belonged Roger Meeson, the well-known barrister, joint author of Meeson and Welsby's *Exchequer Reports*, who died in 1852, and was buried in Overton, county Flint, and Alfred Meeson of London, the eminent civil engineer and architect (b. 1808, d. 1885). The name 'Rhos John ap Madoc' has now been shortened to 'Rhos Madock'.

Attached to the manor of Isycoed[5], but within the township of Dininlle ("infra oppidu' de Dynynlle") was an estate, belonging to Mr. John Eyton, of 57 (customary or 120$\frac{1}{2}$ statute) acres, comprising two

---

5. Annexed to Isycoed because it was a free estate, while the normal holdings of Dininlle were servile.

ABBREVIATED PEDIGREE OF LLOYDS OF PEN Y LAN, DININLLE ISSA

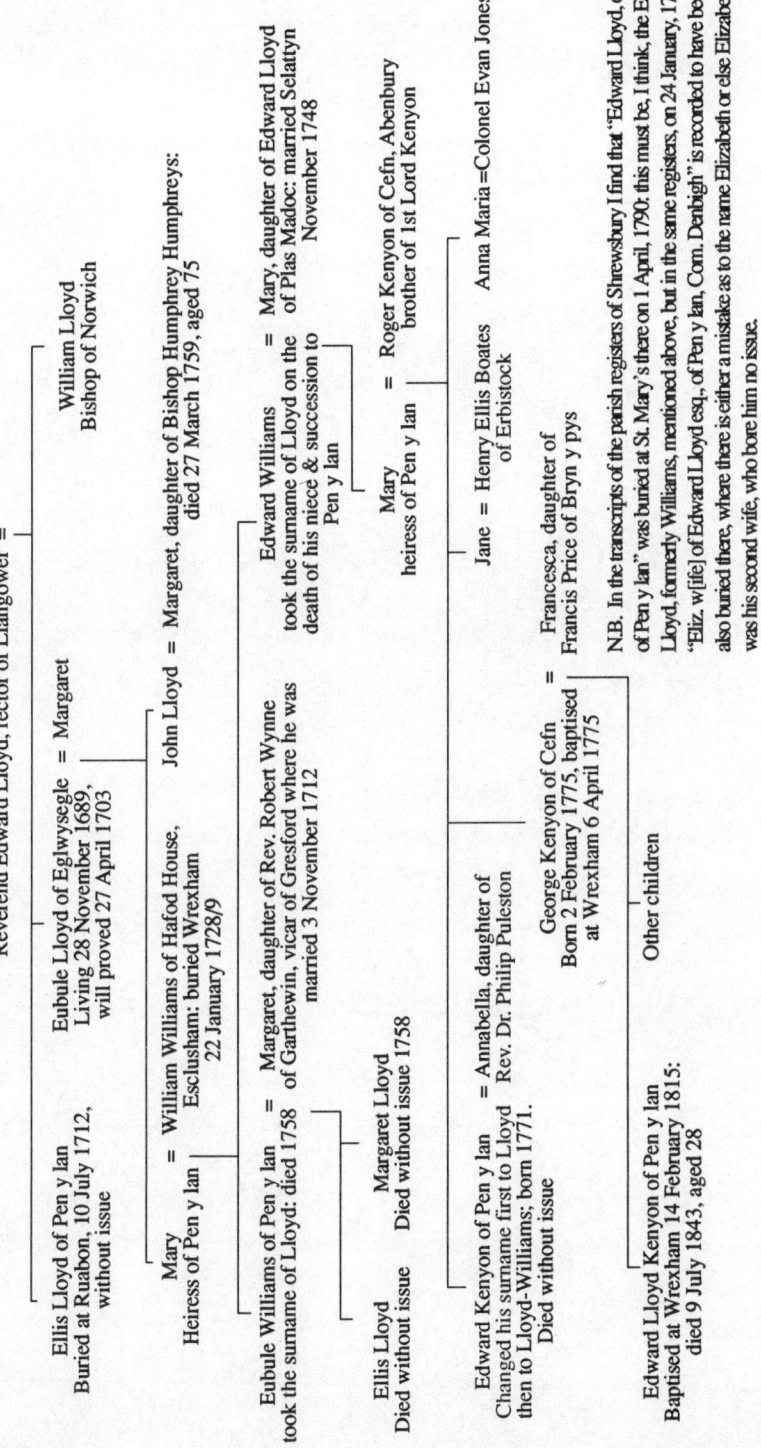

Reverend Edward Lloyd, rector of Llangower =

Eubule Lloyd of Eglwysegle = Margaret

William Lloyd Bishop of Norwich

Ellis Lloyd of Pen y lan Buried at Ruabon, 10 July 1712, without issue

Mary = William Williams of Hafod House, Heiress of Pen y lan Esclusham: buried Wrexham 22 January 1728/9

John Lloyd = Margaret, daughter of Bishop Humphrey Humphreys: died 27 March 1759, aged 75

Mary, daughter of Edward Lloyd of Plas Madoc: married Selattyn November 1748

Eubule Williams of Pen y lan = Margaret, daughter of Rev. Robert Wynne took the surname of Lloyd: died 1758 of Garthewin, vicar of Gresford where he was married 3 November 1712

Edward Williams = took the surname of Lloyd on the death of his niece & succession to Pen y lan

Mary = Roger Kenyon of Cefn, Abenbury heiress of Pen y lan brother of 1st Lord Kenyon

Anna Maria = Colonel Evan Jones

Ellis Lloyd Died without issue 1758

Margaret Lloyd Died without issue

Jane = Henry Ellis Boates of Erbistock

Edward Kenyon of Pen y lan = Annabella, daughter of Changed his surname first to Lloyd Rev. Dr. Philip Puleston then to Lloyd-Williams; born 1771. Died without issue

George Kenyon of Cefn = Francesca, daughter of Born 2 February 1775, baptised Francis Price of Bryn y pys at Wrexham 6 April 1775

Other children

Edward Lloyd Kenyon of Pen y lan Baptised at Wrexham 14 February 1815: died 9 July 1843, aged 28

N.B. In the transcripts of the parish registers of Shrewsbury I find that "Edward Lloyd, esq, of Pen y lan" was buried at St. Mary's there on 1 April, 1790: this must be, I think, the Edward Lloyd, formerly Williams, mentioned above, but in the same registers, on 24 January, 1785, "Eliz, w[ife] of Edward Lloyd esq, of Pen y lan, Com. Denbigh" is recorded to have been also buried there, where there is either a mistake as to the name Elizabeth or else Elizabeth was his second wife, who bore him no issue.

messuages and 28 closes, all the names of which are given in the survey. The most interesting of these may be quoted:- 'Capell Kollen' (Capel Collen *Collen's chapel*), 'Errow armon' (which can mean nothing but *Garmon's erw* or *acre*), and 'Erw Kapel Kwmpas', which we may possibly correct to 'Erw o gwmpas y capel' (*Acre around the chapel*). The names of other fields on this holding were: 'Erw'r gwr Lloyd', 'Kay y gogridd' (Cae'r gogrydd *sieve maker's field*) and 'Kay y gwas newydd' (*field of the new servant*).   But I am particularly interested in Capel Collen, concerning which Edward Lhuyd, writing about 1697, says:- "They call a field where is a cross in Ruabon parish Kappel Kolhen". Now not merely has all trace of this chapel disappeared, but not a single one of the twenty eight field names remains, unless we suppose 'Cae'r groes newydd', which is on the home farm of Pen y lan, to represent 'Kay y gwas newydd' of 1620, or the cross named by Edward Lhuyd as standing on or near the site of Capel Collen.   And there is, not far from Cae'r groes newydd, a little north west of Crab Row, a field called 'Cae Gosper', that is, the *field of vespers*, or *of evensong*, which may preserve some reminiscence of Capel Collen, all tradition of which has been lost with the rapid Anglicizing of the district which has occurred during the last 150 years.

There were two holdings called 'Y Coedleoedd' (*The Woodhouses*)in Dininlle Issa, but although geographically in that township, manorially one of them, then tenented by Hugh ap John ap Edward, was at the time of the survey of 1562 in Morton is y clawdd, and the other in Dininlle manor, was a leasehold tenement of $11\frac{1}{2}$ acres, occupied in 1620 by Thomas ap Edward. At a later date, Matthew ap Rondle ap Edward ap Meredith held the last-named as a freeholder having probably purchased it from the commissioners of James I. His son, John Matthews, a man of some importance, squandered his estate. He lived in Wrexham, his Dininlle house having only one hearth in it. His death is recorded in the Ruabon register thus : "John Matthews, nuper Quaestor panicia de Wrexam sepult' fuit 10 mo die February 1691/2". His wife, Anne, daughter of John Williams, was buried at Ruabon on 24 April 1700. The name 'Coedleodd' in this township is very old for in 1391 "Ieuan ap Madoc duy de Coidlath" in 'Dunninlle' is mentioned.

CHAPTER III

Township of Dininlle Ucha, alias Cristionydd Fechan

There were not in 1620, nor for some years after that date, two townships in Ruabon parish known as 'Dininlle' so that when the township of Dininlle was spoken of, what is now known as 'Dininlle Issa' was meant. The township which is the subject of this chapter, Dininlle Ucha, went by the name of Cristionydd Fechan, of which we still have reminiscences in 'Trefechan', 'Pentre Cristionydd', 'Afon Cristionydd', 'Cristionydd Farm' and 'Cristionydd Mill' but the name 'Dininlle Ucha' does not occur in Norden's Survey of 1620. On the 10 May 1628, Robert Sontley of Sontley, esqr., the younger, sold to Kenrick Edisbury of Marchwiel esqr., and to Edward ap John Robert of Bedwell, yeoman, a cottage, five parcels of land (each called 'kae Eignion') and "a clausure called Maes y Neyodd" (Maes y Neuadd) which Robert Sontley had purchased from the Crown on 22 June 1627, all lying together in "xionedd vechan in the manor of Dynulle". Here the old name is in full use and no Dininlle ucha hinted at. But this extract confirms the explanation already given of the origin of the new name for the township. The greater part of Cristionydd Fechan belonged to the *manor* of Dininlle, and as, with the decay of the manorial courts, holders of the land in Cristionydd Fechan found themselves described in their deeds or 'copies' as tenants of Dininlle, the new name of 'Dininlle *ucha*' was coined to avoid confusion, and make their titles clear.

In 1670, among the list of townships of Bromfield, rated for hearth-tax, is "Trevechan *or* Denynlle ucha". In that year the only person in the township who had more than one hearth in his house was Robert Wynne of Plasdy - called inaccurately in the ordnance map 'Plas du' (*Black-hall*) whereas 'Plasdy' means '*Hall-house*'. Until the great sales by the Crown in the time of James I (after 27 January 1624/5) the tenants of Cristionydd Fechan were either copyholders or 'at will', and accordingly we find that in 1620 only that portion[1] of Robert Wynne's holding which was in the adjoining township of Cristionydd Kenrick and in the manor of Esclusham, was freehold, the rest being absolutely "at the will of the lord". And yet, personally, Robert Wynne was free, being Robert ap Richard ap John Wynn, and a member of the great Puleston family. He probably subsequently purchased from the Crown his lands 'at will' in Cristionydd Fechan, for at a later date all his estate there was wholly at his own disposition. On 17 February 1656/7 Robert Wynne, of Cristionydd Fechan, gent., granted to John Bromfield of Cristionydd Kenrick, gent., and to John Edisbury, of Marchwiel, gent., that capital messuage in Cristionydd Fechan, wherein he lived, and those parcels appurtenant thereto called "Cae ffynnon vair, Maes Lledan (llydan) varl, yr erw brys (in 1620 called 'yr erw bys'), Erw gug, Erw goed, y grogfryn mawr, y grogfryn llwyd" and "y vraithwen" all in Cristionydd Fechan, and two parcels in Cristionydd Kenrick called severally 'y Plasty mawr ucha' and 'y Plasty mawr issa' in trust to certain uses, so that John Wynne, the second son of the said Robert, might enjoy the same capital messuage and closes until Matthew Wynne, Ellen Wynne and Jane Wynne, other children of the said Robert Wynne, should receive their full portions of £40 each, with the proviso that if Robert Wynne, junior, the eldest son, should, after the decease of his father pay to his brother, John Wynne aforesaid, £240, and also the three several names sums of £240 each, the said premises should stand to the behoof of Robert Wynne, the younger.

On 25 February 1669/70 Robert Wynne paid his brother, John Wynne "of Denynlle ucha", the money stipulated who then released the premises. The father, Robert Wynne, the elder, must by that date have been dead, and what became of Robert Wynne, the younger, I do not know, unless he was the Captain Robert Wynne of Maes Mochnant who was buried at Ruabon, 13 July 1717, a suggestion somewhat improbable. However, the point that I wish to insist upon as brought out by the two deeds just summarised is that Mr. Robert Wynne ap Richard, at the beginning of the historical year 1657, called the township in which he dwelled 'Cristionydd Fechan' (or rather 'Christionydd vechan') while his son, John Wynne, at the beginning of 1670, described himself as of 'Denynlley ucha'. We note in short the period during which the new name ousted the old.

Let us now go back to Mr. Robert Wynne the elder (or 'ap Richard').

1. This portion was a parcel of seven customary acres called 'y plasdy mawr'.

On 1 May 1635, he mortgaged two of his fields called 'Tir y Trowsbren' and 'Gwerglodd yr ackre' for £40 to Jane Hughes, spinster, one of the Llanerchrugog Hall family, afterwards of the parish of St. Giles in the Fields, Middlesex, which sum his son Robert Wynne repaid on 15 September 1673.   In 1700, Richard Wynne, gent., was settled in Trefechan and, on 9 July of that year, mortgaged for £40 the close called 'Plasdy mawr ucha' in the township of Crisitonydd Kenrick to Hugh Davies of Esclusham, smith.   He had mortgaged it on 12 May in the year preceding to William Edwards "of Dynnynlle ucha ... milner".

It does not seem possible to carry down any later the history of the Wynnes of Plasdy, but we can trace back their pedigree to an earlier date, giving therewith some interesting information.   In 1620, Robert ap Richard Wynn, whom we have called 'Robert Wynne the elder', had, as a tenant at will of the manor of Dininlle, a messuage, barn, garden, orchard, curtilage, and various pieces of lands[2] some of which are mentioned in the deeds summarised above, and survive to the present day.   Here are the most interesting of them: 'Erw y groe'" (*Acre of the cross*), 'Kae fynnon vair' (*Mary's well field*), 'Maes lledan varle' (Maes llydan marl - *Broad marl field*), 'Yr Erw bys' (wrongly given in the printed copy as 'Erw lys'), 'Y Crogfryn mawr' (*the big gallows hill*), 'y crogfryn llwyd' (*the grey gallows hill*) and a piece of land in Erw Evrog (*Efrog's acre*).   We have already seen that in 1700 one of the closes was known as 'Tir y trawsbren' (*land of the cross tree*).   In 1562, Edward ap Howel ap Edward, great grandfather of Robert Wynne, the elder, held these lands at will in Cristionydd Fechan, and was succeeded four years later, as we learn from a marginal note in the survey, by his son, John (Wynne), and Howel ap Edward of Cristionydd, according to the pedigree at Gwysaney, was a son of Madoc Puleston.   John Wynne will be again mentioned in Chapter V, when we come to speak of Plas issa, his chief house in Cristionydd Kenrick.   Until lately Plasdy still kept traces of its old dignity, but has been partly rebuilt and reduced in size, and by the roadside near the house is the spring - 'Ffynnon Fair' (*Mary's Well*) which is fairly copious.

The other farms in Dininlle ucha are Pant glas, Tai Nant, Hill farm, Y Groes, Yew Tree farm, etc., but I have nothing especially interesting to say concerning them.   And Cristionydd Mill has already been mentioned.

The names of some of the fields of the township, besides those

2. Containing 15¾ customary acres, which with the seven free acres called 'Plasdy mawr' in Cristionydd Kenrick would equal over 44 statute acres.

already designated, seem much more important. 'Cae tan y garnedd', mentioned in 1620, is perhaps represented by, or near to, the close numbered 158 in the tithe map schedule, and therein called 'Cae Carneg': it is on the extreme north of the township, a little south west of Onen Fawr in Morton Wallicorum, but I have never been able to examine it. Another interesting field name in the same schedule is 'Dryll y ddinas' (*the fort patch*) which I once visited but found nothing there worthy of note: moreover, the name is believed to be a misreading of Dryll y ddimai (*the half-penny patch*), a well-attested name here. The three fields called 'Grogfryn' are to the west of Dryll y ddimai, Crogfryn ucha being on the western boundary of the township adjoining the mountain, this part of which was described on an 1825 map as 'Nant y crogrryn (crogfryn) Common' near Pant Glas, on the northern bank of the Afon Cristionydd is a close called 'The helt', an obsolete Cheshire word for a low lying river-side meadow.

CHAPTER IV

Township of Coed Cristionydd

Coed Cristionydd (*Cristionydd Wood*) is a small township which, during the mediaeval epoch, was mostly servile in its tenure, and was a detached member of Manerium Fabrorum (*Manor of the Smiths*) of which more will be said hereafter under Morton Anglicorum, the nucleus of the manor.

In 1670 there was only one person in Coed Cristionydd who had more than one hearth. This was Mrs Dorothy Lloyd, widow, who had also five hearths in two vacant houses in Ruabon township. She was the widow of Edward Lloyd, son of John Lloyd ap Richard (see pp.36) sprung from the same stock as the Lloyds of Plas Bennion. The John Lloyd who married, in 1680, Elizabeth Dymock of Sontley, was one of her sons. The Lloyds of Coed Cristionydd probably lived at Ty Mawr or at Bod Llwyd close to it.

Cefn Bychan, Cefn Station, and Newbridge are all in Coed Cristionydd, but no more seems necessary to be said concerning this township.

CHAPTER V

Township of Cristionydd Kenrick

Coed Cristionydd and Cristionydd Fechan (or Dininlle ucha) were servile townships in mediaeval times. Cristionydd Kenrick, on the other hand, contained many freehold estates and was in the manor or ringildry of Esclusham.

Incidentally, when describing the Plas Bennion property in Bodylltyn, a great deal has been said concerning various holdings in Cristionydd Kenrick which belonged to the Rowlands of Plas Bennion.

In the southern part of the township is the populous village of Cefn Mawr, and in the northern part that of Pen y cae which extends into Dininlle Ucha, while Rhos y medre is on the southern part of the western boundary. Today, the greater part of the township is occupied by iron-works, collieries, brick works, or by the ghastly remnants of such industrial operations but some genuine farm-houses still survive.

In 1562, John Sonlley of Sonlley (now Sontley) by right of his wife, Katherine verch David Lloyd ap John, had a capital messuage here, Plas Ucha, with 300 (customary or 634½ statute) acres, which descended to their son, Robert Sonlley, esqr., and to his successors. David Lloyd was one of the great Puleston family of Bers, his great grandfather, father of Edward Puleston, being Madoc Puleston of that place. John Puleston, father of David Lloyd, was living at Cristionydd in 1500. As Katherine, one of this David Lloyd's daughters, carried Plas Ucha in Cristionydd Kenrick and lands and tenements in Marchwiel, to John Sonlley, so Elizabeth, another daughter, carried Plas Issa in the same township to the John Wynn ap Edward ap Howel Puleston mentioned under Plasdy in Cristionydd Fechan. A third daughter, Elen[1] was, it is said, the wife of Richard Tegin of Bron deg in Esclusham. Plas Ucha is noted in *Powys Fadog* as having been sold to Sir Watkin Williams-Wynn after the disposal of the estate of the Hills, who were the representatives of the Sontleys, but in 1844, it belonged, with 155 acres of land attached,

---

1. If so, she must have been Serjeant Richard Tegin's *first* wife, for I have seen the will of his widow, dated December 1578, proved 7 June 1582, wherein she calls herself "Angharet vz Sr. Mathew".

to the Hon. George Kenyon.

There would seem to have been no fewer than four holdings, each called 'Pen y bryn' (*Top of the hill*) in Cristionydd Kenrick. Two of these, 'Pen y bryn mawr' and 'Pen y bryn bychan', have already been accounted for as forming in 1825 part of the great estate of the Rowlands of Plas Bennion and Gardden Lodge. Pen y bryn Hall, representing the largest of the four, was rather a good and well appointed house when I saw it some twenty five years ago, and had excellent gardens and shrubberies. It was formerly the seat of the Joneses of Pen y bryn, from whom it was sold in 1841 by decree of Chancery in the suit "John Jones versus John Maddock Jones". Over 92$\frac{1}{2}$ acres were then attached to the house, as well as the farm, containing 60 acres, in Cristionydd Kenrick called 'Scybor ucha' (Ysgubor ucha - *Higher barn*) and another farm of 11 acres called 'Bryn y barcut' (*The kite hill*) in Bodylltyn (Ruabon township). The first of the Joneses of Pen y bryn to permanently adopt that surname was Randle Jones son of John ap Edward (alias John Edwards) ap John ap Randle[2] of Pen y bryn. This Randle Jones, who was an attorney at law, recorder of Bromfield and Yale, and agent to the Wynnstay estate, married, firstly, at Erbistock, on 21 February 1703/4, Elizabeth Wynn, one of the illegitimate daughters of Sir John Wynn of Wynnstay by whom he had, besides his eldest son John Jones, six other sons. He married secondly Martha, a daughter of Captain Thomas Jones of Willow House, Wrexham. The Major John Maddock Jones, in whose time the Pen y bryn property was alienated, was the great grandson (son of John Jones, son of John Jones, son of the aforesaid Randle Jones)[3] of the Randle Jones above-named and one of his sisters, Eleanor, became the wife of the Rev. Canon William Williams, of Ysceifiog, whose son, the Rev. William Maddock Williams, rector of Llanfechain, died there in 1883.

But the largest house in Cristionydd Kenrick in 1670, when it was rated to hearth-tax for seven hearths, was that of Mr. Roger Kynaston -

2. This Randle was living in 1620, when he was called "Rondle ap John [ap] David [ap] Llewelyn", and had a tenement and 20 customary acres in Cristionydd Kenrick, and his grandfather was probably the David ap Llewelyn ap John of Cristionydd Kenrick named in 1562.

3. Randle Jones, attorney, of Pen y bryn, died 25 July 1754, aged 63. One of his sons, Thomas Jones (bapt. 5 November 1709) afterwards resided at Plas Newydd, Ruabon, and was still living on 31 December 1777 when he made his will, wherein he mentions his son Rev. Robert Jones, his brother, Robert Jones, and his brother Randle Jones. This Randle Jones, the younger, lived at The Bryn, Ruabon, and died 27 December 1807, aged 70: in his last will he mentions his nephew Richard Lovett (of Belmont, Shropshire) and John Rowlands and Edward Lloyd Rowland, but exactly how these three were nephews to him, I cannot discover.

Plas Kynaston. After the indulgence of 1672 Mr. Roger Kynaston's house in Ruabon (parish) was licensed for Independent worship, Mr. Philip Rogers being also licensed as the preacher there. The Mr. Roger Kynaston just-named must have been the son of Mr. John Kynaston who, on 6 October 1653, was one of the justices of the peace for the Ruabon district, and attended at the quarter sessions for Denbigh on 14 July 1648, Mr. John Kynaston being the son of Roger Kynaston, attorney at the court of the Marches at Ludlow, who married one of the daughters and co-heiresses of Roger Eyton (a son of Edward Eyton of Bodylltyn) of Cristionydd Kenrick, whose house there is said to have been known as 'Cefn y Garnedd'. One of the Kynastons rebuilt this house and called it 'Plas Kynaston'. A 'Roger Kynaston' was buried at Ruabon on 24 July 1641 and a later Roger, eldest son of Mr. John Kynaston, died without issue. The estate, which extended into Coed Cristionydd, passed to his brother Humphrey, who was recorded as living on 13 April 1694, whose sole surviving child, Martha, by marriage with Mr. William Mostyn (son of the Rev. John Mostyn and grandson of Archdeacon William Mostyn of Brymbo and elsewhere) carried it into the Mostyn family, who still owned Plas Kynaston at the end of the 18th century, but, by 1844, it belonged to the Wynnstay property. The estate is now devastated by collieries and spoil heaps. Roger Eyton, one of whose daughters married Roger Kynaston, the attorney, of Ludlow, had in 1620 two tenements and three consolidated holdings in Cristionydd Kenrick, containing 72 (customary or 152¼ statute) acres.[4]

The following are the names of the other larger holders in this township rated for hearth-tax in 1670, with the number of hearths attached:- John ap John (5); William Preese, gent. (4); Mrs Jane Heina (3); and Mary Gervis, David Shone, and Lady Midleton (2 each). Not one of the holdings represented by these names can I identify with certainty.

'Cefn y fedw', the name of the free estate long owned by a family surnamed 'Lloyd' is probably that now called 'Penbedw' (*Top of the birchwood*) in Cristionydd sold to one of the Myddeltons of Chirk Castle and still owned in 1844 by the Hon. Frederick West. Alas, there are no birches at Penbedw now.

A great deal of evidence exists of a family belonging to Cristionydd Kenrick who adopted the surname of 'Morton', doubtless from the adjoining township of Morton Wallicorum, but whose beginning, ending,

4. The present Plas Kynaston is a large red brick building, the front faced with stone and having stone foundations, dating apparently from the latter end of the 18th century.

or exact habitat, in spite of much trouble taken, I have hitherto been quite unable to discover with complete certainty.[5]   Thomas, son of Thomas Morton, gent., of Cristionydd, was baptized at Ruabon, 8 March 1678/9.   Thomas Morton, the elder, went to live in Hope Street, Wrexham, where he died, being buried at Ruabon 4 January 1702/3, when he was designated "esquire". His son, under the name of "Thos. Morton of ye parish of Ruabon, Gentleman", was married at Gresford, 4 July 1706, to Anne, one of the daughters of Kenrick Eyton, of Wrexham, gent. (son of Sir Kenrick Eyton of Eyton), and they had two sons, Thomas, who was baptized at Ruabon, 6 August 1707, and Edward, baptized at Wrexham, 16 July 1708. The wife of Thomas Morton was, perhaps, the "Anne Morton of Wrexham" who was buried at Gresford, 7 July 1727. There was also a Mrs Morton of Cristionydd buried at Ruabon 20 September 1710. A 'Mrs Anne Morton' was married at Wrexham on 9 October 1724 to Thomas Kenrick, gent., of Liverpool. Later on, a Thomas Moreton, clerk, is mentioned in connection with an estate in Cristionydd Kenrick for which by 1794 Edward Eyton esq., of Eyton, paid, as owner, the land tax.[6] Since there is so much obscurity concerning this family and their estate the particulars just given may be found useful. In the Appendix to this chapter something more will be said concerning a possible ancestor of these Mortons.

We have seen, under Bodylltyn, that in 1825 Mr. Edward Lloyd Rowland had a lease of the ironstone upon the Delph estate, and in *Powys Fadog* (Vol. III, p. 123) there is a pedigree of the family of "Bady of Plas yn y Delff" in the parish of Ruabon which I can confirm to some extent. "Owen Badie gen." was buried at Ruabon 7 May 1632, who, according to the same authority, sold Plas yn y Delff to Sir Thomas Myddelton. He was living in 1620, when he had a capital messuage and 40 customary acres in Morton Wallicorum and two other messuages whereto pertained 32 customary acres, or 152 statute acres in all, holding at lease in the same township 15 customary acres of escheat land. Furthermore in the same year he had a capital messuage and 160 (customary or nearly 338½ statute) acres in the manor of Esclusham which, it must be remembered, included the township of Cristionydd Kenrick, and therefore must have possessed much more than what is

5. I venture to suggest Cristionydd Hall as the seat of these Mortons. It was built in 1616.

6. There was an Anne Deacon, wife of Philip Morton, who was buried in Ruabon, 28 December 1624, "Martyn Morton" having been there buried 29 July 1615, and Philip Morton on 3 October 1615.

now known as The Delph farm in the township just named. According to *Powys Fadog*, Owen Bady was son of Roger Bady and grandson of Robert Bady. But it would seem that Owen, or his father, was the first to assume the surname of 'Bady', for I have seen the will of Owen Bady's grandfather who was living at Ruabon in 1566 and called Robert ap John ap David ap Ieuan ap Badye. This will was dated 25 November 1601 and proved on 10 July 1605. Therein the testator speaks of his daughters Elizabeth vz Robert, Maeode vz Robert, Alez vz Robert; of his eldest son, Roger ap Robert, and his other sons William ap Robert, David Lloyd alias David ap Robert, and Edward ap Robert. To David Lloyd, his son, he bequeaths that messuage in Esclusham wherein Thomas ap John Wynne dwelled, and to Edward ap Robert, his son, that messuage and lands in Esclusham, wherein 'John david' dwelled. He does not specify where the house which he occupied was, but merely describes himself as of the parish of Wrexham. The baptism of his daughter Margaret is recorded (10 May 1566) in the Ruabon registers in this form: "Margaret vz Robert ap John ap dd ap Ieuan ap bady". About the year 1815, the Delph farm, Cristionydd Kenrick, was owned by Kenrick Edward Eyton esqr., of Eyton, county Denbigh.

I have seen also another will relating to the township now under review, that of John ap Edward ap Rice, of the parish of Ruabon, dated 13 April 1587, and proved the following September. The testator speaks of his wife, Margaret vz Ieuan, of Griffith ap John, his son and heir, and of Elizabeth vz John, his daughter. He refers to his lands in Cristionydd Kenrick and elsewhere, but does not give the name of his tenement there. A Griffith ap John ap Edward, perhaps his son, was a free tenant of Cristionydd Kenrick in 1620, holding there 18 (customary or 38 statute) acres.

As to 'Rhos y medre', it was already known by that name, which I cannot explain, in 1794. And there seems nothing, worth noting, to add to what has already been said concerning the Acrefair and Trefynant estates.

'Cristionydd' can mean nothing else than the territory of one called 'Cristion'. But it is curious to note that during the mediaeval epoch two of the townships so named should have been occupied in servile tenure, the third only (Cristionydd Kenrick) being free, and still more curious that each one of the three should have belonged to a separate manor.

APPENDIX TO CHAPTER V

Morton Family

It is perhaps possible to trace this Morton family further back although there is an unfortunate gap, which prevents one bridging the gulf, or connecting the earlier with the latter members thereof. On 2 January 1556, Robert ap Jankyn Morton, of Marchwiel, gent., ensealed a long Latin charter in which he conveyed all his lands, tenements, reversions, and rents to feoffees in trust, especially that three closes (cae newydd ucha, cae newydd issa and y gwasgardir) in the township of 'Marghwiell' should stand seized by the feoffees to the use of Joan vz Robert, his daughter *and heir* and afterwards to the use of the lawful heirs of the said Joan and her intended husband, David ap Robert ap Howel ap David ap Griffith, and if the said David and Joan should die without lawful issue, the feoffees were to remain seized of the three closes named until Robert ap Jankyn Morton should pay one hundred marks within the parish church of Marchweil to Robert ap Howel (father of the said David ap Robert). Whereupon the feoffees were to be seized of all the feoffer's lands, etc., to the use of Robert ap Jankyn Morton for life, then to the use of the lawful issue of marriage of the said David ap Robert and Jane vz Robert, or, in defect, to the rightful heirs of the said Robert ap Jankyn, the feoffor. The marriage provided for in this charter of 1556, of which no account is given in the pedigree on page 381 Vol. II of *Powys Fadog*, duly took place and there was issue of it three sons, each of whom adopted a surname connected from the personal name of their great grandfather, namely, John Powell, alias John ap David ap Robert ap Howel, of Tyddyn Gôch, Marchwiel, living in 1621, Robert Powell of the parish of St. Andrew, Holborn, living in 1613, dead by 1621, and James Powell of Marchwiel, living in 1621. Robert ap Jankyn Morton was still alive in 1562 as were his two brothers, John ap Jankyn Morton (who had daughters only) and Griffith ap Jankyn Morton, who, besides certain escheat land held in co-parcenary with his two brothers in Marchwiel, occupied with Philip Lloyd, in right of Katherine vz Thomas, various leasehold lands in the manor of Fabrorum and parish of Ruabon. This Griffith ap Jankyn Morton may possibly have been the ancestor of the Mortons of Cristionydd Kenrick, although the connection, if it existed, cannot at present be proved.

CHAPTER VI

𝔗𝔬𝔴𝔫𝔰𝔥𝔦𝔭 𝔬𝔣 𝔐𝔬𝔯𝔱𝔬𝔫 𝔚𝔞𝔩𝔩𝔦𝔠𝔬𝔯𝔲𝔪

This township is now more commonly called 'Morton Above' or, in Welsh, 'Morton uwch y clawdd' (*Morton above the dyke*). The 'clawdd' indicated in the Welsh name being Offa's Dyke, which forms the eastern boundary of the township.

Morton Wallicorum was during the mediaeval period mainly in the occupation of free tenants, and in the manor of Eglwysegle, while the other two Mortons in Ruabon parish were distinguished by the servility of their tenure, and belonged to other manors.

'Morton' means *Moor-town*, and postulates the existence of a great moor. This moor was the 'rhos', once very extensive, called 'Rhos llanerchrugog' (*Moor of the heatherly glade*), the name at present of a large mining village adjoining on one side of the village of Ponkey ('Ponciau' - *Banks*), and on the other that of Johnstown. Where heather abounded, so would also broom (banadl), and I have often wondered whether the great upland plain was not the feature in the wide tract of diversified country which won for the latter in the first English period (ending about A.D. 1100) the name of 'Bromfield', a designation persisting through the second Welsh period (ending in 1282) and conferring a title on the great lordship marcher so called. This is a suggestion merely thrown out for consideration, but the fact of three adjoining 'Morton' townships is worth noting as indicative of the great extent of the moor. In Bromfield was also Bromhurst (Broom-coppice), the exact locality whereof I do not know, but in the accounts of the lord of Bromfield's receiver from the eve of Michaelmas 1388 to the eve of Michaelmas in the year following, it appears that, during the period covered by those accounts, Einion Gam, the groom, went, with five of the lord's stallions, to Bromhurst, "p' jument ib'm salt'" from Michaelmas 1388 to the 5 of April following, taking for his wages 2d. a day, and that he came from Bromhurst (to Mersley Park apparently) on the 24 July 1389, with four stallions, from which day last-named until Michaelmas 1389, he was paid for 66 days also at 2d. a day.

When, in genealogies and other documents compiled by those Welshmen ignorant of the district, "Burton, county Denbigh" is mentioned, it is sometimes our Morton which is meant. 'Burton' was often written 'Bourton' or even 'Borton'. We have only to assume, quite naturally and probably, that the name 'Treforton' (*Morton township*) had been used by the Welsh people, and there would be nothing then to show, so far as strangers were concerned, whether the radical form of the township name was 'Morton' or 'Borton'. Actually, in the survey of 1562 Edward ap Randall is returned as holding freely a messuage and five closes of 30 acres "in Burton *alias* Moreton Wallicor". But other instances of similar confusion between the two names would be given from the 16th century genealogists.

One of the largest estates formed in this township, after the breaking up of the system of gavelkind, was that of Llanerchrugog, and Hugh ap John ap Ieuan ap Deicws, of Llanerchrugog, was party to a deed dated 16 November 1556, showing the substantial accuracy of the pedigree assigned by genealogists to this family. In the survey of 1562, this same Hugh ap John is described as holding in Morton a messuage and 100 (customary or $211^1/2$ statute) acres of land, while in the survey of 1620 the heir of Richard Hughes (grandson of the said Hugh ap John) is mentioned as possessing in this township, a capital messuage, five tenements, two cottages and 250 (customary or $528^3/4$ statute) acres. It should be said that John, son of Hugh ap John of Llanerchrugog, called himself 'John Hugh', as appears, for example, in his prenuptial agreement, dated 10 January 1551/2, according to which John Hugh was to marry 'Gwenhouer' (Gwenhwyfar) daughter of John Erthig (of Erddig), while his sister 'Katerin vch Hugh' was to marry 'Edward Erthyge', son and heir of the said John Erthig. John Hugh's two sons adopted 'Hughes' as a settled surname, and the grand-daughter of the second of these sons, Parnel Hughes, married Mr. John Payne, whose grand-daughter married Mr. William Higgons, the daughter and heir of whom bequeathed Llanerchrugog Hall to Mr. William Jones, a cousin. But it would be better to show what is really known of the family in the form of a short pedigree. I remember the hall, with a small park attached in the ownership of Mr. Thomas Jones, who lost it by mortgage, and afterwards purchased Plas yn Eglwysegle, alias Plas ucha in Eglwysegle. He was baptised at Wrexham, 16 April 1819, and died in 1894, bequeathing his Eglwysegle estate, itself heavily burdened, to Mrs Willington, the wife of his friend and physician, who sold it to the present Sir H. Ll. Williams-Wynn of Wynnstay. He was a most able, but

ABBREVIATED SKETCH PEDIGREE OF THE JONES FAMILY OF LLANERCHRUGOG

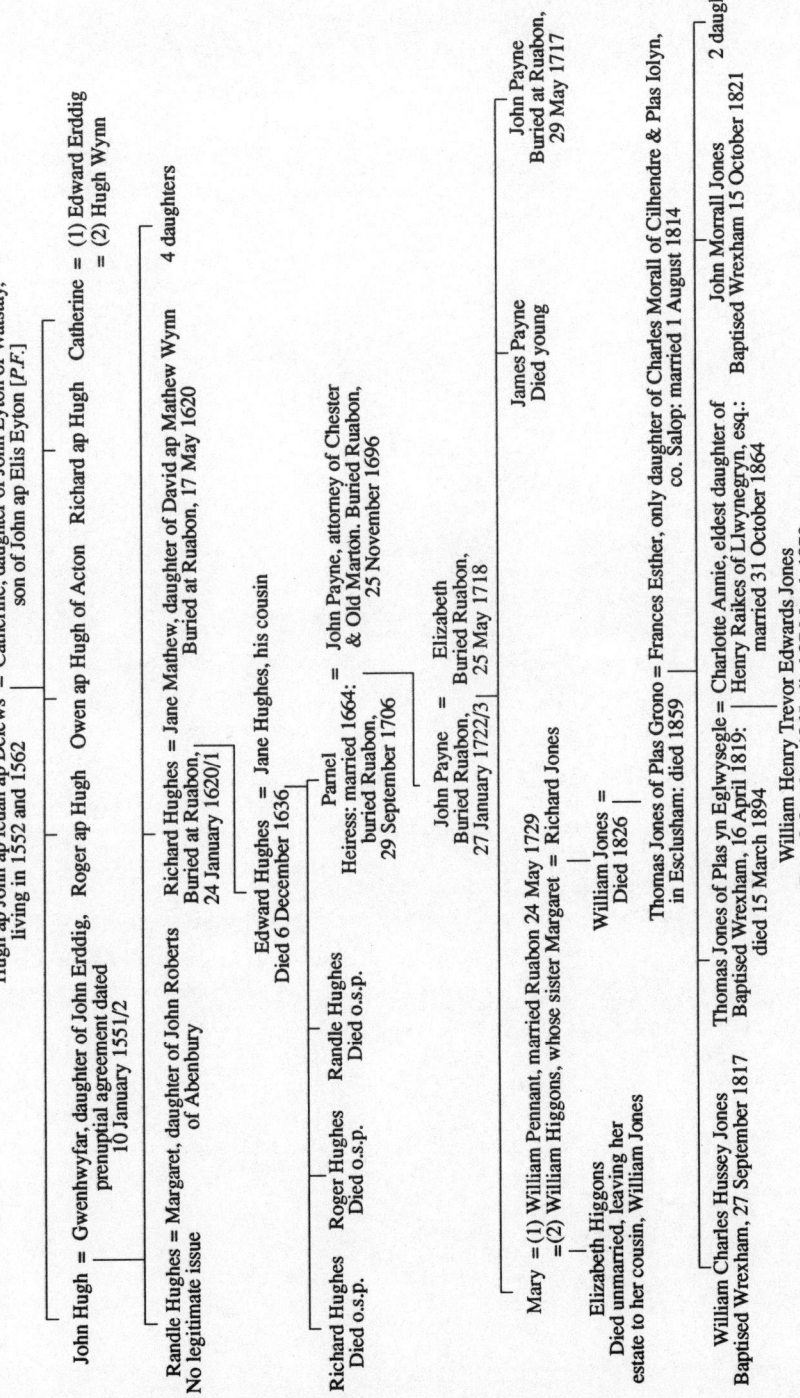

eccentric man, and wrote, among other pamphlets, a quasi-historical treatise on Eglwysegle.

The Mr. Thomas Jones just-named was the second son of his father, who bore the same name. Mr. Thomas Jones, the elder, lived for many years at Plas Grono, near Wrexham, and was busily engaged for many years in all sorts of industrial enterprises, having blast-furnaces and brick-works at Llwyn Enion in Esclusham, besides works at Pant and Aberderfyn in Morton Wallicorum, and leasing for a time the Bersham Iron Works also. His father, Mr. William Jones, is described on 1 July 1796 as "an iron-master" and living at 'Plas Gardden' (Gardden Hall), Ruabon. While Mr. Thomas Jones, the younger, lived at Llanerchrugog Hall, about 100 acres of land were appurtenant to it.

It is impossible to say with certainty which house represented Llanerchrugog Hall in the hearth-tax return for 1670, as the hall was then let to a tenant, whose name is not known. And it is important to point out that, against all precedent, in the return for the aforesaid year the two distinct townships of Morton uwch y clawdd and Morton is y clawdd are treated as one, under the designation of Morton Wallicorum.

Let us now return to the earlier Hughes of Llanerchrugog, who had already begun to diminish their heritage. On 22 June 1626, Edward Hughes, gent., leased for 21 years to John ap John Goch that messuage and those lands then held by the said John, yielding as rent £10 a year and "twoe fatt hens against the feast of Christmas and alsoe twoe daies reaping" (at harvest), but shortly after, on the 23 Novemebr of the same year, sold this tenement with its appurtenances to Kenrick Edisbury, then of Deptford Strand. The names of the eight closes belonging to the farm were given in the deed of sale, of which only two need be quoted - 'y dalwern' and 'Gawirglodd y dalwern',[1] and on the same 22 June 1626 Mr. Edward Hughes sold to Mr. Kenrick Edisbury another tenement with eight fields in the same township, and apparently in the western and upper part of it.

The Hugheses of Llanerchrugog had also very extensive lands in Esclusham, wherein, among other houses, they owned Ty mawr.

It is known that the Sontleys of Sontley had a good house and estate in Morton Wallicorum. On Aug 20, 1550, Robert ap Robert Wyn ap Morgan of Sontley, the father of John Sontley, describes himself as of 'Mortyn Wallicorum', and while old Mr. Robert Sontley (the son of John Sontley) lived at Plas Sonlley (Old Sontley in Marchwiel parish) his son,

---

1. In 1844, a meadow in Morton Wallicorum, owned by the Hon. Frederick West, was called "Gwerglodd dalwern eithaf".

also called Robert Sontley, had a seperate establishment in Morton, so that a deed of 30 September 1625 begins thus:- "Robert Sonlley, [2] the elder, of Sonlley, esquier, Robert Sonlley, the younger of Morton Wallicor' and Robert Sonlley, gent., son and heir apparent of said Robert Sonlley, the younger". In other deeds the estate of the Sontleys in Morton Wallicorum is mentioned, but I have tried in vain to identify it. This is the more remarkable as it turns out that the lands attached to it were very extensive. Thus, in the survey of 1562, 'John Sonlle' is returned as possessing a tenement and 300 (customary or 634$\frac{1}{2}$ statute) acres in Morton Wallicorum formerly of 'Rs ap lln' (Rhys ap Llewelyn). And in the survey of 1620 Robert Sonlley esqr., is declared to have 294 customary acres annexed to his tenement in that township, as well as 16 other such acres, so that the holding of the Sontleys, according to this authority amounted to 655$\frac{1}{2}$ statute acres in Morton Wallicorum alone. But in neither of these surveys is the name of the capital messuage given, nor are the names of the several fields thereto quoted. It is believed that the second Sir Watkin Williams-Wynn bought the Sontley lands in this township about the year 1780, but the Wynnstay estate has no such area belonging to it in Morton Wallicorum as that above indicated. A partial explanation of the problem thus presented is supplied by the Crown Rent Book of 1794 whereupon it appears that the property of the late Mrs Matilda Hill (the representative and descendant of the Sontleys) within the parish of Ruabon lay mainly in other townships of that period, especially in Cristionydd Kenrick and Dininlle Ucha (where was Plas Ucha), as well as in Morton is y clawdd and Ruabon manor. All these or most of these, were supposed to be attached to and lie in Morton Wallicorum where the chief house was. The large acreage above mentioned becomes thus intelligible and possible. But what was the name of the capital messuage of the Sontleys, and afterwards of the Hills, in Morton Wallicorum? This question has hitherto been found unanswerable. It was the unnamed house, rated at five hearths in 1670 for which Mrs Elizabeth Hill (a mistake perhaps for Mrs Anne Hill daughter and heir of the late Mr. Robert Sontley) was then charged. A large part of the township has during the last century been wasted by grievous disfigurements, and tradition is silent or speaks with uncertain voice.

New Sontley Hall, within the precincts of the present Erddig Park,

2. The members of this family, after they ahd adopted a surname. \spelled that name always at first "Sonlley", but afterwards, towards the end of the second quarter of the 17th century, used the modern spelling "Sontley".

Sketch Pedigree of the Sontleys

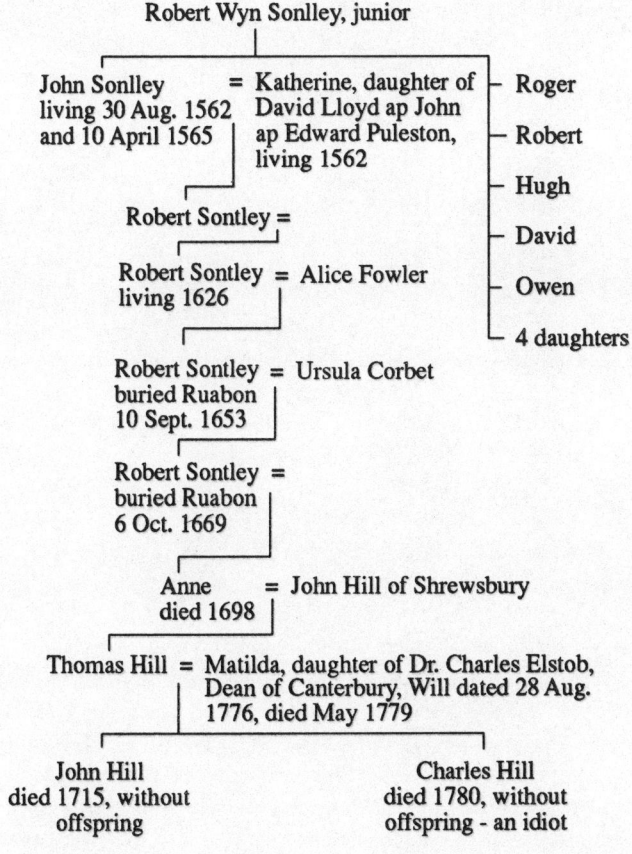

Robert Wyn ap Morgan, alias Robert Sonlley, living 1506 and 1519

Robert Wyn Sonlley, junior

John Sonlley = Katherine, daughter of — Roger
living 30 Aug. 1562   David Lloyd ap John
and 10 April 1565   ap Edward Puleston, — Robert
living 1562
— Hugh

Robert Sontley = — David

Robert Sontley = Alice Fowler — Owen
living 1626
— 4 daughters

Robert Sontley = Ursula Corbet
buried Ruabon
10 Sept. 1653

Robert Sontley =
buried Ruabon
6 Oct. 1669

Anne = John Hill of Shrewsbury
died 1698

Thomas Hill = Matilda, daughter of Dr. Charles Elstob,
Dean of Canterbury, Will dated 28 Aug.
1776, died May 1779

John Hill   Charles Hill
died 1715, without   died 1780, without
offspring   offspring - an idiot

was sold between 1759 and 1766 by Mrs Matilda Hill to Mr. David Roberts, but it seems probable that the greater part of the Sontley estates were not disposed of until long after, probably until both Mrs Hill and her son Charles had died.

In 1562, John Berse, alias John ap John ap William ap Howel, had divers parcels of land in Morton Wallicorum, containing 15 customary acres. This fact is here mentioned so as to establish the identity of John Berse with John ap John ap William of Bersham whose wife, Angharad vz Sir Mathew, subsequently married Richard Tegin esq., of Morton Wallicorum, serjeant at arms, as can be proved by her will. John ap William of Bersham, whose sons took the surname of 'Berse', was living in 1545, and his daughter, Elizabeth, was the wife of Owen ap Hugh, one of the younger sons of Hugh ap Ieuan ap Deicws of Llanerchrugog.

In 1562, John ap David Lloyd ap Deicws had a capital messuage, three tenements and 150 (customary or $317^{1}/4$ statute) acres of land in Morton Wallicorum, together with other lands there, and William ap David Lloyd, his brother, had four tenements and 50 customary acres within the manor of Eglwysegle whereof Morton Wallicorum was a part. And in 1620 the grandsons of the twin brothers, Thomas Lloyd of Plas uwch y clawdd and Robert Lloyd "of Ruabon" were each in possession of a very large estate in Morton Wallicorum and in the townships adjacent. Let us remember the names of the men just mentioned as living in 1620, while we endeavour to identify their holdings and trace their several descents, referring in all cases of uncertainty to the accompanying pedigree, which is based on *Powys Fadog* (Vol. II, p.399, & Vol. III p.55) augmented by information furnished by documents seen by me or kindly supplied by Mr. W. M. Myddelton.

We will begin with Robert Lloyd, described by Norden as being of Ruabon, but by *Powys Fadog* as being "of Plas y Bada"[3], Morton is y clawdd, a name which should possibly be corrected to 'Plas Badi', but which, to date, I have failed to find in any deed or survey. Robert Lloyd was the grandson of the John ap David Lloyd of 1562, and the son of John Wyn Lloyd (described in the Ruabon registers as "John Wyn Lloyd ap John dd Lloyd ap dic ap madoc ap Ithell"). Mr. Robert Lloyd had in 1620 a capital messuage and lands in Morton Wallicorum extending into the townships of Ruabon and Esclusham containing 343 customary acres and a little later had another messuage, formerly of Edward Davies,

3. We can understand why Mr. Robert Lloyd is described as "of Ruabon" since he had a tenement and 16 customary acres of land there which his great grandfather also held, not belonging, however, to the manor of Ruabon, but to that of Isycoed.

with 20 customary acres of land in the same township. These would amount to 790 statute acres. In 1620, he also had 48 leasehold acres in Morton Anglicorum, but no estate is attributed to him by Norden in Morton is y clawdd. Yet, we know that when a little before 1660 he sold all his property in Ruabon parish to the second Sir Thomas Myddelton, of Chirk Castle, knight, he possessed in the township last named a tenement on the site of which Sir Thomas built a handsome new house for his son Charles Myddelton, the present 'New Hall'. The name and site of his capital messuage in Morton Wallicorum remain undiscovered, but he appears to have lived in Ruabon township, where he was a tenant to Mr. Evan Lloyd of Yale, besides having a tenement of his own there.

As to the Thomas Lloyd of 1620, above named, his capital messuage of Plas uwch y clawdd in Morton Wallicorum is now represented by the farmhouse sadly defaced and deteriorated, known as 'Plas yn clawdd'.[4] In 1620, Mr. Thomas Lloyd had a capital messuage and 120 customary acres in Morton Wallicorum, four other messuages there with over 36 such acres, Chamber Wen in Esclusham and another tenement there of 20 customary acres and a tenement in the township of Ruabon with 48 acres, making in all more than 224 (customary or about 474 statute) acres. John Lloyd, the son of Thomas Lloyd of Morton Wallicorum, died without issue surviving, and his sisters sold their portions in their brother's estate to the second Sir Thomas Myddelton, knt., of Chirk, each sister apparently disposing of her right or portion separately. At any rate, Thomas Jones (the husband of Jane, one of Mr. Thomas Lloyd's daughters) together with his daughter and heir sold on 24 May 1662, for £1,000, his capital messuage and lands in Morton Wallicorum with those fields, thereto attached, called "Bron y ffynnon, kae Co......, kae .....dir, Cluttie, kae Rhis, bryn bychan, kae draw, bryn glase, bron yr ychen, kae Clomendie, gweirglodd y kil, gweirglodd ganol, gwern y kidis and Erw y wern". The tenement sold was undoubtedly that now called 'Plas yn clawdd' whereto pertained in 1844 fields known as 'Bryn y ffynnon' and 'Cae'r colomendy', and then belonging to the Hon. Frederick West, as one of the representatives, by marriage, of the Chirk Castle family. Sir Thomas Myddelton also bought, on 24 February 1664/5, from John Rogers for £505 (which John Rogers had purchased from Mr. Robert

---

4. Plas yn clawdd, when I last saw it, was deserted, but it presented towards the Ruabon-Wrexham road a gable of three stories above the ground floor, the gable being composed of timbers, having red brick: the beams of the ceiling in the lower rooms were beautifully moulded, and there was a good but plain oak staircase.

PEDIGREE OF THE LLOYD FAMILY OF MORTON WALLICORUM

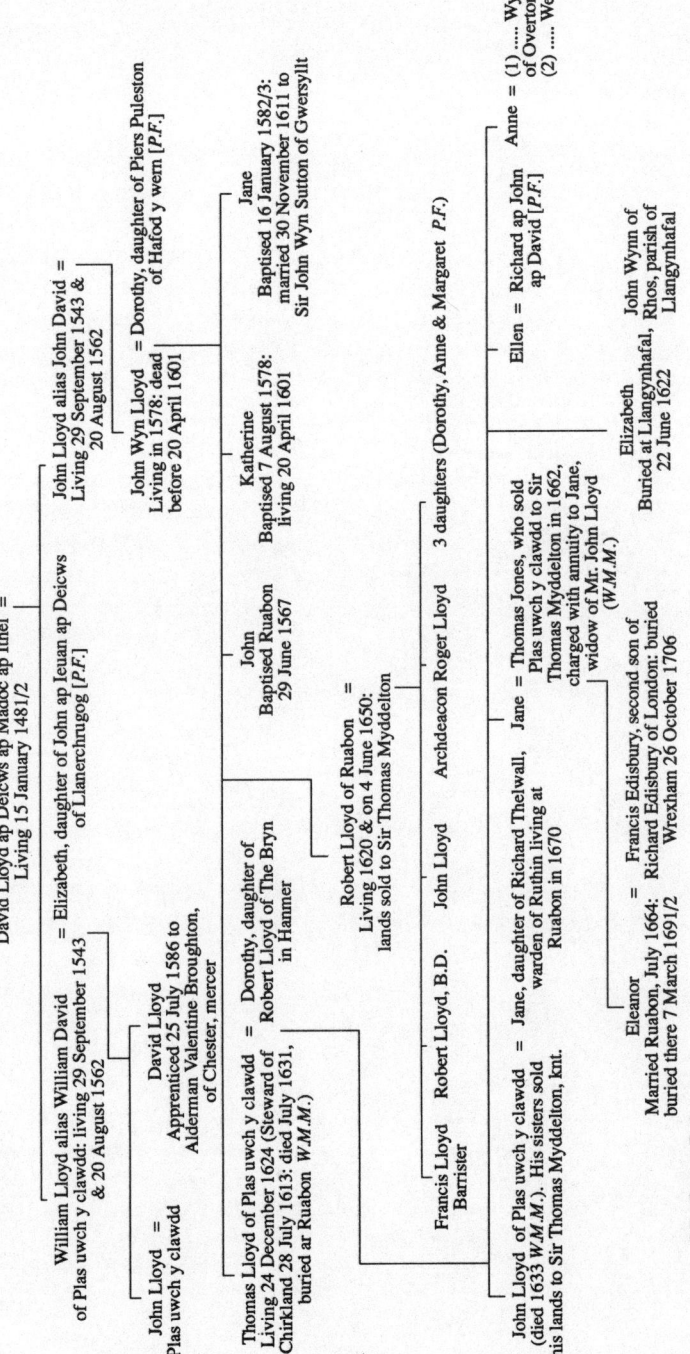

David Lloyd ap Deicws ap Madoc ap Ithel = Elizabeth, daughter of John ap Ieuan ap Deicws
Living 15 January 1481/2   of Llanerchrugog [*P.F.*]

William Lloyd alias William David =
of Plas uwch y clawdd: living 29 September 1543
& 20 August 1562

John Lloyd alias John David
Living 29 September 1543 &
20 August 1562

John Wyn Lloyd = Dorothy, daughter of Piers Puleston
Living in 1578: dead   of Hafod y wern [*P.F.*]
before 20 April 1601

Jane
Baptised 16 January 1582/3:
married 30 November 1611 to
Sir John Wyn Sutton of Gwersyllt

Katherine
Baptised 7 August 1578:
living 20 April 1601

John Lloyd =
of Plas uwch y clawdd

David Lloyd
Apprenticed 25 July 1586 to
Alderman Valentine Broughton,
of Chester, mercer

John
Baptised Ruabon
29 June 1567

Thomas Lloyd of Plas uwch y clawdd = Dorothy, daughter of
Living 24 December 1624 (Steward of   Robert Lloyd of The Bryn
Chirkland 28 July 1613: died July 1631,   in Hanmer
buried ar Ruabon *W.M.M.*)

Robert Lloyd of Ruabon =
Living 1620 & on 4 June 1650:
lands sold to Sir Thomas Myddelton

3 daughters (Dorothy, Anne & Margaret *P.F.*)

Ellen = Richard ap John
              ap David [*P.F.*]

Anne = (1) ...... Wynn
                    of Overton
          (2) ...... Weld

Francis Lloyd   Robert Lloyd, B.D.   John Lloyd   Archdeacon Roger Lloyd
Barrister

John Lloyd of Plas uwch y clawdd = Jane, daughter of Richard Thelwall,
(died 1633 *W.M.M.*). His sisters sold   warden of Ruthin living at
his lands to Sir Thomas Myddelton, knt.   Ruabon in 1670

Jane = Thomas Jones, who sold
           Plas uwch y clawdd to Sir
           Thomas Myddelton in 1662,
           charged with annuity to Jane,
           widow of Mr. John Lloyd
           (*W.M.M.*)

Elizabeth
Buried at Llangynhafal
22 June 1622

John Wynn of
Rhos, parish of
Llangynhafal

Eleanor =
Married Ruabon, July 1664:
buried there 7 March 1691/2

Francis Edisbury, second son of
Richard Edisbury of London: buried
Wrexham 26 October 1706

P.F. - Powys Fadog
W.M.M. - W.M. Myddelton, esq.

Wynn of Llangynhafal), a messuage and lands representing the portion
of Elizabeth, another sister of the last Mr. John Lloyd of Plas uwch y
clawdd, containing cae eithinog, bedw coed, etc.. The remaining
portions into which the said Mr. John Lloyd's estate were divided were
also sold to Sir Thomas Myddelton, a fact which explains the enormous
extent of land owned in Ruabon parish by the Hon. Frederick West, not
in Morton Wallicorum merely, but in Morton is y coed, Ruabon, Dininlle
ucha, Cristionydd Kenrick and other townships of the parish now being
described, all now sold away from the West family.

John (Lloyd) ap John David Lloyd, otherwise known as 'John Wyn
Lloyd', had in 1620 a messuage in Morton Wallicorum with two closes
called 'Bryn y ddinas ucha' and 'Bryn y ddinas issa', together with a
barn and a close called 'Cae lloyd'. The last mentioned name is
preserved in that of the Cae Lloyd Reservoir, belonging to the Wrexham
Water Company. 'Dinas' *may* mean a *fort*, and some twenty five years
ago or more, I made a pilgrimage to Bryn y ddinas but found no trace
there of any defensive spot, though it occupied, as a high plateau, a
splendid natural position.

There is a farmstead on the western side and towards the northern
end of Morton *is y clawdd* called 'Aberderfyn' belonging formerly to
the Myddelton estate, but close at hand, along Aberderfyn Lane, was
another tenement known by the same name, nearly 23 acres pertaining
to which lay in Morton Wallicorum, the rest of its fields being in
Esclusham, and forming part of the Erddig property. The house still
exists, but the lands once attached to it have been wasted in getting coal
and iron-stone or utilized as sites of small houses. In the whole of this
Aberderfyn farm (in Morton Wallicorum and Esclusham) is described as
having 28 acres of land attached, believed to be rich in coal and iron-
stone, being a portion of the lands late of Joshua Edisbury esq., of
Erddig. There was also a smithy there in 1715. "Edward ap Evan of
Aberderfin" was buried at Wrexham on 25 April 1679. 'Aberderfyn'
means *the boundary brook*.

The Yorkes of Erddig also had a small farm of 27 acres called 'The
Caeau' (*Fields*) in Morton Wallicorum. It seems to be that designated
'Tyn y Cae' in the ordnance map. This was sold in 1908 by Mr. Yorke
to the tenant - Mr. Huxley.

On 4 August, 1628, Richard Bayly, of Morton Wallicorum, gent., son
and heir of ffrancis Bayly, late of Morton Wallicorum, gent., deceased,
sold his lands in Sontley to Thomas Dymock, but where his estate in

the township now under consideration was situate or what was the name
of his house there, the deeds do not disclose.

Plas drain (*Hall of Thorns*) has already been incidentally mentioned.
It stands on the north west or mountain side of Morton Wallicorum,
terribly exposed to the force of the wind, so that such trees as grow
there are stunted and bent by the blast. On 28 September, 1619, Richard
Hughes, gent., of Llanerchrugog, mortgaged to "Griffith ap daiud, of
Cristionydd Kenrick, yeoman, and [to] Maria Gruffith and Jane Gruffith,
two of the daughters of the said Gruffith ap dauid", for £220, all that
messuage called "y plas drayne" and two parcels adjoining called 'kae
sovyl issa' (cae sofl issa, *lower stubble field*) and 'bryn llwyd', also those
parcels called 'kae sovyl ucha', 'yr Erw ucha', 'Gwyrglodd y bryn llwyd'
(*Meadow of the grey hill*), 'y kyttir', 'kae hova', and' kae rhedyn' (*fern
field*), all in Morton Wallicorum. This tenement was sold at Michaelmas,
1628, to Mr. Kenrick Edisbury, in consideration of £140 by him paid to
Edward Hughes, of Llanerchrugog, gent., son and heir of the above-
named Mr. Richard Hughes, then deceased. In the agreement relating
to this sale, dated 9 May 1628, the place is somewhat differently
described, namely, as the messuage called 'y place drayne' with two
parcels adjoining called 'y kae ucha' and 'y kae kanol' and *another
messuage* and those two parcels called 'kae sovyl ucha', 'yr errowe
ucha', 'gweirglodd y bryn llwyd', 'y kyttir', 'kae hova', and 'kae
rhedyn'. Griffith ap David was then dead, and the mortgage charged
on the farm, £220, was paid to his two daughters, Maria and Jane
Griffith. Plas Drain continued to belong to the Erddig estate until about
1906, when it was sold to Mr. John Jones, Whitegate farm, Wrexham.
There is a curious description of it in 1715, Thomas Price being then
tenant, and paying £28 a year rent, and all taxes except land tax: "This
tenement lies very cold having hardly a Bush or Tree or any other wood
on it, the fences (such as they are) are made of Stones and Earth". It
is added, however, that there was attached to it "privilege of common
for sheep and young cattle sans number", and "very good coursing,
hunting, ffowling", and the House in convenient enough to receive a
gentleman and his attendance for any convenient time, and that 102
(statute) acres of land belonged thereto. At a later date (1844), nearly
114 acres were annexed to Plas Drain, and some of the old field-names
still remained, such as 'Cutter pella', 'Cutter ucha', 'Bryn llwyd', 'Cae
Offa' (Cae hwfa) and 'Cae rhedy' (Cae rhedyn).

In the preface to the tithe map, as already said in the "Introductory
Remarks", Plas drain farm is treated as a township, but it never was a

true 'tref', or township, and had no constable of its own. Moreover, in
the schedule to the tithe map, as everywhere else, it is described as a
part of Morton Wallicorum. It was called a township merely because
the tithes accruing within it were differently apportioned from those of
the rest of Morton Wallicorum. The tithe map preface speaks of another
area in Morton Wallicorum which it designates as a township and calls
'Tre pwll glo' (*Coal pit township*) the very name of which shows that
it cannot have been an old 'tref', nor is it mentioned as such in any
other of the old parish lists. The same explanation has to be given here
as in the case of 'Tre Plas Drain', so called.

Chapter VII

Township of Morton Is y Clawdd, alias Morton Below

This township was so denominated as being on the east side, or *below* Offa's Dyke, and so distinguished on the one hand from Morton uwch y clawdd, or Morton Wallicorum, and on the other hand from Morton Anglicorum.

During the mediaeval period, Morton is y clawdd was almost wholly in servile tenure, and as late as 1625 the tenants held their lands by leases only. The 'manor of Morton' comprised this township, or the greater part of it, as well as detached servile holdings in other townships.

Many of these leasehold estates, here as elsewhere, were doubtless purchased in fee from the Commissioners of James I in or after 1625, but, so far as can be discovered, in 1620 there were no holders of free land in this township although there is a possibility of free land in Morton is y clawdd being entered under some free manor adjoining.

The manor of Morton, the nucleus whereof was the township of Morton is y clawdd, is described briefly but accurately in the survey of 1562, but in that of 1620 it seems to have been confused with that of Morton Anglicorum. Unfortunately, we can only consult an office copy of Norden's Survey (1620), the original returns for Bromfield having been lost. But in that office copy (Harleian MS. 3696) two separate and different returns for Morton Anglicorum are given. What I suggest is that on folio 122 the title "Maneriu de Moreton Anglicorum" is a mistake in Norden's Survey, and really applies to the 'manor of Morton' which means Morton is y clawdd.

Another point has to be made. According to the genealogists, the descendants of John Lloyd, one of the two sons of David Lloyd ap Deicws, lived at Plas y Bada (Plas Badi?) in Morton Anglicorum, and Robert Lloyd, grandson of the said John Lloyd, sold the house so called to Sir Thomas Myddelton, who rebuilt it. However, as we have seen, the bulk of Mr. Robert Lloyd's lands lay in Morton Wallicorun, a distinct township, and in 1620 there is no mention of Mr. Lloyd holding any tenement within either the manor of Morton or within that of Fabrorum. Still, there is probably some basis of truth in these statements of the genealogists. Mr. Robert Lloyd may have purchased land in fee in or after 1625 in Morton is y clawdd, or if he had land there before that date, and it was free, such land would certainly be attached to an adjoining free manor, such as Eglwysegle, a supposition which would account for the extensive lands entered under his name in Morton Wallicorum in that manor. Whatever the explanation, it is certain that the second Sir Thomas Myddelton purchased a tenement and much land in Morton is y clawdd, formerly belonging to Mr. Robert Lloyd and built thereon a beautiful new house called 'New Hall' rated to hearth tax for 12 hearths. Mr. W. M. Myddelton tells me that during the years 1664 and 1665 payments amounting to £1,154 13s. 1d. were made for building New Hall "with the object of encouraging Mr. Charles Myddelton (one of his sons) and his second wife Jane (daughter of Sir Robert Needham) the famous beauty to settle in the country", and that Mr. G. S. Steinman, F.S.A., writing in 1864, thus described the house:- [1] "over the porch, which is of the period, with fluted columns, are the arms of Myddelton: Argent on a bend vert three wolves heads erased of the field surmounted by an esquire's helmet with mantling. The crest, out of a ducal coronet or, a dexter hand. The motto, "In veritato triumpho". On each side of the helm is a smaller shield, that on the right containing the monogram for 'Carolus' and 'Jana', that on the left the particle 'et'. On a fine old door within the porch are the letters "C.M.", and there is a handsome Elizabethan oak staircase in the house, with high newell posts and pendants. The other interior vestiges of antiquity, chimney pieces, ceilings &c., were all removed some twenty five years ago (about 1839) when the hall was modernised". The old door within the porch was first removed to a back part of the house, and ultimately taken for fuel. The house itself, after it was bought by the late Mr. Henry Dennis from Col. Cornwallis West, was faced with stone, but the entrance hall has still

---

1. The following extracts from the *Chirk Castle Accounts* lately (1908) printed and edited by Mr. W. M. Myddelton, relating to the building of New Hall, may here be quoted:-

15 Aug. 1663: Paid Rees ap hugh, William Rees, and Evan ap Richard for making 104,800 bricks which at iii[s] iiii[d] per 1000 cometh to xvii ixs for the new buildings at Mr. Robert Lloyd's late house in Ruabon" (parish) £17 19s. 0d.

12 Dec. 1665: "Paid hugh ap Owen what he paid to Peter Hayward of wrexham besides the iii[li] formerly paid him and in full for cutting the coate of armes on the Stone at Mr. Charles his house in Ruabon £4 0s. 0d."

Same date: "Paid him more what he paid to Joyners in making Bedsteads, stooles, and some other worke there before the begininge of Novembr 1665 &c. £3 10s. 3d."

the beautiful old staircase, having high newell posts and pendants. The knocker of the old porch door has been placed on the new door.

If we start along the western boundary of Morton is y clawdd (or Morton Below), and walk southwards, we find in the order named the farms called 'Aberderfyn' (to be distinguished from the Aberderfyn in Morton Wallicorum), 'Tan y clawdd ucha', 'Tan y clawdd ganol', and 'Tan y clawdd issa'. The 'clawdd' referred to in these last three names is Clawdd Offa or Offa's Dyke, along the top of which in this area the main road from Wrexham to Ruabon runs. All these four holdings belonged to the Chirk Castle estate and still belonged in 1844 to the Hon. Frederick West, who had more than 400 acres in this township, including the Colomendy in the New Hall neighbourhood.

A little more to the south is Moreton Inn, a good farm with much land attached to it, part of Lord Kenyon's estate.

Lord Kenyon also owns seven fields in Morton is y clawdd on the east side of *Wat's* Dyke, in the northern part of the township, called in the tithe map preface 'Tre Robert Lloyd', (*Robert Lloyd's township*) which do not, of course, constitute a true 'tref'. They *may* take their name from Robert Lloyd of the Bryn in Hanmer township, Lord Kenyon's ancestor, or from Robert Lloyd, of Plas Badi, mentioned in the preceding chapter.

The curiously elongated spur of the township projecting northerly on the west side of Wat's Dyke is also Lord Kenyon's and pertains to Sontley farm.

Sir H. Lloyd Watkin Williams-Wynn has in this township the 'Morton Cock farm', the 'Morton Below farm', and the 'Crymbal Meadows', containing in all about 240 acres. The house called 'Crymbal' with some land (over 13 acres) belongs to the poor of Ruabon.

The Cinders farm, to which pertained 47 acres in Morton is y clawdd and nearly 34 acres in Dininlle issa, was part of the endowment of Ruabon Grammar School, but in 1858 was purchased by the late Sir Watkin Williams-Wynn, subject to £12 a year payable to the vicar.

The Clwt farm belonged to the late Mr. John Roberts, the tenant of New Hall, and contained over 40 acres.

CHAPTER VIII

Township of Morton Anglicorum

Morton Anglicorum and Morton is y clawdd are now generally supposed to be one, but the evidence of the surveys, minister's accounts, and documents of a similar character is conclusive as to their being distinct. The tithe survey of 1844 assigns to them separate boundaries, which appear to be accurate.

Morton Anglicorum had various names. In the will of William ap John David of the parish of Ruabon, made on 26 May 1637, the lands of the testator in 'Mortton Sayson' (*Morton of the English*) within the said parish are mentioned. And 'Morton Saeson' corresponds exactly to 'Morton Anglicorum'. Within the township is the village of Gevelie (Gefeiliau - *Smithies*) and the whole area is sometimes called by the same name. We get the Latin name in the form 'Villa Fabrorum', and since Morton Anglicorum was the nucleus of Manerium Fabrorum or *Manor of the smiths*. we are able to understand why in the surveys Morton Aglicorum is treated under 'Fabrorum' and what is the meaning of that remarkable manor-name 'Fabrorum'. It has been suggested that 'Manerium Fabrorum' was a part of the 'fabric lands' devoted to the sustentation of the cathedral or parish church, and that among "the Fabric Lands in this diocese were the 'Terrae Fabrorum' in Abenbury Vechan, Bodwel Maneria, Coed Cristionydd and Morton Anglicorum in the lordship of Bromfield and Yale. The townships named, or portions of them, were once component parts of Manerium Fabrorum which means, however, *Manor of the smiths*, and has nothing whatever to do with the fabric of either cathedral or parish church.

Before anything further is said, it is necessary to observe that the township of Morton Anglicorum, although mostly in the manor of Fabrorum, was not identical with it, many holdings attached to that manor being situate in other townships, mostly in Coed Cristionydd, but also in Dininlle, Ruabon and elsewhere, the whole manor being in servile tenure.

The surveys of Fabrorum made in 1546, 1562 and 1620 are valuable, but suggest many questions which they do not answer. In 1546, a grain mill with water course is mentioned in the manor of Fabrorum, the site of which we must probably seek in Coed Cristionydd. The survey of 1562 is rather disappointing as to its details, and that of 1620 is puzzling. Morton Wallicorum in the survey last-named is duly treated under Fabrorum, but it is given as though a separate manor, and two somewhat similar but slightly differing accounts are given of it. This fact I explain thus: The manor of Fabrorum was sometimes called that of Morton Anglicorum, from the name of the chief township within it, and a survey was attempted of the township as well as the holdings outside the township belonging to the manor. But not all Morton Anglicorum was in the manor of the same name - Fabrorum - and bits of it were outside. The result was so puzzling that Norden, having in 1620 already made one survey of the township of Morton Anglicorum, made another. I think also that already by 1620 the contents of the two adjoining *manors* of Morton (is y clawdd) and Morton Anglicorum (Fabrorum) were being forgotten, although the bounds of the townships bearing the same name were quite well known, as they are today. But the perusal of the two surveys of Morton Anglicorum, both made by Norden in 1620, still leaves, in many instances, an uncertain feeling in our mind. Nevertheless, many interesting statements, made therein, emerge. We read, for example, of the common called 'Bryn y walley', of which hereafter, of a close called 'Nant y therrell', which name must indicate the dingle still known as 'Nant y tyrel', of 'y Sender ucha', and of 'Gwerglodd vrth y Capell' (*Hayfield by the chapel*).

Of the chapel indicated by the last-mentioned name, we read:- "Rent 4d., out of the waste, at will. The same [Owen Brereton] holds [of the lord] the chapel and two gardens, one called place Robin" and added to this in a later, or, at any rate, in another hand, is:- "They suffer the chappell to decay". Nothing has hitherto been discovered concerning this chapel, but two suggestions may be hazarded. Assuming the building to have been in Morton Anglicorum, and having regard to the name of that township, it is probable that this Morton was once planted with an English colony (perhaps of smiths?) among a Welsh population, and that the chapel was provided for the use of such Englishmen, who gradually became Wallicized[1], and the chapel was suffered to decay,

---

1. By 1620, and indeed at an earlier date, the names of the fields in Morton Wallicorum were become almost wholly Welsh.

because near at hand in Dininlle (Issa) was another chapel, Capel Collen, where such part of the service as was not conducted in Latin was carried on in Welsh, which was becoming the predominant language. Or, Capel Collen itself may have been the chapel in question and attached manorially to Morton Anglicorum, although the field known by the same name and adjoining it was reckoned to be in the manor of Isycoed. The commingling of manors in the same township, in the case of Bromfield, is most perplexing and was a source of trouble to Norden himself in 1620.

The private deeds relating to this township are few but interesting.

On 20 April 1601, Robert Matthews of 'Kyffylle'" (that is, Gefelie in Morton Anglicorum) county Denbigh, gent., William ap John ap Edward of Cristionydd Kenrick, in the said county, 'yeoman', became bound to Katherine Lloyd and Jane Lloyd, daughters of (John) Wyn Lloyd, late of Morton Wallecorum, gent., deceased.

Then on the 10 January, 45 Queen Elizabeth (1603/4) the same Robert Matthews of kyffylie, gent., became bound to John Robert of Esclusham, 'yoman', Edward ap David of 'Abymbere' (Abenbury) 'yoman', Robert ap Nicolas of Llandyrnog, 'yoman', and to John Thomas of Esclusham, tailor, all of county Denbigh, and it is recited that the said Robert Matthews was indebted to John Thomas of Esclusham in the sum of £60, and that the said John Robert, Edward ap David, Robert ap Nicolas, and John Thomas were sureties for Robert Matthews in sums amounting to £100. Robert Matthews mortgaged to the sureties named, for saving them harmless, all his messuages and lands in the "townshippes of Esclusha, morton wallicoru, and kyffyllie" in his own occupation and in that of Robert Lloyd, Howel ap Th..., David Fychan, Mary vz John William, John Thomas, Jane Puleston and Katherine Lloyd.

Here we note, first of all, that Morton Anglicorum bears the alternative name of Gevelie, and next, that it looks as though Robert Matthews had a free estate in this servile township, although this latter conclusion does not necessarily follow from the terms used. He might have merely had a renewable leasehold estate in that township or a free estate in Esclusham. This Robert Matthews' name is mentioned neither in the survey of 1620 nor in that of 1562, but a holding formerly of 'Randle John Thomas' is named in the 1620 survey of Morton Anglicorum, a fact which suggests that John Thomas, or his son Randle, had foreclosed.

The last deed to be noticed is another mortgage made in this case on the 30 May 1638 by John Hope, citizen and armourer of London, to Kenrick Edisbury of London. In consideration of £100 to him paid, John Hope assigned in mortgage to Mr. Edisbury all that messuage and those seven parcels of land in Morton Anglicorum, sometime in the tenure of William Pova and then of Edward Hope, of the yearly fee-farm rent of 9s. 6d. which seven parcels were called 'Tir twin pathog' (Tir twmpathog?), Cae hir icha, Erw grono, Erw tir gwidd, Erw vichan, y wairglodd and Erw hir nessa, together with that other messuage on the north side of Bryn y vallen (Bryn Afallen, *apple hill*) in Morton Anglicorum adjoining, and those three parcels and one fold or hempyard formerly in the tenure of Edward Bennion and then of John Sworton, abutting east on the highway leading from 'Streete yr wich' (Street yr hwch) to Bryn y vallen, south on the highway leading from Bryn y vallen to Gevelie, and north and west upon lands in the tenure of Thomas Hope of the yearly fee-farm rent of 2s. 8d. The first of the holdings so mortgaged can be identified in the survey of 1620, when it was held by Edward Hope, paid a leasehold crown rent of 9s. 6d., and contained 5A 3R 0P, customary measure, although the names of the fields differ from those mentioned in the mortgage. The second messuage named therein cannot be so identified, but there can be no doubt but both these tenements were those belonging to the Erddig estate at or near Crabtree Green, and that this latter name and the 'afallen' or *apple tree* in Bryn y vallen preserve the name of an 'afallen sur' or *crab-apple tree* in Bryn y vallen standing on the boundary between Morton Anglicorum and Eyton. 'Bryn y walley', the name given to a common in, or adjoining, our township, is probably a clerk's mistaken rendering of Bryn yr afallen, or Crabtree Green, in Eyton. Mr. Yorke, of Erddig, has now, I believe, no land in Morton Anglicorum, but Mr. Meller, when he bought the Erddig estate in 1713/4, purchased therewith the two tenements in question, and this is what his surveyor reported in 1715: (1) "John Davies (elsewhere described as "of Gyfelia"), Tenant for 7 years past, Rent 6li and all Taxes. House, 2 bays, Cowhouse, Barn and stable, 5 bays, repaires 1li 10s". Later note: "called Pen y fron, Area 18A 3R 24P. (2) "Swarton has been many years Tenant and lived well formerly on the account of the Bowling Green by his house, where was great meeting of Gentlemen, since that is neglected he's become poor, his [he is] above 70. House, 2 bays, almost down, Rent 2li. 16s. and all taxes, called Crabtree Green, Area 6A 0R 13P". Also five crofts in Morton Anglicorum and *Marchwiel* parish containing 11A 2R 31P. It will be remembered that a John Sworton had been tenant of the second named holding in

1638. As to the statement, made in 1715, that John Sworton's holding at Crabtree Green was in the parish of Marchwiel, we must not too hastily jump to the conclusion that 'Marchwiel' here is a mistake for 'Ruabon', for I have seen an indenture, dated 2 January 35 Henry VIII, between Thomas Hanmer "of pentre mylith" (Pentre meilyn) in the county of Denbigh and Richard Edisbury "of Bedwale" (Bedwell) in the same county wherein the said Thomas let to farm to the said Richard "a mease place or ten^t of hys", with appurtenances, in the township of Morton Anglicorum and in the parish of "Marghwiell". And Archdeacon Thomas has also remarked that "a portion of the tithes of Morton Anglicorum in Rhuabon was formerly paid to the rector of Marchwiel". This seems to mean that a portion at least of Morton Anglicorum was formerly in Marchwiel parish.

I have seen two wills relating to Morton Anglicorum, the first, of William Partyn, the elder, dated 29 Feb. 1642/3, proved 30 March 1643, which I did not abstract, the second of David ap Edward, dated 8 September 1665, and proved 25 October in the same year. David ap Edward speaks of his elder son, Evan ap David, of his other children, Richard, Lettice, Gwenhwyfar, and Anne, of his brother Richard ap Edward, and he constituted his eldest daughter, Lettice vz David, sole executrix.

The names 'Manerium', 'Fabrorum', 'Gefelie' and 'Synder' all point to early mediaeval iron-working.

CHAPTER IX

Ruabon Mountain

In the tithe map of 1844, the common mountain land of Ruabon parish is treated as a separate area, distinct from any one township, but as though appurtenant to the whole parish, and described as containing 2,800 acres. On 16 June 1472, the lords of Bromfield and Yale, had leased for eight years the mines of iron within the parish of 'Ruyabon' from 'Claughwad' (Clawdd Wad - *Wat's Dyke*) to the mountain of 'Glasffrey' (Glasfre). This lease applied only to the commons or wastes, but it practically referred to the entire parish, of which Wat's Dyke was the most obvious feature on the eastern side and Glasfryn or Ruabon Mountain the most conspicuous and well-known place on the western side. Here again, contrary to usage, where the manor or the township was taken as the unit, the parish was regarded for manorial purposes as a single area, and it included Glasfre, but did not include the uplands of Esclusham, which have the same general character as Ruabon Mountain, and are indistinguishable from it by any natural features, all the townships abutting on the whole mountain, and indeed all the townships of Bromfield and Yale being intercommoners, according to general belief and practice, on the entire mountain area. But it is quite clear that the lords of Bromfield recognized that a part of the upland uncultivated ground of the lordship was, for some purpose at least, special to the tenants living within the old ecclesiastical parish of Ruabon. The very name 'Ruabon Mountain' shows this for although it adjoins the parish it does not adjoin the township so called. We have seen that this mountainous district had an earlier name 'Glasfre' (*Green Hill*), a name so pretty that one is sorry that it is now quite lost. It was known in 1472, and known also in 1620, and would be quite distinctive if we were to call it 'Y Glasfre, Ruabon'.

Another point may be touched upon. Almost every township in Ruabon parish had formerly its own common on which geese, donkeys and perhaps a few cattle were turned, which was used also for village games, and other purposes. Nant y belan quarry in 1620 was used "by neighbours thereaboute" "for the makinge of their ovens" [Norden] and is probably the "good quarre of Grinding Stonys yn Ruabon Paroch" mentioned by Leland.

But this and other commons were for the use of particular townships or manors, while Glasfre or Ruabon Mountain was attached to the parish as a whole, according to evidence which, however, conflicts with other evidence presently to be produced. What purposes did Ruabon Mountain and all the similar upland area of Bromfield subserve? In our own time it has been used as a sheepwalk, and people cut heather, gorse and fern there without restraint. Let us now turn to the preambles to Norden's Surveys of 1620, and examine them dispassionately and carefully. The jurors of the *manor* of Ruabon, which included not merely the *Township* of Ruabon, but the townships of Marchwiel and Ruyton, in answer to the 16th article "say that there is no Common wthin this Manno^r that yieldeth any Turfe, furze, or other like Commodite". In other words, the tenants of Ruabon manor not merely claimed the privileges on the high moor, but expressly seemed to disclaim such privileges. The explanation probably is that they had two commons pertaining to their own manor and within Ruabon township, namely, the "rough and rockye common", called 'Nant y belan', for which the tenants paid 16d. yearly to the receiver's bailiff, and 'Nant y glyn ddu', "moorishe and rough, overgrowne with brambles and shrubbes" which the freeholders of Ruabon claimed as "appurtenant to their ffreehold landes". In the preamble to the survey of the manor of Esclusham which contained the township of Cristionydd Kenrick (in the parish of Ruabon), in reply to the sixth and sixteenth articles, the jurors say (6):- "that they cannot sett downe how mutche, or what quantity of commons doe belonge to this Manno^r, for that they are *intercommoners with* ye Manno^r of Minera, Eglwyseagle and Yale, and do not know any certain boundes uppon ye said manno^r." And again (16):- they say that the commons in and about this "manno^r doth yield Turfe, furse, heath, and fearne, wch the tennauntes *and Inhabitauntes* of this and other Mannors adioyninge Doe take and use for fuell as they neede, and thinke ye same doe belong to them as appurtenaunces to their landes and leases". The jurors of Dininlle manor (which contained the townships of Dininlle (Issa) and Cristionydd Fechan (now Dininlle Ucha) in reply to the sixth article "say that they knowe of noe commons or wastes that doe *in perticuler* belong unto this Manno^r", and they make no reply to the sixteenth article. But the

adverbial phrase *in perticuler* supplies the key to all the difficulties raised.
The common was open to all the highland manors at any rate, and in fact
to all the manors of the lordship without distinction, so that the disclaimer
of the tenants of Ruabon manor amounted but to this, that they had no
special common on the high mountain. On the other hand, although in
their presentment the jurors of Esclusham claim such ample privileges
on the mountainous common not merely for the tenants but for the
inhabitants, they are careful to add that such privileges pertain to *their
lands and leases*, so that a mere landless inhabitant had no absolute right,
in the respect named, although in fact such landless inhabitants have
always enjoyed all the privileges on the mountainous area which the
freeholders and leaseholders enjoyed there. The jurors of the manor of
Eglwysegle, which included Morton Wallicorum (now known as Morton
Above) among its townships reply as follows to the 6th and 16th articles:
(6) "As touching their commons they are enter commoners with other
manno[rs] within ye said lordship of Bromfield in a common called
Mynidd ucha (*Upper Mountain*). As for ye quantity they are not able
to expresse it", and (16) "they say that have w'hin that manno[r] upon
the high moore, peate, turfe, furse, and fearne; and that the freeholders
and leaseholders have them for theire severall uses, not paying any thinge
for them, or ever did, to their knowledge". No preambles are given to
Norden's Survey to the other manors (Morton and Fabrorum) containing
the remaining townships of Ruabon parish, but enough has been quoted
for our purpose, and we are able to say that, in 1620, the tenants of all
the manors of Bromfield and Yale had the right to cut peat, turf, furze,
and fern upon the mountainous area, although a part of that area (Glasfre
or Ruabon Mountain) was reserved for the use of the tenants of Ruabon
parish, to whatever manor they belonged. There were two other reserved
portions on the high moor, and until we have referred to these we cannot
understand properly the full function which that moor played in the
economy of the lordship during mediaeval times. One of these portions
was reserved for the use of the lord. It was his "hafod-dir", or summer
pasture, and formed the site of the shielings during the warm months of
the year, of the tenants on his demesne. In 1620, it was described under
the manor of Eglwysegle, being then mentioned as "demean", and not
customary leasehold land and called by the various names "havodd y
weddger"[1], 'Havod y wirgir' and 'havod yr Aggloidd' (*the lord's hafod*).
As 'Havod y wirgir' it is still known. Granted on 8 December 1631, it

---

1. It was called "Havod y Weddgar" in 1706 in the Esclusham Above rate books.

subsequently (in 1699, for example, and long afterwards) became treated
as a detached part of Esclusham Above, and is delineated in the tithe
map of that township made in 1845[2], although not shown in the ordnance
map. But my point is that by whatever name it is called, the word 'hafod'
always enters into the composition of that name. The other reserved
portion of the mountain area was immediately south west of Hafod yr
Arglwydd just mentioned and is described, in the 7th year of Charles I,
as containing various parcels of land, one of which was 'Havod yr estell'
(Hafod yr estyll - *Hafod of the boards*). This area was still apparently
attached to Wrexham Abbot in 1665 but later was treated as an isolated
part of Esclusham Below, in the tithe map of which it is shown, and
declared to contain nearly 122 acres. It is now commonly known as
'The Park', but in the Esclusham Below rate books for 1704, 1707 and
1708 was called 'Hafod' also. The point here again is that this reserved
mountain portion was 'hafod-dir'.

Now we may be quite sure that if Ruabon Mountain had been
enclosed, or capable of cultivation, many houses on it would have borne
names into which the word 'Hafod' entered. In short, the conclusion to
which we are led is that Glasfre served as hafod land for the tenants of
Ruabon parish, just as Brondeg or Esclusham Mountain so served for
those of the rest of Bromfield. It was formerly customary in other parts
of Wales, as in the Hebrides today, for such as had cattle, sheep or goats,
to spend about two or three months in the hills, or to send some of their
women, lads, or herdsmen thither, with the animals for the sake of a
change of grazing. Those in charge of the cattle on the hills occupied
there either shielings or huts of boards, or earthen dwellings.[3] They
used the gorse for fuel, the fern for bedding, plucked whinberries, and
probably often killed for food the moor cocks and grouse that bred there.
They certainly wandered about the mountain without restraint, and during
the long days did much work which could not be executed so easily at
the 'hendref' as the permanent home was called in distinction from the
temporary 'hafod' of the hills. This summer pasture was the special sort
of common provided by the mountainous parts of the lordship. The

2. As containing 204A 3R 21⁹⁶.

3. In the summer of 1889 I visited the upper or summer pastures of the Hebrides, and entered one of
these dwellings, which was a most comfortable room, cut out of the side of a hill, walled with turves,
covered with a wooden frame on which turf was placed, provided with a stove, bedding, shelving, etc.,
and entered from outside by a crooked low passage. The sheiling was in charge of a lad, but I understood
that the women were gone to Stornoway to sell their cheese.

custom of summer-pasturing has so long died out here that its existence on Glasfre or Brondeg cannot be expressly proved, but many circumstances conspire to show that it was formerly used, with all its concomitants, in this district.

I often think, in connection with *hafodau* and summer pastures, of two lines[4] by Huw Morris (Eos Ceiriog) a sweet bard, who died 31 August 1709, aged 87:

> "Tra fo'r oes hafota;
> Ti gei Nef i hendrefa"

A brief account of the subsequent history of Ruabon and Esclusham Mountain must now be given. As the result of previous bargainings, the Crown sold, through the office of Woods and Forests, on 15 June, 1857, to the late Sir Watkin Williams-Wynn "the estate and interest of her Majesty" in various encroachments in the hands of Sir Watkin, then steward of the lordship, containing 7A 3R 36P for £51 2s. 0d; also "all the estate and interest of her Majesty" in various open wastes in the parishes of Wrexham and Ruabon, containing in all 4865A 2R 35P (2091A 2R 10P on Esclusham Common and 2774A 0R 25P on Ruabon Mountain) for £208 11s. 0d., and the sporting rights over the same for £2000, "subject nevertheless to all such rights of common as may be existing over and upon the said lands, or any part thereof except as hereinafter reserved". The reservation relates to any mineral rights which her Majesty might possess in the said lands, other than such rights, digging coal, lead, etc., as were granted 8 December 7 Charles I, 1631, to Collens and Fenn, a reservation under which the Duke of Westminster claims. Unfortunately, the commonable rights on the mountains were not defined, but left to be fought out. The new owners of the soil have not interfered with ancient sheep walks, but in the interest of the shooting, they confine the public to established roads, and forbid the gathering of whinberries, gorse, fern, and heather or digging of turf, and everyone straying from the roads or paths crossing the moor is treated as a trespasser.

4. These lines may be imperfectly Englished thus: "While there be life, summer it; thou shalt get Heaven for wintering (or a permanenr home)"

CHAPTER X

𝕽uabon 𝕮hurch

In the *Taxatis (Pope Innocent's)* for tenths, made about 1253, among the churches of the deanery of Maelawr (Maelor) "Ecc'a de s'o'i Colyem", the church of St. Collen, was tithed at three marks, so that its full yearly value was then £20. The church of St. Collen was Ruabon church, not at that time declared, as the churches of Wrexham and Llangollen were, to belong to the monastery of Valle Crucis, although attached thereto in 1274, as appears from the proceedings in the great controversy between bishop and abbot concerning the nomination of resident vicars. By 1291, when the *Taxatis* of Pope Nicholas was taken, the benefice which had increased in value, was divided into a rectory, worth £12 a year, appropriated to the abbey, and a vicarage, worth £4 6s. 8d. in the gift of the bishop. As Archdeacon Thomas says, no definite record has been discovered concerning the date of this appropriation. It has been suggested, as accounting for this absence of record, that Ruabon church was a mere chapel of Llangollen, and passed into the possession of the monks when a 'portion' of Llangollen church was granted to them in 1232, or in 1238 when the whole church was so granted. All we can say is that it was a parish separate from Llangollen in 1235, and could not therefore have been conveyed under the terms of either of the two grants just named. But, as already said, it had become attached to the abbey by 1274, the bishop having then substantiated his claim to induct the vicar.

It is possible that the parish church of 1253 was the Capel Collen in Dininlle (Issa) still commemorated in 1620 by the name of a field there (see ch. II and ch. VIII), and explicitly mentioned about 1698 by Edward Lluyd, who says that a field where was a cross in Ruabon parish was called Capel Collen. It is further possible that the new church was built on the present site by the monks of Valle Crucis who placed it under the invocation of St. Mary (Assumptu Beatæ Mariæ) the festival of which was on the 15 August. But these are merely suggestions, and the only evidence that can be brought forward in their favour is the former existence of Capel Collen in Dininlle Issa, of St. Collen's wakes, and of the change of invocation.

Before the raising of the level of the present main road, running past the churchyard, the church stood on a hill, as it is seen to stand now from certain positions. An old print shows this to have been the case, and Churchyard (Reprint 1876, p. 89) speaking of the building, says:- "There stands on a little mount a right fayre church", and in 1557 or 1558, Edward ap Roger ap John took of the Crown, for 21 years, one parcel of waste called "y vron dan y vynwent" (*brow beneath the churchyard*) extending in length from a place called the Churchyard stile to a certain bridge there over the river called Avon Cristionydd. Here again the elevated position of the churchyard is indicated.

In the dispute which occurred in the year 1500 as to a certain seat in Ruabon Church of which an account has already been given in Chapter I it was found that the parents of David ap John of Pentreclawdd had occupied that seat for forty years and more, and it was called "the seat of Jankyn ap Adda" which Jenkyn was alive in 1447. The seating of some portion at least of Ruabon church was therefore effected anterior to the Reformation.

But that movement caused many changes in the church. In the Book of Ieuan ap W[illiam] ap D[avid] ap Einws (Llanstephan MS.)[1] are some interesting notes in Welsh which may be here summarized. The new font in Ruabon church, made by "lewys mason" was set up on 15 September 1538; on the 17 March 1548/9 the pulpit was made; on Whit Sunday 1549 mass was discontinued, or rather the service was altered (Ll[yma] o[ed] kjrist 1549 pan droed yr yfferene oi lle av duw svlgwyn), and on 4 January 1550/1, the alter was pulled down [ll. o. k. 1550 pan dynwyd yr allore yn riabon ar IIII o jonor]. The meaning of the "arian gynta" (*the first silver*) being lost on the 12 August 1551, a statement made by Ieuan ap William, is unclear. All these changes were made during the vicarate of David ap Edward alias Sir David Edwards, a pliant parson, whose bastard son, William Lloyd, is mentioned in or shortly after 1562.

In recording these events we have anticipated somewhat, and it is now proper to say that the original returns made in English on the 11th day of May 1535 for the *Valor Ecclesiasticus* of Henry VIII in the case of Ruabon exist and have been printed. The rectory and the vicarage were, of course, valued separately, and will now be copied in full:-

1. See Dr. Gwenogfryn Evans' Report on Welsh MSS, Vol. II, p. 570. The above named Ieuan ap William ap David was constabling Ruabon township in 1554, along with Rondle ap John Ieuan.

"B'n'fic' de Ruavon ex *pte* Reor^e

In p'mis the corn [tithes]	xxiiii^{li}
It the hay (tithes)	x^s
It the offeryng^e the iiii days[2]	xxxii^s
It the Ester Book (Easter)	vii^s viii^d
It lactues [lactuals]	xxiiii^s
It teth egges	iii^s
It hempe & flaxe	xviii^d
It teth gese	iii^s
It pygges	iii^s
It hony & waxe	v^s
It o^r Ladys offeryng^e	ix^s
It the landes	vi^s viii^d
It kyddes	iii^s

Sma xxix^{li} vii^s x^d

John ap Jev^{a}n ap Dic^s
David ap John ap Jankyn
Jev^{a}n ap Lln ap Dd ap Dic^s
David ap John ap David"

The estimated yearly value of the rectory of Ruabon appropriated to the monastery of Valle Crucis was thus £29 7s. 10d. We now copy the items belonging to the vicar:-

Vrontfelde [Bromfield] *The Vicarage of Ruabon*

Inp'imis the corn p^{i}c	viii^{li}
It the hay p^{i}c	viii^{li}
It offeryngs at iiii Tymes in the yer the wholle some	x^s viii^d

2. The four days were Lady day, March. 25; Midsummer day or Feast of the Nativity of St, John the Baptist, June 24; Michaelmas day, and Christmas day.

It the Est^e Booke	xxiiii^s iiii^d
Itm egges, gese & pyggs	iii^s
Itm hempe & flaxe	vi^d
Itm hony & waxe	xx^d
Itm o' lady's offerynge^e	iii^s
Itm the mancion & glebe lades [lands]	ix^s x^d
Itm kyddes p^{i}c	xii^d
Itm for C^{i}soms	xx^d
It holy watter	vi^s viii^d
It for lames [lambs]	ii^s viii^d
It for woolle	ii^s

Sm^a to^{lis} xi^{li} xvi^s [this total is incorrect]
Off that to be alowed ??xye annuell iii^s ix
It ??oxy visitacion v^s iiii^d
nos Dd ap John ap Jenkyn
Dd ap John ap Dd
Jev^{a}n ap Llyen
Johe ap Jev^a ap Dic^s
undecio die mes Maye A^o r.r.H octavi viseio septio."

The offerings to our lady may be noted in both these returns, St. Mary being the patron saint of the church.

The monastery of Valle Crucis (and therewith the rectory of Ruabon) was leased by Henry VIII to Sir William Pickering, knt., of Oswald kirk, and subsequently granted to Sir Edward Wootton, of Bocton Malherbe, afterwards Lord Wootton of Marleigh, who married Heather, Sir William's daughter. Lord Wootton received license (3 October 1614) from James I to sell whatever of his granted possession which he thought fit to dispose of. From him Mr. Edward Lloyd of Plas Madoc purchased the rectoral tithes (corn, grain, and pulse) of Cristionydd Kenrick, and Mr. William Eyton of Watstay the *greater part* of the remainder, and this is why the present owner of Wynnstay is lay rector of Ruabon. The Lloyds of Pen y lan, however, owned the rectorial tithes (three fourths of tithes of corn and hay) of Dininlle Issa and Dininlle Ucha and the tithes of hay in Cristionydd Kenrick, and in 1844 Nathaniel Jones and John Morris, as owners in common, had the rectorial tithes of Coed

Cristionydd, which latter were afterwards sold to William Beamont, esqr., for the endowment of St. Anne's, Warrington (Archdeacon Thomas). The various rent-charges, instead of tithe, within the parish in 1844 were as follows:-

The Vicar	£510	3.	4.
Sir W. Williams-Wynn	£552	11.	8.
Miss Kenyon of Pen y lan	£318	18.	6.
G. H. Whalley, esqr., of			
Plas Madog	£172	10.	0.
Nath[l] Jones & John Morris	£ 42	0.	0.

The vicar had of course, besides the £510 3s. 4d. payable instead of tithes, the rent of the glebe which is rather extensive, over 35 acres in Belan alone adjoining the vicarage, and an acre in Hafod.

Unfortunately, we possess no early description of the church which was altered in 1772, in 1858 and again, in the most drastic fashion, in 1871-2.

The late Sir Stephen R. Glynne, bart., made three visits to Ruabon church, and each time made notes (*Arch. Camb.* 1885. pp. 129-131) and portions of these notes may be here reprinted. On his first visit (date not given) he writes thus: "The church has a west tower, nave, chancel, and side-aisles. The tower is embattled, and has a two-light belfry window, apparently Perpendicular. The church has been much altered, the whole of the original arches and columns removed, and replaced by plain pillars[3], and the greater part of the windows also modernised. At the west end of the aisles remain two Perpendicular windows; and a very good one, of five lights, at the east end[4] of the chancel, has a crocketed ogee canopy. There is an organ in the west gallery, and there are some tombs ... There is *no distinction of chancel*, and the north and south chapels have been rebuilt. The octagonal pillars of the arcades may be original, but the arches and clerestory are modern. There is a private chapel at the east end of each aisle, divided from the rest by Pointed arches on octagonal piers, and from the sacrarium by crocketed smaller arches which may not be original. The south wall is original, and the

---

3. Churchyard (Reprint, 1876, p. 90) speaks of "the pillars large and wide".

4. Churchyard also notes the window "at aulter head of church"..."wherein the root of Jesse well is wrought".

plaster has been removed, but the windows are mostly modern, some not recent, though debased". In 1869 Sir Stephen again wrote: "The original east window has been replaced by a less good Perpendicular one. The tower-arch is Pointed and continuous, but masked by the gallery. Some of the seats have been made open. The Tower is of very poor Perpendicular. The belfry windows have a flamboyant lock. The tower-arch is on pointed corbels". Sir Stephen's last notes were made in 1872:- "The restoration has been completed. The arcades have been replaced: five Pointed arches on pillars alternately octagonal and circular: also a new clerestory, of which the windows are alternately square-headed, and of spherical triangular form. The roofs are all new. A chancel arch is added on marble shafts, and a new east window. The aisle windows are new, Decorated, of three lights: the organ removed to the south aisle, and the Wynnstay seat into the tower. A curious mural painting has been discovered in the south wall, appearing to represent the corporal acts of mercy".

A few additional remarks on Ruabon church may be given. In the wall of the south aisle, a little east of the porch on that side is a pointed closed doorway, against which is built a modern buttress. The mural painting on the same wall inside the church is already fading, but a good drawing of it is given in Lloyd-Williams and Underwood's *Churches of Denbighshire*. A Welsh text, itself becoming dim, has been inscribed across the painting since 1872, of which I have the following copy:"Yn wir meddaf i chwi: Yn gymmaint a'i wneuthur o honoch i un o'r rhai hyn fy mrodyr lleiaf, i mi y gwnaethoch. S. Matth.XXV, 40". Not all the wall on the north aisle is new: within the north porch is a plain perpendicular pointed doorway. But both porches have been built since the last restoration.

In the chancel, on each side of the altar, are two ogee headed recesses for statues, late Decorated or early Perpendicular. Sir Stephen R. Glynne says there was no "distinction of chancel", by which he means that there was no structural chancel, no arch between the nave and ritual choir. This feature was unusual, but existed at Wrexham Church until about the end of the 15th or beginning of the 16th century, and still exists also at Meifod and in many of the plain two aisled churches of Denbighshire and Flintshire.

The earliest existing Ruabon register (of baptisms only) begins on 25 January 1559/60. The register of burials begins on 9 September 1589. In this second register some marriages are recorded.

An attempt will now be made to give as complete a list as possible of the names of the vicars of Ruabon, and here I must acknowledge my indebtedness, in many points to Archdeacon Thomas, whose initials (D.R.T.) I give whenever he is used as an authority. [5]

1404. *Reginald,* son of John Cedewin, vicar of Halkyn.

1414. *David* ap Madoc (D.R.T.).

1430. *Meredydd* ap Rhys (D.R.T.).

-1500. *John Elys,* vicar 2 April 1500, not named by Archdeacon Thomas.

1537. *John Burras,* second son of William ap John ap Einion, by Elizabeth his wife, an illegitimate daughter of John ap Elis Eyton of Ruabon. Younger brother of William Burras, gent., valet to the king.

1539. *David Edwards,* alias David ap Edward ap David ap Robert (so described in the register) rector of Marchwiel and afterwards (in 1556) of Llandegla, almost certainly a member of the family of Croes Foel in Esclusham, and founder of Wrexham Grammar School (see my *History of the Town of Wrexham,* etc., p.105). "Deprived" (D.R.T.).

1570. *David Powell,* D.D. eldest son of Howel ap David ap Gruffydd of Coedrwg, in Llantysilio parish, Yale. He married Elizabeth daughter of Kenrick ap Robert ap Howel of Marchwiel, sister of John Kenrick, gent., of the same, who, after her husband's decease, became the second wife of Edward Eyton esqr., of Watstay. The doctor had six sons and six daughters in all, all but one baptized at Ruabon[6], namely, Jane; Daniel, afterwards of Rhuddallt, already spoken of; Samuel, subsequently himself vicar of Ruabon;Gabriel,who became

---

5. This paper was written by me in 1908 and 1909. Since then the second edition of the Archdeacon's History of *The Diocese of St. Asaph* has appeared, enabling me to give the names of two more vicars.

6. Jane Powell, bapt., 29 May 1571.
Daniel Powell, bapt., 24 October 1572.
Samuel Powell, bapt., 30 November 1573.
Gabriel Powell, bapt., 13 January 1574/5.
Raphael Powell, bapt., 4 February 1575/6.
Michael Powell, bapt., 30 June 1577.
John Powell, bapt., November 1578.
Marie Powell, bapt., 11 February 1579/80
Anne Powell, bapt., 6 October 1582.
Sara Powell, bapt., 21 September 1586.
Martha Powell, bapt., 21 August 1585.

a learned scholar and divine, but died young (1607); Raphael, described in a deed, dated 25 July 1617, as Raphael Powell, of the parish of St. Clement Danes, Middlesex, gent.; Micahel Powell and John Powell, afterwards of Ruabon; Marie; Anne, subsequently wife of Thomas Evans of Watstay; Elizabeth; Sara; and Martha. Dr. Powell was an able man and noted for his many translations, bearing part also in the translation of the Scriptures into Welsh. He had been chaplain to Sir Henry Sidney, and to Henry Earl of Pembroke. Archdeacon Thomas makes him only to have been vicar of Ruabon for seven years (from 1570 - 1578) the vicar during the last twenty years of his life being the Rev. Robert Salusbury, D.C.L., of whom there is no mention in the registers. He died in 1598 and was succeeded, I believe, immediately by his son Samuel. Lewis Dwnn wrote a laudatory elegy to Dr. Powell in 1600, printed in *Byegones* (4 December 1895) in which he mentions his wife, all his children, except Samuel, and his brother Thomas Powell who survived him. Two scathing poems on the doctor, by David Llwyd o Globran and Henry ap Llewelyn respectively, have also been printed in *Byegones* (20 November 1895).

1578. *Robert Salusbury*, D.C.L. son of Sir John Salusbury of Lleweni (D.R.T.).

1598. *Samuel Powell*, a son of Dr. David Powell (See above); buried at Ruabon, 6 August, 1600.

1600. *Piers Williams*, A.M., previously rector of Marchwiel; during his residence at Ruabon, two of his children (Alice, 14 November 1609, and Thomas, 10 October 1610) were baptized there, where also he himself was buried 21 January 1614/5.

1615. *Richard Lloyd,* D.D., previously vicar of Gresford held the rectory of Marchwiel along with the vicariate of Ruabon. Mr. W. M. Myddelton tells me that in 1639 he was tutor to Sir Thomas Myddelton's children. Second son of Howel Lloyd of Penmachno, and brother to Evan Lloyd of Dulassau, he married Jane, daughter of Roderick Hughes of Maes y pandy. The baptism of the afternamed children of his is recorded in Ruabon Registers; Edward (...1615); Thomas and Gilbert (both on 12 September 1617), and Elizabeth (... March 1619). The above-named Thomas Lloyd was afterwards (May

1655) of Staple Inn, London, and among Dr. Richard Lloyd's other sons were the Rev. John Lloyd, B.D., his successor at Marchwiel; the Rev. Humphrey Lloyd, D.D., his successor at Ruabon; and the Rev. Evan Lloyd, M.A., vicar of Holywell. Sir Richard Lloyd of Esless Hall, knt., and Evan Lloyd, gent., of Plas Iocyn in Holt, both near Wrexham, were nephews of his. He appears to have died in 1642, but where he was buried I do not know. Between the time of his death and 1647 Ruabon church was possibly served by itinerant ministers appointed by the committee for the Propagation of the Gospel in Wales.

1647. *Humphrey Lloyd*, D.D., son of the preceding vicar, of the regular series. In the Lords' Journals, under date 10 June 1647, Dr. Aylett was ordered to induct Humphrey Lloyd to the vicariate of Ruabon, from which he was ejected on 16 July 1650 by the Committee for the Propagation of the Gospel. He was restored in 1660, became dean of St. Asaph in 1663, and bishop of Bangor in 1675. He married Jane, daughter of John Griffith of Cefn Amwlch and widow of the Edward Brereton, esqr., of Burras who died in 1644.

1675. *John Robinson*, M.A. previously rector of Llanferres; appointed rector of Erbistock in 1680, which benefice he retained with the vicarage of Ruabon until his death, 19 September 1706. He was buried at Ruabon and "founded the Grammar School in Ruabon and ten almshouses" (D.R.T.). Possibly, he was one of the Robinsons of Brithdir.

1706. *Richard Davies*, A.M. also rector of Erbistock, precentor of Brecon, canon of St. Asaph and of St. David. fifth and youngest son of Mytton Davies, esqr., of Gwysanney: founded and endowed four almshouses in Ruabon: died 25 May 1746, aged 73; buried at Mold.

1746. *Richard Jones*, A.M., previously rector of Worthenbury.

1756 *Edward Davies*, A.M., previously rector of Llanwrin (D.R.T.).

1758. *Lewis Jones*, A.M., married at Selatyn (27 May 1760) to 'Mrs Susanna Williams', half-sister of Martha (Owen) who was the wife of Richard Bulkeley Hatchet, esqr., of Lee, Salop. (see Hon. Mrs Bulkeley Owen's *History of Selattyn*).

1770. *Thomas Trevor*, M.A., son of Roger Trevor esq., of Bodynfol, Montgomeryshire, previously vicar of Oswestry, which benefice he continued to hold with that of Ruabon.. Died 29 February 1784, aged 76. Married, firstly, Elizabeth, daughter of Edward Maurice, esqr., of Trefedryd, Montgomeryshire, and secondly, Anne, daughter of Gabriel Wynne, esqr., of Dolarddyn, and widow of George Robinson, esqr., of Brithdir.

1784. *Philip Puleston*, D.D., also rector of Worthenbury, which benefice he held together with the vicarage of Ruabon. Lived mostly at Pickhill Hall. Seventh child of John Puleston, esqr., of Pickhill, and younger brother of John Puleston of Emral. Bapt. 5 May 1731, married, firstly, at Worthenbury, Mary, daughter of John Egerton, esqr., of Broxton, and, secondly, Annabella, sister of Watkin Williams, esqr., of Penbedw. He had at least three children the youngest of whom, Elizabeth, became the wife of William Wynne, esqr., of Peniarth. He died 27 January 1801.

1801. *Rowland Wingfield*, M.A., previously vicar of Llanllwchaiarn, canon 1819 (D.R.T.), of Rhysnant in the parish of Llandrinio, third son of Mr. Rowland Wingfield of Preston Brockhurst, and the grandfather of Major Clopton Wingfield of Rhysnant, who died in April 1912.

1842. *Richard Bonnor Maurice Bonnor*, M.A., previously perpetual curate of Trinity Church, Oswestry, canon 1850, dean and chancellor 1859 (D.R.T.).

1859. *Thomas Thomas*, M.A., previously vicar of Carnarvon; left Ruabon to become vicar of Llanrhaiadr yn Cinmerch.

1862. *Ebenezer Wood Edwards*, M.A., previously vicar of Nantglyn, one of the sons of the late Rev. William Edwards, vicar of Llangollen, and brother to the late Dean Edwards of Bangor and to the present Bishop Edwards of St. Asaph. Married, firstly, Charlotte Eva, daughter of Thomas White, esqr., of the Manor House, Wethersfield, by whom he had many children, and, secondly, in 1895, Etheldred Mary Anne, elder daughter of the late Simon Yorke, esqr., of Erddig. He died 8 September 1897, aged 67, having already resigned the living through ill-health. There is a window in the north aisle of the church placed there by his children.

1897. *Evan Morgan Roderick*, M.A., previously vicar of Mold: died 16 September 1900, aged 41, and lies buried in Ruabon Cemetery. A marble slab is placed on the west wall in the church to his memory.

1900. *James Sculthorpe Lewis*, M.A., formerly rector of Newtown (son of Evan Lewis, vicar of Llanfair Talhaiarn). (D.R.T.)

APPENDIX I

INSCRIPTIONS IN RUABON CHURCH

HENRY WYNN, died 27 July 1671, aged 69.

JOHN WYNN, (baronet), died 11 January 1718, aged 91. Jane Wynn died 18 February, 1675, aged 43.

EDWARD LLOYD KENYON of Pen y lan, died 9 July 1843, aged 28.

EVAN MORGAN RODERICK, M.A., vicar of this parish, died 16 Sept. 1900, aged 41.

EDWARD LLOYD, Plas Madoc, died 8 August 1760, aged 73.

RANDLE JONES of Bryn, died 27 December 1807, aged 70.

EDWARD LLOYD ROWLAND of Bryn, died 28 July 1829, aged 59.

ELIS LLOYD, esq., descended from ancient family of Aberllefeni, co. Merioneth, died 1 July 1712, aged 77, of Inner Temple.

ANNE ROWLAND, wife of John Rowland, esq., of Plas Bennion, died 17 Dec. 1796, aged 72. John Rowland, esq., died 20 March 1803 aged 87.

EDWARD ROWLAND. esq., of Garthen. died 6 March 1815, aged 63, John Rowland eldest son of above named died 27 May 1815 aged 28, widow of Edward Rowland, esq., died 2 March 1827, aged 49.

REV. JOSEPH VENABLES of Oswestry died 20 June 1825 aged 50, and of Mary his relict, daughter of late Edward Rowland esq., of Garthen Lodge, died 2 March 1827, aged 49.

ROBERT LLOYD, born 4 February 1822, died 8 March 1898, parish clerk of Ruabon for 42 years.

RANDLE JONES, agent to Sir John Wynn, knt., and baronet and to Sir Watkin Williams Wynn, bart., and "recorder of the lordships of Bromfield and Yale" died 25 July 1754 aged 83.

In memory of GEORGE HAMMOND WHALLEY esq., M.P. for Peterborough, died 8 Oct. ... aged 65, and of his wife Anne Wakeford Whalley, died 13 April 1879, aged 63.

WILLIAM JONES, M.R.C.S. (Gwilym Veddyg) died 2 July 1903; practised as physician and surgeon in this district for 44 years. His sons, Evan and Edward Evans Jones, died before him. Marble tablet set up by his widow.

ELIZABETH, wife of Jenkin Lloyd, eldest daughter and heiress of Edward Lloyd of Plas Madoc, buried 12 December. 1758. Tablet put up by Chevalier Lloyd.

N. Aisle window in memory of ANNE ROWLAND of The Bryn who died 17 February 1859, aged 79.

N. Aisle window in memory of WILLIAM JONES of Plas Newydd who died 18 May 1872, aged 51.

N. Aisle window in memory of EBENEZER WOOD EDWARDS, 36 years vicar of Ruabon, born 23 April 1830, died 8 September 1897.

S. Aisle window to the memory of SUSAN HICKS, born 9 Feb. 1839, died 26 April 1891, dedicated by her husband Henry Dennis (of New Hall).

MEMORIALS IN RUABON CHURCHYARD

In memory of REV. JOHN GRIFFITHS of Pen y nant, died 17 Sept.
1774, also of PHOEBE GRIFFITHS, died 19 October 1839, aged 80.

In memory of MARY GRIFFITHS of Pen y nant, died 24 July 1803,
aged 84; also of THOMAS GRIFFITHS of Pen y nant, died 26 April 1808,
aged 97. Near the remains of THOMAS and MARY GRIFFITHS of
Wrexham who died in infancy 1756 and those of EMMA, daughter of said
Thomas and Mary Griffiths who died 26 July 1806, aged 6.

In memory of RICHARD JONES, esq., of Belan Place, died 5 September
1862, aged 78, and of MARY WOOD, daughter of Enoch Wood of Burslem,
esq., who died at Belan Place, 13 Nov. 1857, aged 18.

Brass in monument. JOHN ROWLAND, gent., of Pentreclawdd, who
died 20 April 1843 in 69th year of age.

Rear Admiral SIR JOHN MARSHALL, C.B., K.C.H., of Elm Lodge,
Herts, died 30 September 1850: here buried: lived for the last ten years of
his life at Gardden.

MARY, daughter of Edward & Margaret Jones of [Park Eyton], died 22
October 1797, aged 26 [or 36].

THOMAS, son of Edward & Margaret Jones of Park Eyton died 4 August
1791, aged 14. Also William, their son, died 12 March 1791, aged 18.

EDWARD JONES of Park Eyton, died 2nd February 1747, aged 63;
Mary his wife, died 4 February 1790, aged 80; Edward their son died 3
December 1819, aged 59; Margaret Jones died 9 May 1828, aged 68; Paul
Jones died 21 July 1828, aged 69; W. Jones died 21 March 1832, aged 9.

ERMYNE PARRY, died 6 May 1764, aged 72. Edward Parry of Coed
Cristionydd, husband to said Ermyne Parry, died 3 March 1773 aged 68.
Elizabeth, wife of Watkin Davies, died 29 September 1802. The said Watkin
Davies died 16 April 1803, aged 84.

SARAH YOUDE, only daughter & heiress of Jenkin Lloyd, of Clochfaen, co. Montgomery, esq., and of Elizabeth his wife, daughter and heiress of Edward Lloyd, of Plas Madoc in this parish, and wife of Rev. Thomas Youde died 20 December 1837 in the 93rd year of her age.

First part of the inscription illegible ... Mary Lloyd died 27 June 1779, aged 59 [of Plas Madoc].

Greater part of inscription tooled away on the top but on the side "Anne Lloyd of Plas Madoc died 7ber 23 1755, aged ..."

ANN, wife of Benjamin Poynton [of Wrexham] buried 2nd August 1764, aged 64. Benjamin Poynton, died 2 May 1785, aged 82. Jane Poynton died 14 April 1810, aged 88.

JOHN ROBERTS of New Hall, died 5 May 1781 aged 6.... Also Sarah Roberts, his wife, died 27 February 1804 aged 8...

JOHN ROBERTS, died 10 January 1864, aged 65. Sarah Roberts, died 22 August, 1872, aged 88. Edward Jones, son of John and Sarah Roberts of New Hall, died 29 July 1836, aged 15. Thomas Lloyd, youngest son of above named John and Sarah Roberts, died 23rd January 1842, aged 16. John Williams, second son of John and Sarah Roberts died at Torquay, 23 July 1846, aged 24. William Henry, their third son, died 20 March 1853, aged 28.

SARAH, wife of Edward Roberts of Rhyddallt, buried 12 October, 1762, aged 60.

Obelisk.   1st side: Anne, daughter of John and Anne Rogers, of Rhyddallt, died 6 March 1808, aged 18. Also Edward Rogers, died 24 June 1808, aged 27. Thomas Evans, son of Thomas ... [rest of inscription on this side peeled off].
2nd side: Lewis, their son, died 29 Dec. 1819, aged 12. Edward died 20 Sept. 1827, aged 11. Thomas Evans died 16 Oct. 1828, aged 42.
3rd side: Thomas Evans died 27 Dec. 1856 aged 78.
4th side: Sarah Sophia Evans, died 2nd March 1834, aged 13. Lewis Evans, died 3 October 1851, aged 28.

ANNE, daughter of John and Anne Rogers, of Rhyddallt, who died 6 March in 19th year of her age. Also, Edward Rogers died 24 June 1808, aged 27. Bennet wife of Thomas Evans, died 16 October 1828, aged 42. Sarah Sophia Evans, died 2 March 1834, aged 13. Lewis Evans died 3 October 1851, aged 28.

ELIZABETH LEWIS, died 4 June 1764, aged 76. Also Ann Lloyd, died 2 December 1826, aged 89.

SARAH, wife of Edward Roberts of Rhyddallt, buried 12 October 1762, aged 61.

LIEUT. COL. E. JONES, of Knolton Hall, Overton, son of Rice and Mary Jones, died 20 January ... aged 58. Rice Jones of New Hall in this parish, Captain and for many years adjutant, Royal Denbigh Militia, died 28 September, 1825, aged 67. Mary wife of Rice Jones of New Hall, died 10 Oct. 1831, aged 73.

MARY GRAHAM, wife of C. S. Graham, esq., of Haughton House, Somerset, and daughter of Captain Rice Jones, late of Royal Denbigh Militia, died 2 July 1889, aged 25.

JONATHAN MOORE, buried ... 1789. Richard Moore, of The Park, died 20 March 1820, aged 8[0]. Ann Moore, wife of Richard Moore, died 28 August 1825 [or 1823], aged 70. Jonathan, second son of Richard and Ann Moore, died 11 Sept. 1856 [or 1850] aged 65.

JOHN, younger son of John Parry, esq., of Pen y gardden, died 23 July 1829, aged 11. William Meredith, eldest son of John Parry esq., died 17 Nov. 1832, aged 32. Mrs Elizabeth Parry, wife of Mr. John Parry, died 21 Aug. 1772, aged 63.

ELIZABETH, wife of Richard Jones, Pen y bryn, died ... Aug, 1806, aged 66. Mr. Richard Jones, died ... March 1819, aged 83 [or 85]. John, son of Richard and Elizabeth Jones, died 20 July 1772, aged 4. Sarah, their daughter, died ... 1773 Mary, wife of Benjamin Moore.

THOMAS PRITCHARD of Cae Clapiog, died ... April 1797, aged 43 [or 45].

APPENDIX III

RUABON CHARITIES

Translated from *Crefydd yn Mhlwyf Rhiwabon* by T. Frimston, Llangefni, 1896, printed by Samuel Hughes, 45 High Street, Pendref, Bangor.

(1) 1633. Thomas Nevett, citizen and clothier of London, by his will dated 28 June 1633, bequeathed yearly for ever £105 to the minister of Ruabon for a sermon to be delivered on Good Friday, 40s. yearly to the schoolmaster of Ruabon towards teaching poor children, and 20s. to be divided yearly on Good Friday among 30 poor people. In the same will also 10s. are provided for a Welsh sermon yearly on this occasion.

(2) 1636. By indenture of 7 April 1636, between William Eyton, Ruabon, & Richard Lloyd, vicar of Ruabon, there were dedicated for ever to the poor of the parish of Ruabon the following lands: Tir y stavel fawr, Stavel fechan, y wern gerth, y wern nesa' i'r, Ystryd, Y wern ganol, Y wern fechan in Morton Wallicorum with all barns &c., so as to provide the value of 2s weekly for penny bread (*o fara ceiniog*) to be distributed every Sunday throughout the year before prayers in a convenient public place in Ruabon church, and the like to be parted at the end of the prayers by the overseers of the parish &c between 24 poor persons for ever.

(3) 1677. Cicely Priceley (?Price). Lost. Cicely Priceley of St. Giles, Middlesex, widow, by her will dated 14 July 1677, gave £50 in money to be invested in lands by the vicar and wardens that all the profit thereof of every kind might be parted justly every Sunday among the poor of the parish, in white bread, a penny each [loaf]. This will was proved in the Prerogative Court of Canterbury 13 Oct. 1687. This money was lost in 1704 through being lent in unsafe security.

(4) 1693. By deed dated 2 October 1693 Jane Hughes of St. Giles in the Fields, Middlesex, spinster, gave £200 to be invested in lands, the profits to go to the poor of the parish of Ruabon for ever. The rent upon this at the time £9. On the list of charities we find: "Miss Jane Hughes of

Llanerchrugog, gave £200 to the poor of Ruabon parish to be divided in white gowns on Christmas day yearly." [Translated].

(5) 1703. By will dated 26 November 1703, the above named John Robinson who was vicar of Ruabon gave to his successors in the vicariate from time to time all the land etc., held at the time by Roger Philips yeoman in the townships of Morton Wallicorum and Morton Anglicorum in the two parishes of Ruabon and Bangor, all their issues to be applied thus: £12 yearly to his successors, vicars of Ruabon, to deliver a catechetical sermon every Sunday afternoon from the first Sunday in March to the last Sunday in October, yearly. Also that 12 poor children, from 6 to 12 years old, in Ruabon parish, be provided with coats and caps (a chapiau gleision) and shoes and stockings every Christmas and that such children be dressed with grey coats and caps in and out of school or lose their places, together with the Exposition of the Bp. of Chichester, and to address such in the church on Sunday afternoons, and that on reaching 12 every child to retire to give place to another.

(6) 1746. By indenture of lease and release dated 16 and 17 February 1746, Thomas Wathall, Stryt yr Hwch by John Jones of Ruabon, weaver & Elizabeth his wife of the one part, and the Rev. Richard Jones, vicar of Ruabon, Groom Roberts and John Roberts, wardens, of the other part declare that by deed dated 22 May 1700 that one John Rogers mortgaged to Thomas Wathall and his heirs all his lands in Ruabon for the sum of £140; that the sum which Thomas Wathall received, in money and bonds, was more than £140 together with the property of Elizabeth his wife at the time, and Thomas Wathall acknowledged that the securities taken in his name for £140, had been taken on special trust, that the interest due thereupon due to the use of Thomas Wathall and his wife, so long as they should live and after his day that the £140 and their securities should come to the possession of the said Elizabeth named, her successors, executors and administrators for ever: that Thomas Wathall authorizes the said Elizabeth by this deed by her own will, to give and bequeath this £140 to anything further. By will, dated October 13, 1716, she gave the wardens of Ruabon the sum of £60 in trust, to put out at interest, on land, such interest to be parted in penny bread every Sunday in the parish church of Ruabon, after service to the poor of Ruabon parish.

Consolidated Charities

It was arranged that the sum of £12 8s. 8d. of consolidated charities should be divided in bread to the poor throughout the year thus:- A list is kept of the names of those helped by this charity, as amended, and from time to time 50 names are taken commonly from the list of the parish: a penny bread is given to each of them, every Sunday, by the parish clerk in his house, to which place they are sent by the baker; and 32 from this list receive an additional penny loaf every first Sunday in the month according to the communion gifts made for that purpose.

The
Town, Fields, and Folk of Wrexham
In the Time of James the First

Containing
A Contribution to the History of Ancient Common Tenures under the Manorial System

The Town, Fields, and Folk of Wrexham in the Time of James the First.

IT is proposed to give in this paper some account of a document which affords a great deal of important information as to the condition of Wrexham in the early part of the seventeenth century. In the year 1620 a survey was made of those possessions of Charles, Prince of Wales, afterwards King Charles the First of England, which that prince, as Lord of Bromfield and Yale, enjoyed. This survey was carried out by Mr. John Norden, deputy surveyor to Sir Richard Smith, the Prince's Surveyor General. The results of it are contained in the document which has now to be described,—a document which will henceforth be referred to as "Norden's Survey," or, briefly, as "the survey." A portion of this survey, including the description of Wrexham, appeared several years ago, in successive issues, as an appendix to "Archæologia Cambrensis,"[1] and has thus for a long time been rendered accessible to students of local history. Spite of this, it has never yet received from those of the folk of Wrexham that are interested in the history of their town the attention it deserves. The author has, therefore, ventured to think he might be doing a useful work by giving a succinct account of the principal results which a careful study of that part of the document which relates to Wrexham has yielded.

The survey as a whole consists essentially of a list of the demesnes, freeholds and leaseholds of the lordship, together with the rents due therefrom to the Prince. The names of the tenants are also given, and the nature of the holding belonging

---

[1] The numbers of "Archæologia Cambrensis," in which, under the editorship of the Chevalier Lloyd, this portion was published, were those which were issued between the years 1871 and 1877. The portion of the document which has not yet been printed relates to the manors of Burton, Holt, Minera, Hem, Cobham, Hewlington, the two manors of Yale, and the township of Abenbury Fechan. The survey is for the most part written in Latin.

to each indicated.   Frequently also the names of the fields held
by the several tenants are recited, or the situation of their houses
described.   A great deal of curious but scattered information is
thus given.   These scattered notices, so far as they relate to the
subject of this paper, are here brought together, elucidated, and
made the occasion of such remarks as seem appropriate.

It should be said at once that " The manor of Wrexham "
described in the survey is the manor of Wrexham *Regis*, and
that of Wrexham *Abbot* no account is given.   Since the latter
manor belonged, in 1620, to Lord Wootton,[1] Mr. Norden, as the
surveyor of the Prince, had no business there.   We may bewail
this imperfection of the record, but should remember, at the
same time, for our comfort, that only a small part of the actually
inhabited town of Wrexham lay, at the date named, within the
unsurveyed township.[2]

At the time of the survey the principal streets of Wrexham
Regis were already in existence, though they were not in every
case called by the names they now bear.   High Street, Hope
Street, Abbot Street, Church Street, Henblas Street, the road to
Rhosddu, Chester Road, and the Beast Market are, however,
distinctly mentioned in the document by those names.   Lamb-
pit Street, Charles Street, and Brook Street were then called
respectively   " Lampint,"   " Beast-market Street,"   (or " High "
Street, see page 14,) and " Glan yr afon."   The names by which
College Street, Town Hill, Yorke Street, Mount Street, and
Tuttle Street were then known do not appear, but the streets
themselves are distinctly indicated.   Wrexham Fechan ("Little
Wrexham") was still regarded as a distinct hamlet, separate
from Wrexham itself, which is in general carefully distinguished
as " Wrexham Fawr " (Great Wrexham).

The general account thus given of the streets of Wrexham in
the early part of the seventeenth century will now be supplemented by a more detailed description of them.

---

[1] Edward, Lord Wootton of Marleigh, son-in-law of Sir William
Pickering, to whom at The Dissolution of the Monasteries the estates
of the Monastery of Valle Crucis were granted.

[2] The *manor* of Wrexham Regis included the two townships of
Wrexham Regis and Wrexham Fechan, now reckoned as one.   The
manor of Wrexham Abbot is conterminous with the township of the
same name.   Sir Watkin Williams Wynn is *steward* of the first-named
manor and *lord* of the second.   There are probably in the archives of
Wynnstay documents which are not less valuable for the history of
Wrexham Abbot than Norden's Survey is valuable for the history of
Wrexham Regis.

, And we will begin with HIGH STREET. Here in front of the
" Shirehall" stood the High Cross. To the houses on the south
side of the street belonged gardens, which stretched to the
churchyard, and there was at least one garden on the other side.
Doubtless the most notable building in the High Street of 1620
was "Ty Mawr." ("The Great House") a tenement on the south
side with shops held by Valentine Tilston. Its rent exceeded
by more than three times that of any other in the same street,
and yet amounted to only thirty-two shillings and eightpence a
·year. On the same side of the way John ap John, the clothier,
paid two shillings and tenpence for his house, shop, stable,
and courtyard; while twelvepence was the yearly rent of the
messuage, shop, and curtilage in the same street, leased to Hugh
Meredith, Esq. The lowness of these rents, paid by tenants
holding under leases, strikes of course at once the reader's
attention, but become perhaps sufficiently intelligible in view
of the explanation given below.[1] The position of the messuage

[1] The comparatively high purchasing power of money in the early
part of the seventeenth century, as well as the fact that the payment
of rent was not the only obligation to which the leaseholders were
liable, must of course be borne in mind as substantial sets off against
the lowness of the rents mentioned in the survey. But the true
explanation of the insignificance of the latter must be found in the fact
that they were *customary* rents, and the leases the result of a " composition" made by the crown with tenants who, as copyholders,
claimed to possess " estates in possibility." It may be of interest to
give here the history of this " composition," together with a brief
account of the obligations, other than rent, due to the crown from the
leaseholders, as well as of some of the contingencies incident to the
tenure of the latter. As the result of a dispute between Queen
Elizabeth (as Lady of Bromfield and Yale) and the copyholders of the
lordship, who claimed an ampler property in their holdings than the
Queen's advisers would admit, the tenants holding by copy of court
roll agreed in the year 1562 " for the establishinge of their new
estates " to pay a certain sum of money as fine to the crown, and take
out leases which were to run from " 40 years to 40." These leases
recognised, it would appear, the ancient customary rents of the copyholders, and imported, as was afterwards ascertained, the heritability
of their property in the same, but did not cover the timber and
minerals on their estates, which were reserved to the crown. The
leaseholders were liable, on the renewal of their leases, to pay a fine
amounting to two years' rent. They were bound also to effect all
necessary repairs to their tenements, and to re-erect them if they
decayed or were destroyed, so that if, through failure of heirs, or
neglect to fulfil the stipulated and customary engagements, their estates

last mentioned—that of Mr. Meredith—is accurately known. It stood where now stand the premises of Mr Strachan. The property remained in the possession of the Meredith family until the year 1880, when it was purchased by the present possessor. The existing building was erected by Mr. Thomas Meredith, of Pentrebychan, in the year 1738. The land extending between Mr. Meredith's messuage and the end of Hope Street was called "Tir Gwalchmai." (See page 18.) This land is mentioned under the same name so early as 1573, and appears to have been then open ; but formed in 1620 the site of three tenements belonging to Sir Henry Salusbury—tenements which are represented to-day by the shops of Mr. Dutton, Miss Whiting, and Mr. Edisbury. The old shop at the corner of High Street and Chester Street, now in the occupation of Messrs. H. & T. Jones, was doubtless in existence at the time of "the survey." and represents possibly the property described as consisting of a tenement, shop, and curtilage "at the corner of High Street turning to Lampint," held by Roger Roydon, Esq. This Roger Roydon was of Is-y-coed, and the same that was afterwards a captain in the Royal army. In High Street also stood, in 1620,

"escheated," or became forfeited to the lord, the latter might resume them in a condition as good as when first granted. Finally, the leaseholders shared with other tenants of the lordship in the obligation to pay fines on alienations or surrenders, to render "myzes" when due, to perform suit of mill (see page 45) "serve at the Leete and Lawe dayes," and discharge other duties. The fine levied, when the tenant alienated his holding, or a portion of it, was a year's rent of the same. Myzes were due whenever (by the death of the lord ?) the lordship changed hands. The tenants had managed to escape the payment of the curious "custom-money " called "amobr," which was in this district a fine of five shillings, whenever a tenant gave a daughter in marriage. And they were not liable to the render of "king-silver " or "head-silver."

The customary leaseholders constituted, in 1620, the great mass of the tenants of the lordship. There was, however, another class of leaseholders, represented in Wrexham by a single tenant, holding portions of the demesne, under leases of 21 years, at rents not regulated by custom. Thirdly there were, but not in Wrexham, tenants at will. And lastly must be mentioned the free tenants, whose property in their holdings was much more absolute than was that of the other class of tenants, and who held their lands, and all that was thereupon, to them their heirs and assigns. subject only to the payment of a small chief rent, to the rendering of the services and customary payments mentioned, and to certain incidents which need not be here specified.

the " Red Lion " and the " Crown ;" these houses were probably taverns, though this conclusion does not necessarily result from the fact that they carried signs, since the tradesman of 250 years ago was as careful about hanging out his sign above his door as the modern tradesman is of painting his name there.

The SHIREHALL stood on the site of the present building. On the ground floor were nine or ten shops or stores, and above, a series of solars or lofts ("sollers vel lostes")[1], as well doubtless as a grand chamber for the Great and Quarter Sessions, and for the Lordship and Manor Courts. Nine of the shops (or the nine shops) below were held by Mr. Thomas Goldsmith at a rent of fifty shillings a year ; they had, in 1562, been held by William ap Robert, at twenty-eight shillings and eightpence, William Roydon having at the same time, it would seem, a tenth shop there. Since the "new hall" ("aula nova") of an older survey (which Mr. Norden cites, and from which the last-named particulars are taken) can hardly be any other than the building just mentioned, we may surmise that it had been in 1562 only recently erected. In the same older survey it is once spoken of as " The Common Hall" (" 9 shopas subt' co'em aulam "). This, also, is evidently the building which, in an extract quoted by Norden from the Records of Holt Castle, is called " The Hall of Pleas." In this extract, at any rate, a piece of land is described as " adjacen' ante plitorum ville de Wrexham," where " plitorum"; is plainly an abbreviation of " placitorum," and " ante" a misprint for "aulæ" — " adjacent to the Hall of Pleas of the town of Wrexham." The Shirehall probably also included, or had appendant to it, the Lord's Prison. If that prison is not mentioned in the account given of the Hall in the survey, this may be because, being maintained by the lord, it would yield no rent to him, and its name thus have no place in the record. Wherever it was situate, we know it to have been called "Y Siambr ddu," " The Black Chamber," and we may be very sure that it right well deserved that name. In the " True Report of the Life and Martyrdom of Mr. Richard White " (see page 12), the gaol at Wrexham is spoken of under the name just given, and described as "a vile and filthy prison." In this prison Mr. White was confined, and from it was dragged to execution. The lane which runs along the northern side of the Hall, and which we now call " *Back* Chamber Street," is mentioned in the only two references

[1] Although these "solars or lofts" are not expressly described as belonging to the Shirehall, but only as being above the shops next the High Cross, it is extremely probable that they did, in fact, belong thereto.

made to it in the *older* parish registers[1] under the name "*Black Chamber* Street." Now it seems evident that we have in this older form of the name (assuming it to be correctly given in the register) not merely a reference to the old "Siambr ddu," but also a confirmation of the correctness of the suggestion as to its position which has been made.

Though the "TOWN HILL" does not appear to have been called, in 1620, by the name it now bears, there can be little doubt that it was then in existence as a public street. It is evidently the street described in one passage as leading to "Glan yr Afon," and in another as leading to Oswestry. It is, in fact, the only main way within the bounds of the township having the direction named which is not otherwise specified. Opposite the Shirehall there, and next the shop of Thomas ap John Robert (see page 11)—probably, therefore, where now stands that of Mr. Phillips—was the shop of Richard Benjamin, butcher (see page 11). A kiln and other structures are mentioned as situate in the same street; but the most noticeable building was that which had already stood for nearly a hundred years, and which still stands—the house with curiously-carved sills and beams, now known as "The Hand Inn." It is described as a "fair tenement." Two shops and a courtyard belonged to it, and it was held, together with a lot of adjoining property, including three cottages in Abbot Street, by Edward Davies, at a total rent of eleven shillings.

By "GLAN YR AFON," the east side of the present Brook Street, were three or four cottages with gardens, and apparently a kiln.[2]

Returning from Glan yr Afon, we could, if we had accompanied Mr. Norden and the jury on their round, have passed up College Street, then probably called "Cefn y cwm," a name it still bore within living memory, and so have ascended the steps and crossed the stile (both steps and stile are specially mentioned) into the churchyard. At the foot of the steps was a kiln, with chamber, cellar, and other buildings, the annual rent of which was eightpence! Close to it, and next the west end of the churchyard, was a tenement leased to Sir Henry Salusbury, of Lleweni. Mr. Norden is careful to give Sir Henry his full title of "knight and baronet." At the top of the steps, and, as it would seem,

---

[1] I have not searched the registers that are later in date than the year 1789.

[2] Both Abbot Street and Glan yr Afon were doubtless much more populous than the above description would suggest. Only that portion of each of the two streets is, of course, noticed which lies within the township with which Norden was concerned.

within the churchyard, stood a house held by Mr. John Jeffreys (see page 47).

We pass now out of the churchyard by the Lychgate, into CHURCH STREET. Thomas ap Richard held here, at a rent of two shillings, the house, shops, and cellars where now stands the shop of Messrs. Jones and Company, while the site of Mr. T. C. Jones' premises was occupied by the "tenement, shops, cellars, and other necessary buildings" held by Thomas ap John Robert, at a rent of six shillings and eightpence. David ap John Robert, the brother of the Thomas just mentioned, held a great deal of leasehold property in the Wrexham of that day, and was one of the jurors who accompanied Mr. Norden in his rounds.

From Church Street we now cross into Hope Street.

HOPE STREET must, in 1620, have presented an appearance very different from that which it presents to-day. Only four or five shops are mentioned as situate in it,[1] but there were several gardens and other pieces of land, an orchard, a kiln, several barns, cottages, and two or three large houses. Bryn-y-ffynnon House is incidentally referred to as "the tenement of Edward Jones," but (being assumed to be situate outside the township bounds) is not specifically described. Of the piece of land, however which had formerly belonged thereto, and which extended from Bryn-y-ffynnon House to Hope Street, a detailed account is given, the dove-house that stood upon it being particularly mentioned. This piece of land had been purchased of Edward Jones[2] by Thomas Trafford, Esquire (see page 35), the Receiver for the Lordship of Bromfield and Yale, who had enlarged it by the addition of three acres from "Eslom" (see page 32) adjoining. In this added portion an orchard had been planted, and gardens and walks laid out. Mr. Trafford's house seems to have stood in the detached portion of Esclusham, in which the old Vicarage is situate. In the genealogies the Trafford family is described as of "Treffordd" in Esclusham, but where precisely Treffordd was does not appear. The footpath leading from Hope Street to Bryn-y-ffynnon, which is described by Norden as bounding one side of Mr. Trafford's property, is plainly the present PRIORY LANE. The Talbot Inn, in Hope street, was probably in existence at the time of the survey—perhaps it was the house belonging to Richard Benjamin, of Town Hill (see page 10),

---

[1] Of these, three belonged to the "fair tenement" of Edward Davies on the north side of the Shirehall, where now is the shop of Messrs. Jones and Thornley.

[2] Perhaps Edward Jones, the hatter (see page 48).

which is described as situate at the corner between Upper and Lower Hope Street, and opposite the house of Mr. John Jeffreys (see page 47). If this identification be correct, the house just mentioned, which was evidently on the west side of the street, must have stood somewhere between the shops of Mr. Pritchard and Mr. Rogers. It was a large house, and there belonged to it gardens, orchard, stable and barn. The kitchen adjoined a garden which was situate in Receiver's Street.

As to the position of RECEIVER'S STREET just named nothing definite has been ascertained. It is mentioned in an earlier survey, made in the year 1562, and must, therefore, have been in existence under the name by which it is designated in Norden's survey at least 58 years before the date of the latter. But it is never named in the Parish Register, and the memory of it is now wholly forgotten. It would seem, however, from the way in which Norden speaks of the street, that it must have led from some part of Hope Street down towards the river bank. That one portion of it was quite close to the detached portion of Esclusham in which the old Vicarage now stands, is at any rate clear. We should naturally identify it with Priory Lane if the latter were not distinctly described in the survey as a footpath. Receiver's Street, on the other hand, seems to have been a street of some importance, and to have contained several large houses. Here were the "fair tenement" ("pulchrum tenementum") of Ralph and Thomas Edwards, and the "handsome tenement"- ("speciosum tenementum"), with other necessary buildings, of Robert Sontley, Esq. This Robert Sontley was of Sontley Hall, now called *Old* Sontley, and had been twice Sheriff of the County. Sir Hugh Sontley, a former vicar of Wrexham, was his uncle. Although the vicar was called " Sir Hugh," he was no knight ; but it was common in the sixteenth century to give the title of " Sir," to priests and curates. Several illustrations of this practice might be given from Shakespeare's plays (which are a mirror of Elizabethan manners), but it may be sufficient to point out that " Sir Hugh Evans " is the name of the " Welsh parson " in " The Merry Wives of Windsor." A contemporary writer represents Sir Hugh Sontley as a most cruel persecutor of Roman Catholics, and by a pleasant little touch calls up the vision of him before us, as " riding on his ambling mare from his parish church upon a Sunday morning." This notice is taken from a MS. found in the mission house of the Roman Catholic Chapel, Holywell, entitled " A True Report of the Life and Martyrdom of Mr. Richard White, Schoolmaster."[1]

[1] It has been printed in the 3rd volume of Lloyd's " History of Powys Fadog."

The name which QUEEN STREET bore at the time the survey was taken does not appear. Later in the century it was called colloquially "Spotty," or "Sputty,', from the "Yspytty"—a piece of land abutting upon it whereon, in 1620, no house stood. Norden simply describes the street in question as "the lane between Hope Street and Lampint." It contained a few cottages and gardens, two barns, and a small shop.

The way called "Y PLACE HEN"—the modern HENBLAS STREET—is mentioned. But a garden is also described as stretching from High Street quite away to Lampint, and this could hardly have been so described if there had been at that point any intermediate street. "The Henblas" could not, therefore, have been a *thoroughfare*, It was probably only a way leading from Queen Street to a spot between the present Lambpit Street and Henblas Street, where perhaps had once stood a large house called "Yr henblas" ("The old hall,") and where at the time of the survey stood a kiln.

"LAMPINT," as the present Lambpit Street is nearly always called in the survey,[1] was, it would seem, a somewhat thickly-peopled street, chiefly inhabited by the poorer classes. Nearly all the tenements are described as cottages, and a good many of them are mentioned. But it could not have presented the dismal appearance it now shows, for almost every cottage had its garden, croft, or courtyard. There were two orchards there, and no fewer than nine barns, one of which is described as of five bays, also a bakehouse and smithy, so that the street must then have been a tolerably busy one, in which something was always going on to feast the eyes and afford subject for the tongues of the gossips of that day. The 'great pool" ("pwll mawr") in this street is also referred to, and the messuage having the sign of "The Bull." One of the barns in Lampint is described as "adjacent to the school house." This school house can be no other than the Grammar School, in Chester Street, where it had recently been founded by Mr. Valentine Broughton, of Chester. Whether the Grammar School be the same school as that mentioned elsewhere as held freely with a garden of one rood area by the churchwardens at an annual quit-rent of twopence is open to conjecture. At the east end of Lampint, and at the corner of that street and Chester Road, was a free tenement belonging to Mr. Hugh Meredith, together with two gardens.

---

[1] It is only once called there by the name it now bears. But from the 16th century downward both names—"The Lampint" and "The Lambpit" (generally spelled "Lampit")—have been in use.

This house was almost certainly the predecessor of that now called "The Seven Stars," which has only recently passed out of the hands of the Meredith family (see page 47).

In CHESTER STREET itself were very few houses indeed; but on each side of it stretched away to the township bounds what had formerly been actually, as they were then still called, "the common fields" of Wrexham, or "Wrexham fields," or "the town fields." Concerning these town fields much will be said hereafter. But let us now continue our description of the town streets.

In some passages of the survey Norden, treating the present CHARLES STREET as an extension of High Street, calls it by the latter name, but elsewhere he gives it the distinctive title of BEAST-MARKET STREET. On the north side of this street were two or three crofts and pieces of ploughed land (portions, apparently, of the old town-fields) and most of the houses had gardens attached to them.

The BEAST MARKET, or "Forum Bestiale," was a large open area, having doubtless the same general outline as at present. At its lower end was a great pool, and the "forum" itself was surrounded by houses, barns, gardens, orchards, and fields. One of these last, called "Cae'r cigyddion," (the butchers' field) is described in the survey as "ex oc'i'entali parte fori bestialis," "on the western side of the beast market." It is almost certain, however, that this field was on the other, or eastern side of the market, and that we have in "oc'i'entali" ("western") a transcriber's mistake for "orientali" ("eastern"). Norden, in fact, elsewhere tells us that "Kaer kyddion" ("Cae'r cigyddion") was adjacent to "Cae bychan"—a field which, from another document (see page 41), we know to have lain on the eastern side of the area in question. It would scarcely have been worth while to take so much trouble, as in fact has been taken, in ascertaining the precise position of the old "butcher's field" if there had not been strong reason to suspect that it formed the main part of the area which is now occupied by the Smithfield or new cattle market, or was at least adjacent to that area.

"The street below the churchyard," now called "YORKE STREET"—a comparatively modern name—was lined with houses, cottages, and gardens. A barn and three kilns are also mentioned as being situate there. These latter were, it must be supposed, malt-kilns, since lime-kilns would hardly have been built in a peopled street. If so, it is very plain that a great deal of malting must have formerly gone on in Wrexham, for on looking through the survey it is found that no fewer than twelve kilns ("ustrinæ") are mentioned as situate therein. In this connection may be related a story told of the Rev. Walter Craddock, a former curate of Wrexham, It is said of this eloquent preacher that he was driven from Wrexham, after a year's residence here, by the maltsters of the town, who were angry at his success in preaching down intemperance. But it is doubtful whether there is any truth in the story, and the form of the entries relating to the kilns suggests the conclusion that most of the latter belonged rather to private persons who prepared malt for their own use than to maltsters who made it for sale. Canon Thomas fixes the period of Mr. Craddock's residence in Wrexham between the years 1628 and 1631. His name does not appear in the parish registers. In a passage in the survey of 1562, which itself seems to be an extract from a record dating from the year 1528, "the market next the churchyard" ("mercat' jux'a cemiter'm") is mentioned. The suggestion that the market-stead thus indicated was no other than the way now known as " Yorke Street," is worthy perhaps of attention, and this the more if the statement is true which has been made, that "Yorke Street" was once called "Marchnad-y-moch," or "Pig-market." In this same street stood also the house of "Thomas Goldsmith, gentleman," the holder of the shops beneath the Shirehall and a great deal of other leasehold property in Wrexham and throughout the Hundred[1] (see pages 9, 28).

Not far distant, "next the little hill there called " Bryn," was the fair newly-built house of Sir Richard Trevor, of Trefalun. A garden and stables belonged to it, together with three cottages which faced the street leading towards " y bont bren." This " bont bren," or "wooden bridge," was probably a predecessor of the present PONT TUTTLE (Pont Twthill or Twthill Bridge), so that it seems likely that Sir Richard's house was either identical with Plas Gwern, the ruins of which still stand behind the " Nag's Head," or was situate between Plas Gwern and " the Mount."

---

[1] The following particulars relating to the family of Mr. Goldsmith may possibly prove interesting. This gentleman had apparently no sons. His daughters Ermine, Mary, and Dorothy were the wives respectively of Richard Benjamin, butcher, of Town Hill (see pages 10, 11), Randle Jones, Esq., of Llwynon, and Mr. David Edwards, of Stansty. In applying, in November, 1660, for a lease of the shops beneath the Hall, Peter Edwards describes himself as a grandson of the last lessee. Mr. Goldsmith's widow married Mr. Robert Bellot, a son of the Roger Bellot who in 1620 had a lease of the mill and tolls of Wrexham (see page 45).

The house upon "the Mount" called "Plas Steward" must have formed, after that of Sir Richard Trevor, the principal feature, in 1620, of what Norden calls "the street leading from the churchyard to the Green." It was occupied by Hugh ap Robert, a flourishing currier and glover. Seven other houses or cottages are mentioned as situate in the same street.

As to "the Green" itself, Norden speaks of it as though in his time it was still a piece of open common, and not yet a settled street. We read of "one cottage and garden pertaining to the same on the west side of the Green." Before the end of the century, however, a thickly-peopled street had already grown up upon it. This is the present Salop Road, still popularly known as "The Green."

"Plas yr Esgob"—"The Bishop's Hall"—is described in the survey as "a fair tenement, with garden and courtyard," held by Susanna, Lady Puleston, but no hint is given as to its position. It was probably the same house in which, nearly a hundred years before, Bishop Parfew or Wharton had been accustomed to reside during his visits to this town. The Bishop spent much of his time here, and had actually endeavoured to get Wrexham made the head of the diocese, in the place of St. Asaph (see Thomas's "History of the Diocese of St. Asaph"). The Lady Puleston, who in 1620 held Plas yr Esgob, was the widow of Sir Roger Puleston, of Emral, and a daughter of Sir Roger Bromley.

The "Parc y llys"—"Court Park"—mentioned in the survey was not at the date of the latter, spite of its name, a park at all. It consisted of three pieces of land and a meadow, containing in all 24 acres. On the property were a barn and other buildings, but no house. Nor apparently had there been any house there when the survey of 1562 was taken. We cannot identify Parc y llys with the land belonging to the house now called "The Court," since the latter is situate in Wrexham Abbot, while Parc y llys must have lain in Wrexham Regis. It was doubtless the land on which the "llys-dy," or court house, of Wrexham Regis had formerly stood. This court-house is mentioned in an old document published in the first volume of Lloyd's "Powys Fadog." It had belonged, together with the tolls, rents, and other revenues of Wrexham, to Beatrix Countess of Arundel. On the death of that lady, in the year 1440, the jury empanelled to assess the value of the profits enjoyed by her, returned "the court-house" of "Wryxham" as of "no value." This "llys-dy" was ultimately superseded by the building called "The Court of Pleas," the predecessor of the present "Town Hall."

A few remarks upon some of the names of fields mentioned by Norden may here be made.

And we will take first "Kae Denter." This is plainly "Cae'r deintyr"—"field of the tenter-hooks," and an indication of the former manufacture in Wrexham of some kind of web, probably of flannel. It is extremely likely that in the name of the "Tenters Fields" which lie on both sides of Tenters Lane, we have another such indication. It should be added that there is also a "Cae deintyr" in the township of Erddig,[1] and that there are several other similarly-named fields in the neighbourhood.

There is another field name mentioned by Norden, which, since it throws light on a point of some interest, may here be referred to. It is generally stated that Wrexham church is dedicated either to Saint Giles or to Saint Silin. That it was under the dedication of Saint Giles in the year 1494, at any rate, is plain from the terms of the will of Guttyn Meredydd (given in the 1880 volume of "Archæologia Cambrensis"), who directs his body to be buried in "the church of Saint Giles, abbot and confessor, Wrexham." But that a building earlier in date than the present one was dedicated to Saint Silin is very probable, and it is interesting to note in this connection that a field in Acton, apparently next Croes Eneurys, just outside the township boundary, was at the time of Norden's survey still called "Erw Sant Silin"—"Saint Silin's Acre." Llansilin in Denbighshire, and Eglwys-silin in Montgomeryshire, are other place-names in which this Saint Silin is commemorated.

As to "Croes Eneurys," this is generally written "Croes yn Eiris"—a form manifestly corrupt, and one which carries no meaning. Pennant writes it "Croes Oneiras," which latter would mean "the Cross of Oneiras," or "of Goneiras," but no such name as this last is known. Professor Rhys, of Oxford, has, however, been good enough to say that "Croes Eneurys" is probably the correct form of the name; that "Eneuris," or "Eneurys," is met with in the "Liber Landavensis" (Book of Llandaff) as the name of a priest or "presbyter;" and that there are other examples of its occurrence. Croes Eneurys must have surmounted the grave, or marked the preaching station, or indicated the bounds of the lands of the person whose name it bears, or, since it seems to have stood on the border-line of the townships of Wrexham and Acton, it might have been intended to mark that border-line, and to commemorate the name of him who set it up to fulfil that function.

[1] It is the field next to Y Felin Buleston Bridge, which is traversed by the path leading from Ruabon Road to Esless Mills.

To return to Saint Giles.   This saint was said to have received a wound in his foot which he refused to heal.   Thus he established a relation with the lame, and became recognised as the patron of cripples.   Now it seems not unlikely, in view of this relation, that there was some connection between the dedication of the parish church of Wrexham to Saint Giles and the existence of two "Cripples' Fields" in the neighbourhood.   These were situated in Marchwiel and Esclusham.   Both are mentioned by Norden.   The latter is still so called, and lies on the main road between Wrexham and Ruabon, nearly opposite Croes Foel, and on the right-hand side of the trackway leading to Hafod y bwch.   "The Cripples' Field" of Marchwiel has not yet been identified.

The following other mediæval Welsh personal names are still, or were formerly, preserved in the field-nomenclature of Wrexham :—

GWALCHMAI in "Cae Gwalchmai" and "Tir Gwalchmai," ("Gwalchmai's field," and "land"[1] or,, perhaps, "Hawk's field" and "land.")

ERDDYLAD in "Kae Erthelad" ("Cae Erddylad" "Erddylad's Field") and perhaps in "Acker Artheladd" ("Acre Erddylad"— "Erddylad's Acre").

IORWERTH in "Plas Iorwerth ap Einion"—"Hall of Iorwerth ap Einion."

TUDOR in "Groft Tuddir" ("Tudor's Croft").

IOLYN in "Plas Iolyn" ("Iolyn's Hall").

DEICWS in "Cae Dicus" ("Cae Deicws" "Deicws' Field").

"Tir Gwalchmai" was the name of a piece of land the position of which has already been described (see page 8).   "Cae Gwalchmai lay in Wrexham Fechan.   So also did "Acre Erddylad," while "Cae Erddylad" was situate by the side of Chester Road, apparently just within the corner of the present Acton Park.   Erddylad was the wife of the Guttyn Meredydd whose will has already been referred to.   It seemed worth while to mention this, though, of course, we cannot be sure that this Erddylad was she whom the field-names just indicated commemorated.   To "Plas Iorworth ap Einion" and "Groft Tudor" reference will hereafter be made.   Plas Iolyn, the name of two fields on the south side of Ruthin Road, and on each side of Watts' Dyke (much cut up by the railway), preserved, and still preserves, the memory of a large house—"Iolyn's Hall"—that

---

[1] In the Parish Register appears in the year 1635 the following entry : "Jana filia Edwardi Gwalgmai 18° die Januarii." [baptizata fuit].

once stood there, and of which there are other evidences.[1] "Cae Deicws" is opposite the front of the Cobden Mill.[2] But in speaking of Plas Iolyn and Cae Deicws we have wandered into Wrexham ~~Regis~~ and Bersham.

Many of the fields of Wrexham Fechan[3] mentioned by Norden bore in his time names by which they are still known. It is interesting to find "Yr hirdir" (The Longland), "Cae'r porth" (or Gatefield), and "Cae Dibbin" distinctly referred to in the survey. "Cae Dibbin" ("Dibbin's field," or perhaps "Cae dibyn"—"Cliff field") is the name of a field on the King's Mills property, just behind Mr. John Francis' house. In "Kaer skybor" —"Cae'r ysgubor" ("barn field")—the mention of which follows immediately upon that of "Cae'r porth," we have probably a reference to a predecessor of the old barn in Bryn y Cabanau Lane. "Cae'r groes" was probably the name of the field still called "Cross-field," which lies on the side of Whitegates Lane, opposite the Iron Church. The name "Cae'r garnedd" shows that there was formerly in Wrexham Fechan a "carnedd," or grave-heap of stones, big enough or distinctive enough to be recognised as such. Could this "garnedd" have been that from which afterwards the house now called "Hillbury" was named? The name of the two fields which lie in the corner between the upper part of Bennion's Lane and the field-path which connects Percy and Sontley Roads is given in the tithe-apportionment maps as "Pen y gilio." This is doubtless intended for the same name as that which appears in Norden's survey under the name "Pen y geilied," or "Pen y geilyed"—a corruption, apparently, either of "Pen y gwylied"—"the head or hill of watching," or of "Pen y geilwad"—"the caller's or summoner's hill." The latter of the two explanations just offered seems on the whole that which should be preferred. "Pen y geilwad" is probably the brow

---

[1] Similarly there must have been formerly a large house called "Plas Tomlin"—"Tomlin's Hall"—on the north side of the church-yard, for Norden quotes an older record in which a piece of land having that name is described as there situate.

[2] One of the old bells in the church tower was called "Cloch Ddeicws" "Deicws' bell."

[3] We must rid ourselves of the notion that the name "Wrexham Fechan" was always confined to the little stretch of street to which it now exclusively belongs. That street represents, evidently, the actual village, or ordered group of dwelling-houses, in which most of the inhabitants of old Wrexham Fechan lived, but the *township* of Wrexham Fechan included, it would seem, all that portion of the present Wrexham Regis which lies on the right bank of the Gwenfro.

from which it was customary to summon to their meals in the farmhouse adjoining tne labourers that were at work in the fields. It is still (the writer is informed) usual in some parts of North Wales to call the hands to dinner by blowing a horn on a hill near the house. Such a hill might very well be called "Pen y geilwad." [1]

Of the names of fields in Wrexham mentioned by Norden, all but two are Welsh. Nothing could show more clearly than this fact how predominantly Welsh the *agricultural* part of the community in 1620 still was, or until recently had been. Nor is the force of this observation very much weakened when we have to admit that some of the words (as "groft," "acrau," "clai,") entering into their names are really English words in disguise. For the forms which disguise those words are Welsh, and the names which the latter compose could only, therefore, have been given by a Welsh-speaking people.

We come now to speak of the old "TOWN FIELDS," or arable lands, distinctly called in an earlier record (of date 1562) "the COMMON FIELDS" of Wrexham. [2] Norden mentions by name most of the closes that composed these fields, and not only distinctly describes the position of some of them, but indicates more or less clearly the position of others. The names of the more important town closes occur also in various deeds of lease and sale which have been examined, and inferences as to their situation have been

---

[1] Reference may here be made to two closes in Wrexham Fawr whose name Norden gives as "helltie," with which may be mentioned a field in Cristionydd Fechan referred to in the survey under the name "heltye." These both stand doubtless for the plural of "helt," a field-name rather common in this district. The Wrexham "helltie" are possibly the same two fields as those which Mr. Thomas Bury tells me are called "hiltre" in a deed in his possession. These two fields, though not actually situate within Wrexham Fawr, directly adjoin it. They stretch between High Town and the brook, and abut upon the latter. They are intersected by Rivulet Road, and the Gas-works stand upon a portion of one of them. The three or four other "helts" known to me are also river-side fields, but this fact may have no relation to the name they bear. What that name means is not known. The suggestion has been made that it is possibly a Welsh form of the English "holt"—a wood. But it is not certain that this suggestion is the true one, and the word is here mentioned in the hope of eliciting other suggestions as to its true form and meaning.

[2] "Robertus ap John ap Madocke 11 seliones p'estim' 6 acr' terr' et past in co'ibus campis." And again :—"6 selion terr' in co'e campo."

thence derived. Finally, in fixing the bounds of the general
area in which these closes lay, recourse has been had to certain main principles of research, deduced from the examina
tion of a great many other town fields in this neighbourhood.
Thus it has been found possible, not only to ascertain the
general extent of the old common fields of Wrexham, but even
to determine, except at two or three points, their limits on
every side. They included a considerable tract of land on the
eastern side of Chester Road and southern side of the Rhosddu and Rhosnessney Lane,[1] and stretched from the road
first named westward as far as, or nearly as far as, the
boundaries of the township, that is to say, to the site of

---

[1] It will be noticed that I have not included within the common
fields the land which lies *north* of the Rhosddu and Rhosnessnay Lane,
and which reaches thence to the Acton border. For, as to one portion of this land—that long irregular piece of meadow (see map)
compassed by the Wrexham boundary and extending thence to Cross
Eneurys—it is plain that this, at any rate, could never have formed
part of the common *ploughland* of Wrexham. Otherwise, it could
by no means have acquired the two names—"Acton Moor" and
"Gwaun y terfyn" ("Layland of the boundary")—by which it was
formerly known. Moreover, it is actually described, in 1562, as
"subbosc"—"underwood." And with regard to the remaining portion
of the area mentioned—represented to-day by that part of Acton
Park which lies within the township of Wrexham, and including, in
1620, among other fields, those called "Kae wad," "Cae Erddylad"
(see page 18), and "Cae tan y wern Acton" ("field below Acton
alder-marsh")—this cannot with any *certainty* be identified with any
of the common closes mentioned by Norden. "Cae tan y wern" was
undoubtedly included within the Town Fields of Wrexham, and was
itself one of the Town Fields, but with this "Cae tan y wern *Acton*"
does not appear to have been identical. Nevertheless, "Cae tan y
wern Acton," which was held by Mr. Jeffreys, included "a parcel"
which was demised to another tenant, and as this is *in general* (see
page 23) a mark of fields formerly common, it is not impossible that
the portion of the township that lies within the present Acton Park
had been aforetime part of the common ploughland that adjoined.
And in view of the position—between that common ploughland and
the township bounds—of the *whole* of the tract of land mentioned in
this note, it seems extremely likely that it had been at an earlier date
subject to rights of common of some kind. As to "Kae wad," this
is clearly the same field that is elsewhere called "Kae wedd" and
"Kay Wadd," so that we may suppose the true form of the name to
be either "Cae hwyad" ("duckfield"), "Cae'r wedd" ("field' of the
yoke)", or "Cae'r wadd" ("molefield").

Hey, to Spring Lane, the site of the Great Western ....ay Station, Watt's Dyke, the portion of the brook nearest the Dyke, and to "The Walks," including the land north of Grove Road called by Norden "Tale y gyfer,"[1] (see map), and the Grove district generally, the land on both sides of Rhosddu Road as far south as the Yspytty, the land on both sides Regent Road ·as far south as Bryn-y-ffynnon, and the land on both sides the new Saint Mark's Road.[2]

Stretching eastward from Chester Road the common fields probably extended as far as the eastern boundary of the township. That they touched that boundary at one point of its course, and approached it very closely at other points, is, at any rate, quite clear. Southward they stretched at least as far as the present Holt Street, and apparently across the site of it to the backs of the houses in Beast Market Street (now Charles Street). Extending also across the present Holt Road, they took in two fields called "Cae'r pant"[3] and "Bryn gwaun," on the east side of Farndon Street and the Beast Market, and perhaps two or three other fields adjoining them. The extension southward just given to the common arable lands of old Wrexham would seem to be justified by the fact that "Cae'r pant" and "Bryn gwaun," and apparently also a field in Beast Market Street, possessed, like all the closes

[1] "Tale y gyfer" probably stands for "Talar geifr"—"The Goats' Headland." It is, in fact, once actually called "Tal y *geifr*" in the survey; and that the name was supposed to contain the word "geifr" ("goats") seems plain from the fact that the two closes into which the field was afterwards divided were called respectively "Goats' Field" and "Goats' Meadow" (see map).

[2] It can be proved that the common fields comprised within the area west of Chester Road, mentioned above, touched the town boundary along a great part of the course of the latter, and it is probable that they touched, within the same area, that boundary along the whole of its course.

[3] "Cae'r pant" ("the field of the hollow") is mentioned in the parish terrier under that name. It extends from Farndon Street eastward in a direction parallel with Holt Road. The field whose name is given above as "Bryn gwaun" ("the layland hill ')—so-called, perhaps, from the common which adjoined it—appears on the survey under the several forms—"Bryn gwian," "Bryn gwyan," and "Bryn gwain." If I am wrong in preferring the last of these forms to the first two, the name should perhaps be written "Bryn y Gwion"—"Y Gwion's Hill." We might then add another to the list of old Welsh personal names enshrined in our field nomenclature (see page 18). One of the lords of Iâl (Yale) bore this name.

situate within the Town Fields, a characteristic[1] which has now to be described.

The Town Fields were all divided into "parcels," lying parallel each to each, and held by different tenants. These parcels varied in width, according as they included several "selions," or butts of land, or a single selion or butt, and they were of all sizes from an acre and a half to eight perches. They were divided from the parcels on each side either by "balks," or strips of unploughed grass, as was generally the case in England, or else by lines of "mere stones," as "quillets" in common fields are in this district marked off one from another to this day. The parcels described by Norden were, in fact, no other than what we now call "quillets," and this is the name by which they will henceforth be spoken of. They were held, some under lease,/and some as free, but in either case were assumed to belong, in the last resort, to the manorial lord, who granted and gave. And they represented the strips into which the common ploughed fields of Wrexham were aforetime divided for distribution among the several members of the community.

Let us now pass from the general account just given of the early condition of the common fields of Wrexham, to a more particular description of them.

Of those of the inhabitants of Wrexham who in 1620 possessed quillets in the common fields, some held many of these, and a few but one. And when many quillets belonged to a single owner, these were in general widely scattered over those fields. This is a characteristic which is very clearly indicated in the survey. Thus, we read: "Dorothy Ellis, of Alrhey, widow, holds a messuage, garden, and shop in the High Street, also nine parcels of land pertaining to the same in the fields of Wrexham, namely, one parcel called Kae Claii in Maes y dre issa, one parcel in Kae tan y werne ucha, one parcel in Kae tan y werne issa, one parcel in Kae bychan, three parcels in Pant y crydd, two parcels in Tale y gyfer, and one small parcel in Kae Martin." The extract just given affords not merely an example of the scattering of the quillets over the cultivated area, but also an example of something like the *average* number of them held by each owner or tenant. The list now to be given is intended to show the occasional *accumulation* of the quillets in the hands of a single person, but at the same time supplies an additional and very striking instance of that remarkable dispersion of them to

[1] Until November, 1880, "Cae'r pant" still possessed this characteristic.

which attention has been called. In the enclosing of adjoining parcels to which the list bears witness, we see also the beginnings of the process which led ultimately to the formation of a new group of fields, and to the possession of the whole of each field by a single person.

LIST, COMPILED FROM NORDEN'S SURVEY, OF THE HOLDINGS
    BELONGING, IN 1620, TO JOHN JEFFREYS, ESQ., IN THE
    FIELDS OF WREXHAM.

In MAES Y DRE UCHA : Two parcels whose contents are not stated, and one parcel of three "selions."

In MAES Y DRE ISSA : A parcel called " Erw glai;" a parcel called "Perth y Benglog;" a parcel called "Tyroyth Kymmion" ("Tiroedd ceimion"—crooked lands) ; a parcel of six selions ; six other parcels ; three small crofts ; another small croft next " Perth y Benglog;" a close called "Place yerwarth ap egnion" (see page 31) ; and a close called " Perth y Benglog."

In MAES Y DRE (without distinction made of "ucha" and "issa") : One parcel of six selions and three other parcels.

In CAE MARTHIN FYCHAN : One parcel.

In PWLL Y WRACH : Four parcels (two of them free) ; also two closes called " Pwll y wrach" and " Y wrach," which were doubtless inclosed quillets taken out of the larger field bearing the same name.

In ESLOM · A parcel of four selions.

In TAL Y GYFER : Six parcels [two of them free).

In CAE BYCHAN : One parcel, and also a close called by the same name, and probably enclosed therefrom.

In PANT Y CRYDD : Four parcels.

In CAE TAN Y WERN ISSA : Two parcels.

In BRYN GWAUN : Two parcels of three selions each.

In PANT Y GLOVER : Two parcels.

In HIRDIR MAWR : One parcel.

Also a parcel adjoining "Hirdir mawr ;" a close called " Hirdir bychan ; " a parcel called " Kay yr on " (see page 31) ; a parcel near "Cae'r on;" a parcel called "Errow y street;" a parcel opposite " Gwaun y terfyn ; " a close called " Cae newydd " (see page 31); and four selions in Wrexham Fechan called " Erwau'r ysgubor."

It may well have been that, with the exception of the lord's portion, the shares which each quillet-holder, or, at any rate, which each quillet-holder *of the same rank*, possessed in the fields of Wrexham were originally equal. But when once these shares ceased to be at regular intervals re-distributed, such an inequality as that which has just been noted would inevitably tend to become established. The wealthier owners would hasten to buy as many quillets adjoining their own as the holders of them could be induced to sell. And this is what

Mr. John Jeffreys, in his anxiety to "found a family," had, in fact, been doing. But though we may suppose that the shares of the several occupiers in the common arable lands were originally equal, we must not conclude that the various quillets comprised in those shares, or even that the various butts comprised in those quillets, were all of equal area. As a matter of fact, the Wrexham quillets varied in size not only as the number of butts in each quillet varied, but also as the length of the fields varied in which they lay.[1] The equality supposed may, however, have been approximately secured by assigning to every householder of the same grade an equal share in each of certain groups of fields within the cultivated area. And this was possibly one of the results which the scattering of the quillets belonging to each holder over the fields of Wrexham was intended to secure. Such a scattering of the quillets over the village domain, supposing it to have been established with the object named, would then serve a further purpose. It would become at once possible to enforce a common system of cultivation, and, in doing so, to treat every quillet-holder alike. And such a common system of cultivation, when the lands held by each tenant were intermixed after the fashion described, was plainly necessary. In England and on the Continent, the equality of the holdings and the uniform and systematic treatment of them were secured by dividing the arable area into three fields, and assigning to every holder of equal rank an equal share in each. Each of these fields was then *in turn* subjected for two years to a similar succession of crops, and in the third year lay fallow. That one of the three fields which in the first year remained uncultivated bore in the second year wheat or rye, and in the third barley, oats, or some other crop; while in the same year each field was treated differently according to the routine of cultivation agreed upon. Now the number of closes within the cultivated area of Wrexham was in 1620 rather large, and it has not been found possible to group them so as to correspond to the "three fields" of the arable marks of England and the Continent. Norden does, indeed, seem to suggest that one group of closes lay within "Maes y dre issa"—"the *lower*

---

[1] It has been stated that the quillets were of various sizes, from an acre and a half to eight perches. Mose of those, however, whose area is given may be arranged in one or other of three groups, which include respectively parcels containing an acre, a half acre, and a quarter of an acre each. As to the selions, or butts, whose size is stated, these varied from two perches to a quarter of an acre in area.

town field," and another group within " Maes y dre ucha"—
"the *upper* town field." And here we have perhaps two of
the three *main* fields we are in search of. But the classification
thus begun is not sufficiently specific, and does not go far
enough to be of much value. Nevertheless it seems reasonable
to suppose that the town fields here were subject to regulations
as to the threefold succession of tilths and fallow similar to
those which prevailed elsewhere. We have, in fact, but to
look at a map of the township to have this conclusion directly
suggested to us.

There are, as is very well known, five detached portions of
Wrexham Abbot lying within Wrexham Regis. The detached
portion which includes the greater part of Abbot Street and the
land on both sides the same, seems to have contained the old
court house of Wrexham Abbot, and to be identical with the
ancient precincts of that house. But it is with the four other
" portions," situate *outside* the actually inhabited town, with
which we are now solely concerned. It will be shown hereafter that the first and most extensive of these is no other
than a portion of the *common pasture* of old Wrexham, and it
must now be pointed out that the three detached portions
remaining lie within the area which formerly constituted the
common fields of Wrexham. It is a natural inference that
when the older and greater Wrexham was, in the year 1200,
divided into two manors, the first of the four detached portions just mentioned was the share of the old common pasture
assigned to the new manor of Wrexham Abbot, while the
detached portions of the same manor in Holt Street, Holt
Road, and Beast Market constituted the share in the old
common fields which was similarly assigned.[1] But in the
assignment of three distinct fields, instead of a single field
equal to their total area, we have the required proof of
the existence, in the Wrexham of 1200, of the threefold succession of crops and fallow which has been described. And
in this connection the fact that the Vicar had until recently a
quillet in each of these three fields, is one of great significance.
It should be said, on the other hand, that while two of these
three arable " portions " are approximately equal in area,

---

[1] These four detached portions are represented in the annexed map—
the portion in the common pasture coloured purple, and the three
portions in the common fields coloured yellow. All of them will
shortly be absorbed under the provisions of the " Divided Parishes
Act." There was, in 1620, a detached portion of Wrexham Regis in
Pentrefelin.

and contain about two acres each, the third is a mere strip, consisting of a single quillet and containing only half an acre of land. But it is extremely probable that this third portion has been reduced to its present area by the *subsequent* formation of Holt Road, which bounds it on its north side.

It has been already said that of the quillets that lay in the fields of Wrexham, some were held by free tenants and some by leaseholders. And it may now be added that the quillets held by free tenure and the quillets held by lease were so intermixed that almost every field within the ancient cultivated area contained some of each. The question as to the precise original status of the two classes of tenants named, is one the answer to which the early records of the manor can alone supply. That the leaseholders should pay a higher rent than the free tenants for their quillets is what we should naturally look for. The free tenants whose rents Norden gives paid, in 1620, at the rate of from 2d. to 4d. an acre, while the rent of the leaseholders ranged from 5d. to 5s. 6d. an acre.

Two parcels within the common fields are described in the survey as *pertaining* to the tenement of Richard Benjamin (see page 10), nine to the tenement of Dorothy Ellis (see page 23), and four to the tenement of Hugh Meredith, Esq., in Lampint (see page 13). And there can be no doubt that the possession of a group of plots in the fields of the village was at first absolutely dependent, here as elsewhere, upon the occupation of a certain tenement in the village itself, to which they *pertained*, but in 1620 the old cultivating community had long since been broken up, and the condition named had become no longer indispensable.

The question as to the generic name by which the quillets in the common fields were known to the folk of old Wrexham is one of some interest. The English-speaking portion of the population would seem in 1620 to have called them "parcels." This, at any rate, is the conclusion which is suggested by the fact that in the Latin of Norden's survey they are described as "parcellæ." The more specific word, "quillets," did not come into use until a later date, and then the customary descriptive phrase applied to a parcel in Wrexham Fields became, in legal documents, "a quillet or so many butts of land lying and being under known meres and bounds in a field commonly so-and-so called." Some of these quillets had already, at the time of the survey, acquired distinctive names. And nearly all these names contained the word "erw"—"Erw gam,"

"Erw fechan," "Erw glai," "Erw'r stryt," "Erwau'r pwll."
When we come to speak of the common fields of Wrexham
Fechan, we shall in like manner find that two quillets there
were called, respectively, "Erw goch" and "Erwau'r ysgubor."
Thus it would seem that, as the English inhabitants of old
Wrexham called the quillets in the common fields "parcels," so
the Welsh inhabitants called them "erwau." (The word "erw"
is properly applicable to a piece of ploughed land having a
definite area; it is now used as the equivalent of the English
"acre.") These inferences accord completely with the word-
ing of two deeds, dated 1602 and 1625 respectively, in which
certain quillets in Wrexham Fields conveyed thereby are
described as "errowes or parcels of land."

The result just reached is very important, because if the
quillets in Wrexham Field were formerly commonly called
"erwau," this could only have been because an "erw" was
understood to be the *normal* area of each, whatever the *actual*
contents of many of them might in 1620 have been.[1]

In view also of the original theoretical area of the quillets
thus indicated, it may be well to say that one of the closes
lying within the town fields was at the beginning of the 17th
century called "Acrau hirion"—"The long *acres*," and so
continued to be called as late as the end of the last century.
In 1620 all this field, save "one little parcel," was leased to
Thomas Goldsmith, but in an indenture (preserved among the
Pentrebychan deeds) dated eighteen years earlier, "foure
severall errowes" are described as lying therein. It is
apparently the close within which the house called "Beacons-
field" now stands.[2]

[1] The average area of "quillets" in the neighbourhood of Wrexham
at the present time is *half* an acre.

[2] If "Acrau hirion" be not the close above indicated, then it must
be that adjoining it, which was afterwards called "The Soldier's field"
(see map). And to whichever of these two fields the name "Acrau
hirion" is assigned," the name "Y borthgrey" must be given to the
other. Now this latter name is one which calls for some notice. The
form in which it appears in the survey and in other documents can
hardly be correct. "Y borth" would mean "the ferry." and it is
difficult to believe that at or near the Borthgrey any ferry could ever
have been. But in transcribing documents of the 16th and 17th
centuries, "e" is often mistaken for "o," so that it seems likely that
the form "Borthgrey" was due at first to a transcriber's blunder.
Perhaps the true form of the word should be "Y berthgref"—the
strong bush. This would, at any rate, be a *possible* name. Towards
the end of last century this field came to be called "Boch y dre."

It would seem that quillets were also once called in Wrexham "drylliau" (plural of "dryll"—"a piece") and "ysgythrau" (plural of "ysgwthr"—"a cutting.") The quillet in "Cae'r pant" belonging to the glebe was, at any rate, called "*Dryll y ficer*"—"the Vicar's piece," and the name "Ysgythrau" was given to two fields in Wrexham Fechan which there is reason to suspect had aforetime contained quillets (see page 36).

Not a single one (or not more than a single one) of the quillets that formerly lay in the fields of Wrexham now remains. Four, however—those belonging to the Vicar—were still in existence so late as November, 1880, when they were sold by public auction. Three of these have already been described, the fourth was situate in Rhosddu Road. In the tithe-apportionment map of 1844 four others are represented, namely, two in "Cae'r pant," and two in Grove Park. The two latter (represented in the annexed map) were then the property of the late Sir Robert H. Cunliffe, and are apparently the same that had belonged earlier in the century to Mr. Meredith, of Pentrebychan. In the year 1800 the Meredith family possessed three other quillets in Wrexham, one of them in a field in Rhosddu Road, near the Dissenters' Burial Ground, and two others lying along Chester Road, one of them on the west side of that road, and the other directly opposite, in the "Town Field" (see page 30). Of the two quillets last named the following interesting description occurs in one of the Pentrebychan deeds, dated March 25th, 1800:—"Two pieces of land, formerly in one, and *lately divided* by the turnpike road leading from the town of Wrexham to the city of Chester, called by the name of Erw clay."

The quillet just mentioned, "Erw glai" (see page 24), is again noticed in a very curious list of quillets belonging in 1731 to the Pentrebychan family. A copy of this list, which is entitled "Acct. of Parcels of land in Wrexham in other ground uninclosed," is here given :—

"In MAES Y DRE : Two buts and four pikes.
"In the ground of RICHARD ABRAHAM : Four buts.
"In MR. HANMER'S FIELD : Three buts and four pikes.
"In late HARRY JONES' CARPTER LAND : A small piece for which Rd. Arthur received 6d. yearly.
"In THE FIELD BY NEW CHURCHYARD, likewise the ground of John Hughes, brazier, and Acton lands : Five buts.
"ERW CLAY : A small field entire, and part of the hadland."

The "new churchyard" here mentioned is the Dissenters' Burial Ground in Rhosddu Road. "Hadlands," or headlands, are the strips of unploughed land at the two ends of a field on which the ploughing teams are turned. "Pikes," according to Halliwell ("Archaic and Provincial Dictionary"), are the "short butts [in a field] which fill up the irregularities caused by hedges not running parallel." Mr. Holland, of Frodsham, who has supplied this quotation, says that such short butts in the corners of fields are in Cheshire called "cuttings."

Now it is important to note that not one of the *modern* quillets mentioned in the two paragraphs preceding lies outside the limits of what we now know to have been the old common fields; and if we were to draw a boundary line which should enclose them all, we should map out at the same time a considerable portion of those fields. The question naturally suggests itself whether we should be justified in regarding any other ancient *arable* area which contains quilleted fields as representing the old common ploughland of the township in which that area lies. The author thinks it possible to show that such a conclusion would be abundantly justified, and hopes in due time to publish some notes on the identification of the common lands of the older village communities, in which the proposition indicated will, among other propositions, be advocated.[1]

It has already been stated that the name "Maes y dre" seems to have been applied not to the common fields of Wrexham generally, but to a certain area within them, and that this area was divided into an "Upper" and "Lower" portion—"Maes y dre ucha" and "Maes y dre issa." Of these two portions the latter lay certainly on the east side of the present Chester Road, and it appears from the Parish-map that the name "Town Field" was in 1844 still given to nearly the whole of that triangular area, divided into fields, which is bounded on one side by the Chester Road, on another by the road running along Acton Park wall towards Rhosnessney village, and on the third by the well-known footpath which connects the two roads just mentioned. One of the closes lying within "Maes y dre issa" was called "Perth y benglog,"

---

[1] I may say that I have found distinct traces of the former existence of a system of associated tenure, similar to that formerly existing in Wrexham, in thirty other townships situated within the Hundred of Bromfield and the adjacent parts of Denbighshire and Flintshire. A summary of the results obtained from the researches that have been made into the former condition of these townships will be included in the forthcoming paper to which reference has been above made.

" The bush of the skull." With this, we may be sure, some fatal incident now forgotten was connected.[1]

As to the position of " Maes y dre *ucha*," the only hint that is given in the survey is contained in the statement that a field called " Pant-y-crydd " (" The Shoemaker's Hollow ") lay within it. But this hint is sufficient. For " Pant-y-crydd " is known (from one of the Pentrebychan MSS.) to have been situate on the west side of Chester Road. The present Vicarage stands either actually within its limits or quite close to those limits. But, if Norden is right in including " Pant-y-crydd " within " Maes y dre ucha," the distinction of " upper " and " lower " between the two portions of " Maes y dre " must have been purely conventional, since there is no noticeable difference of level between the land on the one side of the road and the land on the other. Perhaps the knowledge of the exact course of the old Chester Road might do away with the difficulty. Whether other fields on the west side of that road belonged also to Maes y dre ucha we do not know. But it may be as well to state, with as much detail as the materials at our disposal will allow, what these other fields were.

Proceeding, then, along the road named, from Pant-y-crydd northward, we should come, on the same side of the road as that on which the latter lay, first to " Pant-y-glover " (the glover's hollow), then to " Cae newydd " (" The new field," belonging wholly to Mr. Jeffreys), and finally to "Tale-y-gyfer." This last stretched, as we know (page 22), along the township bounds to Rhosddu Road : the Dissenters' Burial Ground seems to have been taken out of it. South of Tale-y-gyfer (but on which side of the road last-named is not clear) was " Kay-y-Synor " (" Cae'r swynwr "—the Wizard's field). Lastly, adjoining the Yspytty was " Cae'r on " (" Field of the ash tree "). (See page 24.)

It may be fitting to continue the topographical description which has been thus begun.

We come, then, next to the lands between the Rhosddu and Regent Roads. The southern portion of this tract (the neighbourhood of the present Argyle Street) was occupied by " Cae bychan" (" The little field "). Going northward came another field, or other fields, which cannot be identified. And lastly,

---

[1] This close seems to have included a piece of land which went by the name of " Plas Iorwerth ap Einion"—" Hall of Iorwerth ap Einion"—so called, probably, from a house bearing that name which adjoined (see page 24).

stretching from somewhere near the present Grosvenor Road, to the site of the railway station and of Mr. Thomas' timber-yard, was a large piece of land called "Pwll-y-wrach" ("The witch's pool"). A portion of this area—a field next Mr. Strachan's nursery—is still called by the same name. Within this field is a "flash" or pond—(see map)—doubtless the pool after which the field was named. How did this acquire the name it has so long borne? Can it be the pool in which our foregoers dipped those unhappy hags who by their ugliness or other unlovely qualities were deemed to be in league with the devil? There is another "Pwll-y-wrach" near Cowbridge, in Glamorganshire.

Finally, the land *west* of Regent Street must be dealt with. The southern portion of this area, lying next Bryn-y-ffynnon, and stretching between road and river, is represented in the survey by a name which appears under the several forms— "Maes Eslom," "Estane," and "Estome." Of these, the first is the form for which there is most authority, though it is the one which lends itself to explanation least readily of all. "Eslom" is not explicitly mentioned by Norden as one of the common fields, but in the fact that it included in 1620 two or three parcels held by different persons (see page 24) we have a sufficient warrant for saying that it must have been afore-time one of those fields.

The land lying *north* of Maes Eslom, and extending thence between Regent Road and the brook towards Watt's Dyke ("Clawdd wad") is not directly referred to in the survey. But we may infer from its position that it had formed, originally, at any rate, an integral portion of the common arable area. And it seems very likely that two of the "town fields" mentioned in the survey— "Cae tan y wern ucha" and "Cae tan y wern issa"— were here situate. The former of these is, in fact, described as lying "against" Cae bychan. In later times, and down to our own day, this tract (across which Bradley Road has recently been carried, and whereon the Lager Beer Brewery is now being built) has borne a very interesting name, "Twmpath-y-cryddion"—("Shoemakers' Mound"). What this name may be taken to import will be discussed hereafter. Meanwhile, the mention of it affords the occasion for referring in detail to several names conforming to the same general grammatical type, which have already received a passing mention. These names containing reference to certain ancient crafts and callings were, within the tract representing the common fields of Wrexham, rather thick upon the ground, and they occur also frequently within the ancient cultivated areas of other townships within this district. Now there is good reason to believe that names of the class indicated, *so occurring*, have, *when really ancient*, in the *majority* of cases, a very interesting explanation.

The early village community was self-supporting and in no wise trusted to the operation of free trade for the supply of its wants. The craftsmen that it needed it took care to provide, paying its shoemaker, smith, or other worker not in money or in kind but by the appropriation to him of certain lands in the village domain. The several *officers* of the community, the reeve, the herdsman, even the priest, were provided for in the same way. So that it is not impossible that the field which so late as the beginning of the present century was still called "Pant-y-crydd"—the "Shoemaker's hollow"—may have contained a portion of the land which the early Wrexham community once assigned in the common fields to the man or the men who made and mended the village shoes.

The words just used have been chosen with care, and it is important to note what they really imply. We are not to imagine that the shoemaker's share in the arable area lay all together in one field, or that it consisted in anything else than quillets dispersed over that area. We are to suppose (assuming the correctness of the explanation offered) that at

[1] I cannot refrain from quoting here certain passages from the third of Sir Henry Sumner Maine's lectures on "The Village Communities of the East and West." Sir Henry points out that "in India the village communities include a nearly complete establishment of occupations and trades for enabling them to continue their collective life without assistance from any person or body external to them." Among the occupations, those of the village headman, the Brahmin and the accountant, the blacksmith, the harness-maker, and the *shoemaker* are mentioned. "But the person practising any one of these hereditary employments is really the servant of the community as well as one of its members. He is sometimes paid by an allowance in grain, more generally by the allotment to his family of a piece of cultivated land in hereditary possession. Whatever else he may demand for the wares he produces is limited by a customary standard of price very rarely departed from. *It is the assignment of a definite lot in the cultivated area to particular trades which leads us to suspect that the early Teutonic groups were similarly self-sufficing.*" See also a very interesting article on "Allotments to Early Village Officers," by Mr. G. Lawrence Gomme, in "The Antiquary" (Vol. III., pp. 252-256.)

the time of the last assignment of portions in the common fields a definite number of quillets was assigned in " Pant-y-crydd " to an equal number of shoemaking families and a like number of quillets to the same families in at least two other closes. If to each of these latter a name having a similar import to that of " Pant-y-crydd " was not also given this was doubtless because these closes possessed already titles that were appropriate, and because like-sounding names could not conveniently be given to distinct fields situated within the same area. We need not consider that the whole of either of these closes was appropriated, even at first, to shoemakers. ,It would be sufficient that Pant-y-crydd should contain the shoe-makers' portion to secure for it the name it bore.

It is possible to find within six miles of Wrexham a case in which the maintenance of an important village functionary is still *in part* provided for by such an assignment as in the last paragraph has been supposed. Within the limits of the old village fields of Erbistock is a close called " The Parson's Field," which, under the corresponding Welsh name, " Cae'r person," can be traced at least as far back as 1620. Of the seven quillets into which this close is divided, three belong to the Rector, who owns also, as such, nineteen other quillets dispersed over the ancient cultivated area. And these, with two small fields within the same area, constitute the glebe.[1]

The three quillets belonging to the Vicar of Wrexham, one in each of the three fields of Wrexham Abbot, might be cited as a perfect example of the assignment to a public official of a definite group of lots within the town fields, if we could be quite sure that all three of these quillets had come down together from medieval times.

Two other of the town fields of Wrexham bore names containing reference to trades and callings. These were " Cae'r swynwr" ("The wizard's field,") and " Pant y glover" ("The glover's hollow"). If, however, the explanation above given be applied to the former of these, we should have to ask whether a wizard, as well as a shoemaker and a priest, was esteemed by the early Wrexham folk an essential part of the communal outfit. And with regard to "Pant y glover," it should be pointed out that the trade of a glover is not one of those ancient callings, important to every member of the community, to which the explanation referred to applies. Such a name

[1] The rectorial or vicarial glebe-lands of almost all the parishes around Wrexham contain a number of scattered quillets.

could hardly have arisen under the same conditions as those
with reference to which "Pant y crydd" might have acquired
the name it bore. Still, it should not be forgotten that the
making of gloves was a leading industry in Wrexham from
somewhat early times, and remained so until a late date.
Three glovers are mentioned in "the survey" (see page 48),
two of whom were evidently well-to-do, probably, therefore,
master-glovers, having other glovers in their employ. Twenty-
eight glovers are mentioned in the parish register during the
five years between October, 1677, and October, 1682. Nor
should we omit to notice another close which seems to have
lain within the same general area—"Cae'r Receiver" (the
"Receiver's field"), though this was not, properly speaking, a
"town field," but rather, apparently, a group of adjoining
quillets enclosed by one of the earlier Receivers of the manor.
The Receiver was an officer of the manorial lord, charged with
the duty of receiving and accounting for the rents of the
tenants (see page 11).

We may now give closer attention to a name—"Twmpath
y cryddion," or "Shoemakers' mound"—which has already
(page 32) been briefly referred to. Now, the fact must not be
overlooked that the land bearing this name lay, like Pant y
crydd, within the limits of what were once the common fields,
and may therefore have included an allotment having a like
origin to that assumed to have been situate within the close
just mentioned. But the form of the name seems rather to
suggest that it belonged to a guild of Wrexham shoemakers,
the members of which, having no common hall, held their
meetings around the mound of which the name, "Twmpath y
cryddion," still preserves the memory. And there are other
facts which should be taken in connection with this suggestion.
On one side of Crispin Lane is a piece of land, now traversed
by the Great Western Railway line, which was formerly called
"Crispin field" (see map), and on the other side of the same lane
(whose name is thus explained) was a large field (on the north
side of the present Race Course) known as "Crispin croft"
(see map). The triangular croft in the apex of which Crispin
Lodge has been built, and whose base forms one side of Stansty
Park, is called "Crispin meadow," while a second "Crispin
field" lies opposite to it on the other side of the Mold Road.
Now these several closes, or three of them, seem to have been
connected with a tavern which once stood in Stansty, called
"The Crispin Inn."[1] But St. Crispin was the patron saint of

[1] It twice appears in the parish register under the name "Cris-
pianus."

shoemakers; and it may very well be that in the name of this inn we have another indication of the former existence in Wrexham of some such incorporated society of these craftsmen as has been supposed.

Whatever be the explanation of the names which have been cited, they are, it cannot be denied, very curious and interesting.

WREXHAM FECHAN had also its tract of common arable fields. One of these, called "Maes Wrexham Fechan" ("Wrexham Fechan field") was, like the Town Fields of Wrexham Fawr, divided into quillets or groups of "selions" (=butts) held by different persons. Two quillets lying probably in the field just named bore specific names—"Erw goch" ("Red acre") and "Erwau 'r ysgubor" ("The Barn acres.") Since "Groft Tuddir" ("Tuddir's or "Tudor's croft") and "Cae newydd" or "Cae Cocksuite" ("The New" or "Cocksuite's field") contained also two or more "parcels" of land, it would seem that these closes had aforetime been included in the common fields of Wrexham Fechan. So had probably the close called "Acrau"—"The Acres." The name "Skithrey," borne by two other pieces of land in Wrexham Fechan, stands almost certainly for "ysgythrau"—"the cuttings" (plural of "ysgwthr"), and indicates in that case that the fields to which it was applied had themselves been *cut* up into quillets. [1] This name has been met with, at any rate, attached in other townships to closes which lay within the common fields of those townships, one of which closes was actually cut up in the way indicated. If this assumption be correct, and the "Ysgythrau" of Wrexham Fechan were a part of the common arable lands of that township, then it is possible to indicate the general position which those lands occupied. Since the former adjoined Glyn Park (see page 44), the latter must have lain on the right-hand side of the Ellesmere Road, as one goes towards the King's Mills.[2] Close to these, and perhaps formerly included within them, seem to have been "Cae'r deon" and "Kaer eyrregh," which latter is probably "Cae'r eurych,"—the tinker's or goldsmith's field. Just, in fact, as in the

---

[1] One of them was, in 1620, actually divided into "moities."

[2] There is some reason for suspecting that these common fields extended at one time townwards along the road mentioned as far as Bennion's Lane, so as to take in Cae'r porth (Gate-field), Pen y geilied (page 19), and other closes. But the situation of the several fields of Wrexham Fechan, mentioned in the survey, is indicated so vaguely that no conclusions based upon their relative positions can be regarded as absolutely certain.

fields of Wrexham Fawr we had several examples of the class of field-names referring to trades and callings, so we seem to have in those of Wrexham Fechan another example of the same class. As to the other field-name just mentioned, if we take the word " deon " in the sense in which it is now always used, and translate " Cae'r deon " as the " Dean's field," we shall get a name obviously of considerable importance in connection with the ecclesiastical history of the parish and district. There were formerly a great many fields in the Hundred bearing this name, and there are still a " Cae Deon " in Sontley, a " Tir y Deon " (" Dean's land ") in Stansty and apparently a " Tir Deon " in Burton. Whether we are to believe that the office of Rural Dean, now purely honorary, was formerly otherwise, and that the several fields mentioned indicate some of the lands once belonging as endowments to the Rural Deanery of this district, is not clear. Canon Thomas, in view of the great variety of ecclesiastical endowments, sees no reason why there should not have been such appropriations as those supposed; but makes at the same time the interesting suggestion that these " Dean's fields" may be connected with the possible residence in Wrexham of the Dean of St. Asaph during the time (1402-1482) that his cathedral lay in ruins.[1] To the former actual residence of Bishop Parfew in this town reference has already been made (page 16). It may, however, be not altogether out of place to point out that " Cae'r deon " should possibly be translated " The Strangers' field." " Deon," at any rate, had, it appears, this meaning in old Welsh, and the word is so used in the famous song called " Hirlas Owain," which commemorates a battle fought in this neighbourhood,[2] and which suggested to Mrs. Hemans the stirring stanzas published with her poems under the name of " The Hirlas Horn."

[1] In this connection should also, perhaps, be mentioned the tradition which relates that the parish church of Wrexham was formerly served by a college of clergy, The lands belonging to the dean presiding over such a college, or chapter of canons, might, of course, very well be called by such names as those quoted above. There is a house in the churchyard called " The College," and there are others in two townships adjoining known by the same name. These names lend, it is true, a certain likelihood to the tradition ; but it seems desirable, before that tradition is accepted, to ascertain when it first arose and what evidence beyond the names cited can be adduced in support of it.

[2] The Battle of Gaerddin, or Gardden.

We have now ascertained with tolerable precision the general position and extent of the common arable lands of old Wrexham. But where was the COMMON PASTURE? Doubtless, here as elsewhere, there was common of pasture over the fallow fields of the third year, and over the stubble of the other fields after the crops had been garnered. But there was also a continuous and ample tract of permanent pasture, on which the cattle of the community were wont to graze. This tract had in 1620 been for some time enclosed, but its former existence is, in the survey referred to, and a point within it indicated. It is plain from this reference—which will be discussed presently—and from other considerations, which will appear as we proceed, that the *main portion* of the old common pasture stretched southward from a line which roughly coincides with the present Holt Road to the brook, and eastward from the fields at the back of the Beast Market, and from the brow south of Smithfield Road, to the detached portion of Wrexham Abbot in which the Town Depôt and Spring Lodge now stand. This detached portion, also, it must have originally included. For common lands, it may safely be said, reached always to the township bounds,[1] and this bit of Wrexham Abbot lay within the bounds of the older and undivided manor of Wrexham. It seems, in fact, as already has been suggested (see page 26), that when, in the year 1200, that older and greater Wrexham was divided into two manors, the detached portion of Wrexham Abbot just mentioned was the portion of the old common pasture which was assigned to the manor last named.

"The Green," which is the older name of the present Salop Road, suggests the former existence there of a bit of open common (see page 16). And it may very well be that this bit of common, properly called "The Green," was in fact that portion of the old common pasture which became, so to say, entangled in the town. With the main portion of that common pasture the Green would then be connected by the narrow strip of land which lies between the brook and the ridge on which the house called "The Caeau" stands. The name "Caeau" ("The Fields," or, more strictly, "The Closes") seems to imply that the lands to which it was given had been enclosed, at a late date, from a tract formerly open and uncultivated.

[1] When *open* common pastures did not reach to the township bounds, this was because the common wood, itself a kind of common pasture, lay along those bounds.

The general area thus assigned ·as the site of the old common pasture of Wrexham is represented on the annexed map by the portion coloured green. It is the area to which several indications point. And it is the area which two passages in Norden's survey directly suggest. Let us now consider these two passages. In the first of them a piece of land called " Pwll yr vwde," adjacent to " Bron pwll yr vwde," is described as having formerly been common pertaining to the town of Wrexham, but as being then enclosed therefrom and held of the Crown by letters patent. Now if we could identify this piece of land we should fix one point at least within the old common pasture. Where, then, was " Pwll yr vwde ?" There is no evidence of any field in Wrexham having ever been so called, nor does the name itself carry any obvious meaning. The letter " v," however, is often used in the survey, and in other documents of the period, where " u " should appear. Replacing, then, the former letter by the latter in the name " Pwll yr vwd," we get " Pwll yr uwd."[1] Now there is good reason to believe that " Pwll yr wydd " ("Goose-pool "), the current Welsh name for the house more generally called " Spring Lodge," is a corruption of an older name, and that this older name is no other than " Pwll yr uwd." [2] The house just mentioned is never called "Pwll yr wydd " in the early parish registers, but always " Pwll yr ywd," and this is the name by which, even in our own times, old inhabitants have still spoken of it.[3] Since it is plain that the actual " Pwll yr uwd " and the house which took its name from it could not have been very far apart, it follows that we must seek the former in that portion of Wrexham Regis which lies nearest the latter. But it is possible to determine the position of " Pwll yr uwd " with still greater precision. Norden tells us that it was adjacent to "*Bron* pwll yr uwd " or " Pwll-yr-uwd *Brow*," and that the latter lay partly in another manor. The

[1] The final " e" is once omitted.

[2] " Pwll yr uwd " would mean "porridge pool." It would be idle to speculate as to how this name came to be given. The name of a hill in Ruabon appears elsewhere in the survey under the form " Bryn yr vwd," wherein again for "vwd" we should almost certainly read " uwd."

[3] Since the above was written I have noticed a contemporary reference to Pwll yr uwd House under its true and ancient title so late as 1786. The first mention of its modern name—Spring Lodge—that I have met with occurs under date July, 1810. Charles James, Esq., then lived there.

only "brow" to which this description can apply is that which overlooks the Town Depôt; and there can be very little doubt that we shall be right in regarding as "Pwll yr uwd" the level space which stretches between the foot of that hill and the entrance to the Depôt. The field on the opposite side of the Holt Road, which also overlooks the level space just indicated, seems to be that which Norden calls "Cae'r fron" ("Field of the brow"). (See Map.) But from one of the Pentrebychan manuscripts (date 1602) we learn that the full name of this field, which is described as "lying betweene the high waie leading from Wrexham toward Rhosenessnie and the land called y borthgrey on the north end," was "Kaer vron pwll yr vwd,"[1] that is "The *field* of Pwll-yr-uwd brow." Thus all indications point to the area marked on the annexed map, or to some area directly adjoining, as the site of the pool under discussion. It is very likely that the hollow close on the *north* side of Holt Road, opposite the Town Depôt, as well as the trough in which the Depôt itself stands, was *also* called "Pwll yr uwd."

A very interesting point in connection with "Pwll-yr-uwd" will be touched on hereafter (page 41). Its present interest for us, however, lies wholly in the statement contained in the passage from the survey already quoted, that it had aforetime formed part of Wrexham Common. Another passage throwing light on the extent of that common has been above referred to. This passage must be now considered.

Norden distinctly describes "The Dunks" as *moorland*— "the mores called Gwern dunck." That these "mores" are what we now call "The Dunks" (see page 46) is certain. The mention of them occurs in connection with the account that Norden gives of the boundaries of the township, and their position is therefore readily determined. It is true that the Dunks are situate not in Wrexham Regis, but in the detached portion of Wrexham Regis already mentioned; but we may be sure (since the division of Wrexham into two manors is of comparatively recent date) that the common pastures of the two townships were formerly one, and lay afterwards side by side, so that to fix the position of one is to fix the position of the other.

The general extent of the old common pasture of Wrexham may thus be regarded as determined with some approach to precision.

---

[1] In the document mentioned "v" is also used instead of "u." Thus, "Maes y dre ucha" is written "Maes y dre vcha."

To that common pasture an incidental reference of considerable interest occurs in one of the Pentrebychan manuscripts. The manuscript referred to, which is a deed of sale bearing date 1573, conveys a messuage in High Street (the messuage which belonged afterwards to Mr. Hugh Meredith—see page 8)—and four parcels of land in the town and fields of Wrexham pertaining to the same. The first of these parcels is described as being called "Kae byghan" (see page 14), and stretching in breadth between the lands of John Hugh and the lands belonging to the Vicar of the parish church of Wrexham, and in length from the Beast Market to "*the place called Rhosnesni*," and to other lands. It thus appears that the common pasture of Wrexham was formerly called "Rhosnesni," or, rather, that it was regarded as a portion of the tract of moorland bearing that name. That this tract occupied a part of the township of Acton was already plain from the existence of the hamlet called "Rhosnessney" situate within that township; that it extended into Abenbury so as to approach or surround the farmstead there called "Hullah" ("Yr hwla"—see map)—might appear from an entry in the Parish Register, [1] and that it stretched from Acton and Abenbury westward almost to our own doors we now know. In view of this last-named fact, the explanation of the name "Rhosnessney" as "Rhos nessa i ni" ("the rhos or moor nearest to us") becomes at once invested with a certain likelihood.

On the town moor we should naturally expect to find the town gallows. And Norden distinctly tells us that the field called "Pwll yr uwd," whose position we now know, had actually been, before it was enclosed, "the place of execution for malefactors."[2] The hill which at the time of the survey was called "*Bron* pwll yr uwd," is mentioned in the tithe map schedule under the name "Bryn y fwyell"—hill of the *axe*. It can scarcely be doubted that we have in this latter name a

---

[1] The following is the entry referred to:—[April, 1697] "1. Peter Ellis of whola or Rosenesney was Buryed." That we are to take this as implying that Hwla was a part of Rhosnessney, and not that Peter Ellis lived *either* at Hwla or Rhosnessney, appears from entries relating to other townships in which a similar form Is used.

[2] Doubtless it was here that Mr. Richard White (see page 9), thirty-six years before the date of the survey, bore so nobly the horrible death which the interested zeal of men less worthy was permitted to inflict upon him. If so, not all were malefactors that suffered at Pwll yr uwd.

MAP REPRESENTING OUTLINES OF CERTAIN FIELDS I

see correction p35 of Town Fields

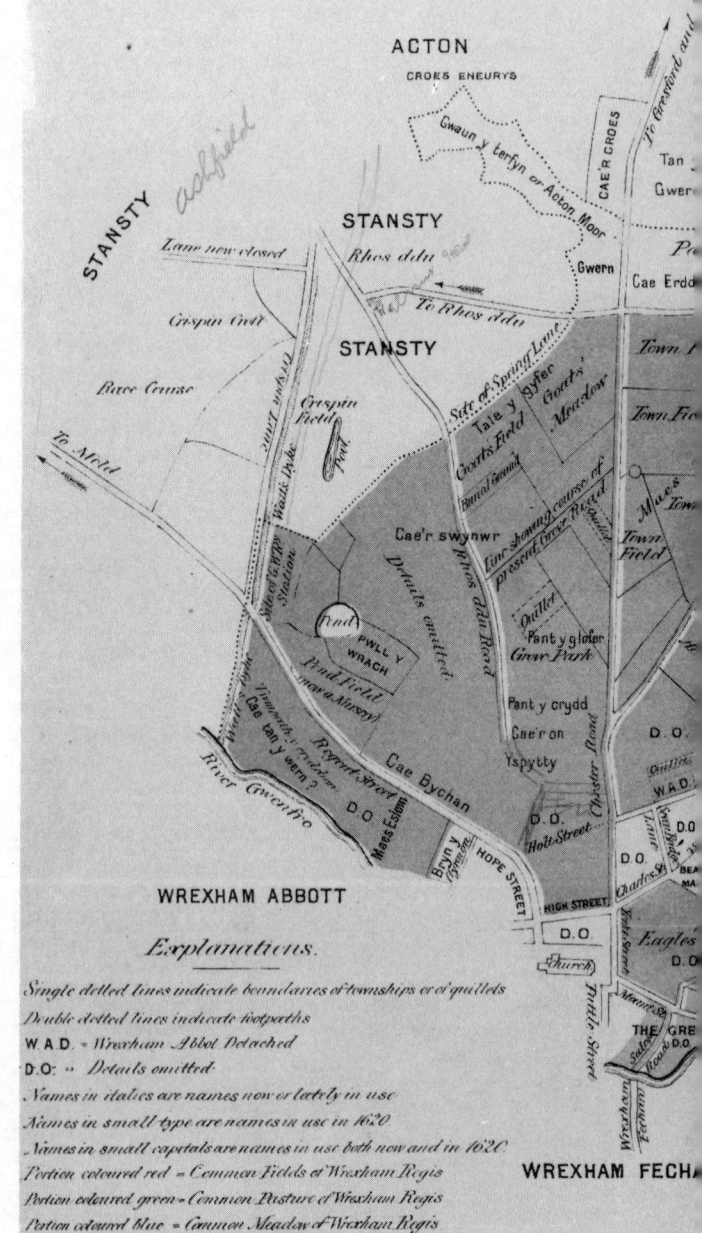

ACTON

CROES ENEURYS

Gwaun y terfyn or Acton Moor

CAER CROES

Tan
Gwern

STANSTY *ashfield*

STANSTY

Lane now closed

Rhos ddu

Gwern

Cae Erdd

Crispin Croft

To Rhos ddu

STANSTY

Race Course

Crispin
Field

Croft

Site of Spring Lane

Tate y Syfer

Goats
Meadow

Town F

Town Field

Courts Field

Burial Ground

Line showing course of
present Grove Road

Maes

Town

Cae'r swynwr

Site of Gaol &
Station

Pwll

PWLL Y
WRACH

Pond Field
now a Meadow

Details omitted

Rhos ddu Road

Town
Field

Quillet

Pant y glofer

Grove Park

Pant y crydd

Cae'r on

Yspytty

D.O.

D.O.

Hand Walk Drib

Walk Drib

Byegate Street

Cae
tan y vern?

Maes Eshim

River Gwenfro

Cae Bychan

D.O.

D.O.

Quillet

W.A.D.

Bryn y Grug

Chester Road

Holt Street

D.O.

D.O.

Charles St

BEA

MA

Bryn y Grug

HOPE STREET

HIGH STREET

D.O.

Eagles

D.O.

WREXHAM ABBOTT

D.O.

Church

Yorke St

THE GRE

Brittle Street

Wrexham Fechan Road

Salop Road

THE GRE

D.O.

Explanations.

Single dotted lines indicate boundaries of townships or of quillets

Double dotted lines indicate footpaths

WAD. = Wrexham Abbot Detached

D.O. = Details omitted

Names in italics are names now or lately in use

Names in small type are names in use in 1620.

Names in small capitals are names in use both now and in 1620.

Portion coloured red = Common Fields of Wrexham Regis

Portion coloured green = Common Pasture of Wrexham Regis

Portion coloured blue = Common Meadow of Wrexham Regis

Portion coloured yellow = Common Fields of Wrexham Abbot

Portion coloured purple = Common Pasture of Wrexham Abbot

WREXHAM FECHA

Scale :- 6 inches to the Mile.

reference to the fatal functions which were formerly wont to be discharged on the space below.

Let us now continue our account of the common lands of Wrexham.

No evidence has been found of the former existence in Wrexham *Regis* of a COMMON WOOD ; if there ever was such a wood in the township it must have occupied that area on the northern side of the latter where the common fields did not reach the border (see page 21). The portion of that area called "Gwaun y terfyn" is actually described in 1562 as containing "underwood." But it seems not unlikely that the common wood of *old* Wrexham was situate in that portion of it which afterwards became Wrexham Abbot, and within the area which in 1620 was called Glyn Park. Some confirmation of this opinion is to be found in the statement of Mr. Norden's jurors that the underwoods in that park the tenants " doe take and use for tinsell [kindling or firewood] as need requires." (See page 45.)

In this wood of Glyn the inhabitants of Wrexham Fechan were we may suppose intercommoners with those of Wrexham Fawr. If this supposition be correct, the common fields of Wrexham Fechan would stretch from the inhabited village to the edge of the common wood, and the common wood from the outer hem of the common fields to the border of the township. Such a position would, at any rate, be a normal one both for the former and the latter.

But the area over which the cultivating and associated householders of old Wrexham exercised rights of use would have been inadequate to their requirements if it had not included a COMMON MEADOW as well as common fields and a common pasture. There is, indeed, no reference to such a meadow in the survey of 1620 ; but this may have been because it had already been appropriated to the use of the lord. How much more readily such an appropriation might be effected in the case of the common meadow than in the case of the common fields will appear presently.

Meanwhile it may be well to point out what the conditions of tenure in the common meadows of England and the Continent were. Those conditions varied very much. But, speaking generally, it may be said that at the beginning of the growth of grass the meadows were portioned out into as many parallel strips, generally called "doles,"[1] as there were persons

---

[1] This word " dole " must not be confounded with the Welsh "dol," which signifies " a meadow," and which is pronounced in the same

entitled to receive them. To each portioner one of these strips
was then assigned, the assignment being determined either by
lot or in accordance with a definite scheme of rotation. But
the portioners held their plots no longer than the end of the
hay harvest, so that on old Lammas Day all their *several*
rights in the common meadow were determined, and the latter
became for the rest of the year an open and free common of
pasture for the cattle of the tenants and inhabitants. Also,
frequently, once in three years, each of the common meadows
in turn lay fallow.

Now it is plain that a holding which was enjoyed for only
four or five months out of twelve was much more precarious
than one which was occupied continuously ; and we must not,
therefore, be surprised if the attempts of the lord upon the
common meadow were more successful than were his attempts
upon the common fields.

Putting aside for the present the question as to whether
there was ever in Wrexham a tract of land with which the
right of common in meadow was connected, let us inquire
whether there formerly existed here an area which was
regarded as permanently devoted to the raising of hay. It
would seem that there was actually such an area. Norden
describes as "meadows" three closes which were called
respectively "Gweirglawdd fawr" ("Big hayfield"),
"Gweirglawdd fechan" ("Little hayfield"), and "Gweirglawdd hir" ("Long hayfield"). Two of these lay east
of the church and adjoined, and we may be almost certain
that the third was not far distant. The name of the first
can be traced as far back as 1562. Other pieces, also, of
meadow, two of which, described as "parcells," were possibly
enclosed "doles," seem to have lain within the same general
area. The evidence is not complete, but as far as it goes it
appears to show that east of the church was situated a tract
of land which in 1620 was used for the growing of hay, and
which in earlier times had also been so used. It is probable
that the general extent of this tract of meadow is, on the
whole, accurately represented on the annexed map by the
portion coloured blue.

But it would be strange if the arable land of old Wrexham
being common fields, and the pasture land common pasture,
the meadow land were not at the same time common meadow.

way. The "doles" of the common meadows are simply the portions
of the latter which are yearly *dealt* out, or assigned to those who
have rights therein.

GLYN PARK has already been mentioned, and it is now time to give a fuller account of it.

At the time of "the survey," Erddig Park was not in existence, or, at any rate, was not in existence under that name. But a large part of the present park had formed a portion of an earlier enclosure called "Glyn Park," which, in 1620, had been disparked, ploughed, and divided into several holdings. This park was formed by the valley or "glyn" (whence its name) through which the Clywedog, in its course from the Ruabon Road to King's Mills, flows, and included, besides, a considerable area of level land on the Wrexham side of the Glyn. It appears, indeed, that the Sontley and Erddig Roads, from the point at which (near the present Bath Road) they diverge, lay wholly within it. Its total area was 350 acres. The name of the house called "Coed-y-glyn" is a reminiscence of it. A rough plan of this park was made by Mr. Norden, and has been recently published in the third volume of Lloyd's "History of Powys Fadog." Within the Ruabon Road end of the park the river had been divided into two watercourses, and a mill built on each. On the plan, these mills are represented as distinct buildings, but in the survey they are described as being under one roof. They are represented to-day by the building called Y Felin Buleston. A farmhouse is described as situate near the mills. It is plain from the plan that this farmhouse is the same that we now call Little Erddig. The park had been some time before leased to Peter Warburton, Esq., of Lincoln's Inn, who had assigned his interest therein to Dr. Yale, from whom it had come to Mr. Richard Davies, a silk mercer, of London. One or other of these had unlawfully cut down the trees in the park so that at the time of the survey only a few scrubs were standing, and about twelve acres of underwood ("hasell, allders, withie, and thornes") on the hills. The lower part of the park is described as "boggyd." The rent of the whole is returned at seventy-nine shillings and eightpence a year.

The Erddig Park of our own times has been formed by re-enclosing a part of old Glyn Park, and adding thereto portions of the townships of Erddig and Sontley.

Mr. Norden prefaces his entry relating to Glyn Park with the following important note:—"This is not leased frome 40 yeres to 40 yeres but as demean." The extent of the old town-fields has been ascertained: a probable conjecture as to the position of the common pasture and of the common meadow has been formed, and now we possess in the passage quoted a

clear indication of the position of "the demesne." We are
clearly to take the word "demesne" here in its *narrower* sense
as indicating that portion of the manor which, before the latter
fell to the Crown, the lord held in his own hands. The
position, however, of the park, in relation, first to the
boundaries of Wrexham Fawr and Wrexham Fechan, and,
secondly, to the assumed position of the common fields of the
township last named, suggests the possibility of its having been
at a date still earlier the common wood of old Wrexham (see
page 42). It should be said, however, that while such evidence
as there is favours the suggestion thus made, that evidence is
very far from being conclusive.

Just as at the Ruabon Road end of old Glyn Park the stream
had been divided into two watercourses, so had it, according
to Mr. Norden's "plan," been divided just outside the other,
or Shrewsbury Road end of the park. And once more, on each
of these watercourses stood a mill. One of these was called
" Mr. Puleston's Mill," the other the " Prince's "—the predecessors of that we now call " The King's Mills." Of the first
of these no mention can be found in the survey, but the second
is described as newly built and as let to Robert Puleston, Esq.,
of Hafod y wern. Mr. Puleston held, therefore, both mills, but
of the second was only sub-tenant, holding it under Mr. Robert
Bellot to whom it had been leased for £10. 6s. 8d. a year.
At this mill Mr. Norden records "all the tenauntes and inhabitants of this manno' of Wrexham are bound to grind."
The Prince's Mill was, in fact, as we might infer from its name,
the town-mill for Wrexham Regis, just as the Abbot's Mill in
Pentre'r felin (now the Zoedone Works) was the town-mill for
Wrexham Abbot. The latter is still popularly called " The
Town Mill." The Prince's Mill was otherwise called
" Y Felin Newydd " (The New Mill) : the group of houses that
grew up around it thus coming to be known as " Pentre'r felin
newydd "—"The hamlet of the New Mill." Then, to dis-
tinguish this hamlet from the " Pentre'r felin " in Wrexham
Abbot (now called simply " Pentre felin ") the latter was
named " Pentre'r felin Abad "—" The hamlet of the Abbot's
Mill." And these names were still in use a hundred years
ago.

The same Mr. Bellot to whom the Prince's Mill or Felin
Newydd had been leased, farmed, for £10. 6s. 8d. a year, the
tolls of the fairs and market of Wrexham. Among the tolls
he was entitled to levy were " pickage " and " stallage,"
pickage being a charge for breaking the ground, and stallage

a charge for setting up stalls thereupon.   Markets were in 1620 kept on Mondays and Thursdays, and fairs held on the 12th of March, the 5th of June, and the 8th of September.

Mr. Bellot was a nephew of the Bishop Bellot who lies buried in the chancel of Wrexham Church, and lived, it is believed, at Plas Power, then called " Ty Bellot." ·

Situate somewhere upon " Gwern dunck " and along the boundary of the township, was a hill called " Bryn Tunck." It is plain that "Gwern dunck " and " Bryn tunck " contain the same word, and probable that this word is no other than· " twnc."   Now " twnc " was a tribute paid to the chief by the ancient Welsh freeholders or " uchelwyr."   It appears from a passage in the " Record of Caernarvon " (quoted in the 1847 volume of " Archaeologia Cambriensis ") that a particular " vill " mentioned therein paid as " twnc " to the Abbot and Convent of Bardsey eighteenpence in money and certain measures of barley.   In the same passage the expression— " From every Rander whence Twnc is paid "—occurs.   It seems then very likely that " Gwern dwnc," once much more extensive than now,· constituted aforetime, together with other lands, a " Rhandir ' or Division-land, which yielded " twnc " to the chief.

It should be pointed out that the name " Gwern dwnc " preserves for us the memory of a condition of society earlier than that we have above described.   The ancient cultivating community of Wrexham, on whose doings so much light has now been thrown, though exclusively Welsh so far as race and speech were concerned, was yet organised strictly according to the English or Anglo-Norman manorial type.   But the name which the Dunks still bear carries us back to a time when there were as yet no manors in Bromfield, when the relations between higher and lower were not of a feudal kind, and when the Saxon, if he had already come hither, had not yet come to *stay*.

It may be fitting to give here a brief account of those of the

[1] In the portion of Abenbury which surrounds Abenbury Lodge, and adjoins The Dunks, are fields having such names as " Garden *Dunk*," " House *Dunk*," " Flood *Dunk*," " Footpath *Dunk*," " Lane *Dunk*," and " Far *Dunk*."   Several of these fields are represented on the annexed map.

chief tenants [1] of Wrexham Regis mentioned by Norden that have not been already dealt with.

JOHN JEFFREYS, Esq., was the son of Jeffrey ap Hugh, of Wrexham, and the first of the family to bear the surname which afterwards became identified with it. He held at the time of the survey, besides the Acton estate, a great deal of leasehold property in Wrexham (see page 24). Doubtless his position as one of the deputy stewards of the lordship, gave him opportunities of acquiring this kind of property on easy terms. He lived, as already has been intimated (see page 12) in Wrexham, but his son, who succeeded to his estates and bore the same name, took up his residence at Acton. This John Jeffreys the second was the father of George Lord Jeffreys, of Wem (better known as "Judge Jeffreys"), and grandfather of the Sir Griffith Jeffreys, who rebuilt Acton Hall, and whose widow, Dame Dorothy Jeffreys, is still by her charities remembered among us.

HUGH MEREDITH, Esq., was the founder of the Pentrebychan branch of the Merediths. At Pentrebychan, however, he does not seem to have ever lived. In 1620, and for some time before and after, he resided in Wrexham, either in that tenement of his in Lampint, which became afterwards "The Seven Stars," or in his other house in High Street, which has been already described (see page 8). He had previously lived in London and at Llwynon. He was "Keeper of the Original Seal for the Counties of Denbigh and Montgomery," and became, in 1621, High Sheriff of Denbighshire. He died at some date between the years 1624 and 1626.

ROGER ELLIS, Esq., and DOROTHY ELLIS were respectively son and widow of Humphrey Ellis, Esq., of Alrhey Hall, Bangor, and the latter was a daughter of Edward Jones, Esq., of Plas Cadwgan, in Esclusham, who was put to death on a charge of high treason in the year 1586.

GABRIEL GOODMAN, Esq., was doubtless a member of the Ruthin family of that name. He was buried at Wrexham on the 30th of May, 1641.

NICHOLAS AP JOHN EDWARD, held some freehold, and much leasehold, property at the time of the survey. His "mansion house" is mentioned, but no hint given as to where it stood.

EDWARD CREW, Gentleman, another considerable leaseholder in the Wrexham of 1620, was member of a family to which

---

[1] By "chief tenants" is meant those who held most land or houses, or paid the highest rents, or those who, without being large holders, bore distinguished names.

Sylvanus Crue, the engraver, belonged, and which had afterwards for several generations representatives in the towns
of Wrexham and Holt.   He died in January, 1636, and was
buried at Wrexham.

RALPH AP ELLIS was a blacksmith who lived in Lampint.
He held several cottages and various pieces of land in the
Town Fields.   Geoffrey ap Ellis, another blacksmith, whom
we may suppose to have been Ralph's brother, seems to have
lived in "the street below the churchyard."

The reference just made to the two blacksmiths mentioned
in the survey may now, in conclusion, be appropriately supplemented by the following list of the names and callings of the
other tradesmen of whom Norden speaks.   These were :—
Hugh ap Robert, the currier and glover ; John David, the
glover ; Griffith Jones, the joiner ; Ralph Lloyd, the shoemaker ; Hugh David, the baker ; Robert ap Hugh, the butcher ;
Richard Benjamin, the butcher ; John ap John, the clothier ;
Roger Powell, the "waker," or fuller ; David ap Hugh, the
silk-weaver ; and Edward Jones, the hatter.

All the main points of interest which Norden's survey
presents have now been touched on.   The direct statements of
that survey have been supplemented by the statements of
other documents, and by deductions drawn from the field names
which Norden mentions, or which have been gleaned from
other sources.   Important information relating to the Wrexham
of the time of James the First has thus been obtained, and a
series of inferences thence derived as to the condition of the
Wrexham of earlier times.   Many of the subjects thus discussed involve points of so much difficulty—points which have
never been touched by any previous historian of Wrexham—
that the author cannot hope to have wholly escaped mistakes
in his treatment of them.   But he has spared no pains to
secure an accurate presentment of the matters dealt with, and
has been especially careful to distinguish between what is fact
and what is merely speculative and inferential.

CORRECTIONS

Page 125, line 4 from top of page, for "Wrexham Regis" read "Wrexham Abbot."

Page 126, line 5 from bottom of page, for "suggestion" read "explanation."

Page 127, line 5 from top of note, for "Cross" read "Croes."

The portion of the common fields between Chester Road and the present Regent Street is accidentally represented on the accompanying map as reaching to the back of High Street. In reality, this portion did not extend further southward than the Yspytty. It is perhaps necessary to add that only those streets are given on the map, the direction of which it was necessary to mark in order to fix the positions of the fields represented.

Offa's and Wat's Dykes

OFFA'S AND WAT'S DYKES.*

By Alfred Neobard Palmer.

The following notes relate to those portions only of Offa's and Wat's Dykes which traverse the hundred of Bromfield and the parishes of Chirk, Hope, and Mold.

I do not propose to treat of those points relating to the dykes which have already been handled by other writers, and are matters of common knowledge. Those who desire to become acquainted with what has been said of those portions of the dykes not here dealt with are referred to the articles of the late Rev. H. Longueville Jones in the 1856 volume of *Archæologia Cambrensis*,[1] to the article by Professor Earle in the 1857 volume,[2] and to that by Dr.

---

[1] "Offa's Dyke and Wat's Dyke," *Arch. Camb.* for 1856 (3rd Series, vol. ii.), pp. 1–23, and "Offa's Dyke," No. ii., in the same volume, pp. 151-4. See, too, in the immediately following pp. 155–8, the remarks on "Offa's Dyke," by the Rev. Jonathan Williams, forming part of his *History of Radnorshire.*—E. P.

[2] "Offa's Dyke in the neighbourhood of Knighton," by Professor John Earle, *Arch. Camb.* for 1857 (3rd series, vol. iii.), pp. 196–209. See also the note by the Editor (Mr. Longueville Jones), pp. 209–10, and that by Mr. Thomas Wright, pp. 311-2 of the same volume. A letter by "E. B. C. G." on the remains of Offa's Dyke on and about Titley, Herefordshire, will be found in *Cambrian Quarterly Magazine* for 1833 (vol. v.), p. 421.—E. P.

---

* A paper read before the Honourable Society of Cymmrodorion on Wednesday, April 29th, 1891.

Edwin Guest in the 1858 volume of the same serial.[1]
What I aim to do is to put on record the materials I have
myself collected relating to the dykes, scanty as those
materials are.

It may be desirable, however, first of all, to subject to a
brief but careful examination those documents, already
known and available, which contain the earliest references
to the two dykes, or to one of them, and to inquire how far
those documents and references are trustworthy, so as to
learn whatever is possible from those sources, concerning
the origin and purpose of these wonderful works with which
in this paper I propose to deal.

As to Offa's Dyke, its construction by Offa, King of
Mercia, as a boundary between his own territory and that
of the Welsh is well attested. Thus, there is its name,
which, both in its Welsh and English form, attributes it to
him. The oldest reference to the dyke is by Asser, who,
it must be remembered, was a Welshman from *Mynyw* or
St. Davids (*Asser Menevensis*), and who wrote only about a
hundred years after Offa's death. This is what Asser
says: "There was of late in Mercia a certain strenuous
king, and a formidable one among all the kings about him
and the neighbouring countries, Offa by name, who ordered
to be made, between Britain and Mercia, the great dyke
from sea to sea."[2] There was a very early MS. (the
ancient "Otho, A. xii.") of Asser, which was destroyed in

[1] "On the Northern termination of Offa's Dyke," by Dr. Edwin
Guest, *Arch. Camb.* for 1858 (3rd series, vol. iii.), pp. 335–342.
[2] The following are Asser's actual words: "Fuit in Mercia
moderno tempore quidam strenuus, atque universis circa se regibus
et regionibus finitimis, formidolosus rex, nomine Offa, qui vallum
magnum, inter Britanniam atque Merciam de mari usque ad mare
facere imperavit." *Annales Rerum Gestarum. Ælfredi ab. An.
DCCCXLIX. ad An. DCCCLXXXVII., Auctore Asserio Menevensi,*
as printed in *Monumenta Historica Britannica,* vol. i. p. 471. The
passage will be found at p. 10 of Wise's edition.

the Cottonian fire in 1732, but which had been printed by
Wise at Oxford ten years before. Knowing that one of
the printed editions of Asser [1] contains many interpolations, I was once doubtful as to the genuineness of the
passage quoted relating to Offa's Dyke, but Mr. Egerton
Phillimore kindly undertook to look into the matter, and
wrote to me thus : "In the edition of Asser given in the
Monumenta Historica Britannica, all the passages which
can be shown by a comparison of the different MSS. and
editions not to have been in the old Cottonian MS. are
placed in brackets, but the passage about Offa is not among
them, therefore it evidently *is* the genuine work of Asser."

Mr. Phillimore has also called my attention to a passage
in *The Life of St. Oswald*, written in the year 1162, and
printed in The Works of Simeon of Durham. [2] The following is a translation of the passage : "This place [Maserfeld]
is distant from the dyke of King Offa, which divides
England and North Wales, scarcely half a mile, from
Shrewsbury quite seven miles, and from Wenlock Abbey,
towards the south, about sixteen miles. The aforesaid
dyke King Offa formerly constructed, entrenched within
the defence of which he abode the more securely from his
Welsh enemies. For, in his time, continual strife existed
between him and the Welsh, so that he could by no means
get the upper hand of their assaults or ambushes, except
with this protection. From sea to sea, therefore, it hemmed
in almost all his land towards Wales, and he fixed that
dyke to be the boundary of the land of either." [3]

---

[1] The edition (1574) of *Asser's Life of Alfred*, by Archbishop
Parker, with interpolations from some *Annals*, falsely ascribed to
Asser—*The Pseudo Asser*.

[2] Rolls edition, 1882. This *Life* is attributed by Thomas Arnold,
the editor of the Rolls edition, to Reginald of Durham. Introduction,
p. xli.—E. P.

[3] "Distatque locus iste a fossa regis Offæ, quæ Angliam et

In the foregoing passage, it will have been observed, Offa's Dyke is said to divide *North* Wales from England, and yet to run from sea to sea.[1] Mr. Phillimore, therefore, suggested to me that perhaps by "North Wales," what we know now as Wales, as distinguished from "West Wales" (Cornwall, and parts of Devon), was intended by the writer. It will be remembered that from about the seventh to the tenth century the whole, roughly speaking, of what is now known as "Wales," was called by the English "*North* Wales," while they gave to Cornwall and a large part of Devon the name of "West Wales." But when the Life of St. Oswald was written these appellations had lost their original meaning, and I have sometimes wondered whether, while borrowing from Asser the statement that Offa constructed a dyke from sea to sea, the author of *The Life* was not in possession of other information relating to *Wat's Dyke*, which exists in North Wales only, and attributed this to Offa also. In that case he would, of course, confound the two dykes, but he would also be an early witness to the existence of Wat's Dyke, and to the tradition which ascribed it, as well as the other dyke, to King

Waliam borealem dividit, miliario non ferme dimidio, et Scropesbyri miliario integre septimo, ab abbatia vero Waneloc versus plagam meridianam miliario circiter sextodecimo. Fossam prædictam rex quondam Offa effecerat, cujus munimine vallatus securius ab hostibus suis Walensibus commanebat. Nam suo tempore juge certamen inter illum et Walenses extitit, quod nullatenus eorum impetus vel insidias nisi hac protectione devitare prævaluit. A mare ergo usque ad mare, pœne totam terram suam versus Waliam præcinxit, et fossam illam utriusque terræ terminum fore constituit." *Vita Si Oswaldi*, cap. xiv., printed in Simeon's *Works*, Rolls edition, i. 353.

[1] Really at present to a point on the Wye opposite Bridge Sollers. From this point to Chepstow, it is probable, the Wye formed the frontier of Offa's dominion. But I do not speak with any authority as to the dyke in South Wales.

Offa. In any case, we have in the *Life of St. Oswald* a twelfth century reference to the great dyke between England and Wales, and to its being named after King Offa, whichever dyke he meant.

Simeon of Durham himself also speaks of Offa's Dyke thus: "Beorhtric, King of the West Saxons, took to himself in marriage Eadburh, a daughter of a king of the Mercians, Offa by name, *who ordered to be made between Britain and Mercia the great dyke*, that is, *from sea to sea*.[1] The words which I have italicized are a *verbatim* quotation from the true Asser (see the quotation in note 2 on p. 66 before), and Mr. Phillimore tells me are printed as such in small type in the Rolls edition of Simeon's works.

Although in the *Annales Cambriæ*, the *Anglo-Saxon Chronicle*, and the oldest or Strata Florida edition of the *Brut y Tywysogion* many particulars are given of the devastations of Wales by Offa, no mention is made in any of these works of the construction of the dyke which has for so long borne his name and which he beyond question ordered to be made.[2]

The poet Churchyard's statement in his *Worthinesse of Wales* (A.D. 1587) that the space between the two dykes was "free ground," wherein the Danes and Britons met and made "trafficke," is, so far as I know, quite unattested, and is, therefore, until such attestation be forthcoming, wholly unworthy of attention. Even the sixteenth century

---

[1] "Rex autem Brichtric occidentalium Saxonum accepit sibi in conjugium Eadbergam quæ filia regis Merciorum, nomine Offa, *qui vallum magnum inter Britanniam atque Merciam*, id est, *de mari usque ad mare facere imperavit.*" Simeon Monachus Dunelmensis— *Historia Regum.* Works, ii. p. 66, Rolls edition, 1882.

[2] It is worth while noting the local names for Offa's Dyke recorded by Professor Earle in *Arch. Camb.* for 1857 (vol. iii. p. 197) as existing in English Radnorshire between Knighton and Presteign, viz. *Heyve Deyttch, Have Deytch,* and *Hof Deytch.*—E. P.

Book of Aberpergwm knows nothing of this "neutral ground" theory, on which subsequent writers have been so eloquent.

It has been suggested that the dyke now called " Clawdd Offa " was already in existence before Offa's time, and was merely utilized by him as a boundary. But we must remember that the dykes have undergone the wearing influences—what the geologists would call the "degradation"—of more than a thousand years. When first constructed, therefore, their embankments must have been very much higher, and their ditches deeper than they are now. In particular, the larger of these two dykes, if it existed before Offa's days, must have been so stupendous, that it is inconceivable it should not have had already a distinctive name, or that it should have been attributed, both by Welsh and English, to King Offa. The first English period was, in fact, the time when it was by no means unusual to construct boundary dykes such as these. Cases in point are: *Wansdyke*, with its dyke on the north side, which was probably constructed by the West Saxons,[1] and *The Devil's Dyke*, with its ditch on the western side, which certainly formed one of the defences of the East Angles against the Mercians. It is true that when Offa's Dyke passes a Roman station (as at Caergwrle), or actually traverses a Roman settlement (as at the Ffrith), it has been found to contain Roman coins, fibulæ, inscribed altars, brooches, pins, rings of gold, silver, and copper, part of an inscribed lamp, &c., or even to cover a hypocaust,[2] but all

---

[1] That Wansdyke is post-Roman is manifest since it covers Roman remains.

[2] See Lewis's *Topographical Dictionary of Wales*, edition 1850, article " Hope." I once examined very hurriedly part of the hoard described by Lewis, which is now preserved at Nant y ffrith, and can vouch for the presence in it of coins of Domitian, Marcus

this only shows that the dyke has been constructed since the Romans left the country.

We have seen that the evidence is incontestable which points to Offa having constructed the dyke called by his name as a boundary between his own territory and that of the Welsh. That Wat's Dyke was also intended to mark the boundary between the Welsh and Mercians, and that it was constructed by the latter, seems certain from its resemblance to Offa's Dyke, the ditch in both cases being on the western and not on the eastern side of the vallum. The facts now to be named are also interesting as pointing to these conclusions. In the township of Bistre, in the parish of Mold, through which Wat's Dyke runs, there is a field on the east side of the dyke called "English field," while adjoining it, but on the west side of the same dyke, and in the township of Hartsheath, are two fields named in the Tithe Survey of 1837 *Coitia Bruton.*[1] These names show that more than fifty years ago Wat's Dyke was traditionally regarded as a national boundary, although it had for centuries run within Welsh territory, and had a Welsh-speaking population east of it. I ought to say that in the parishes of Hope and Mold, and especially in the latter, *coitia, coetia,* or *coitié* is one of the commonest of

Antoninus, and Trajan. Mr. R. V. Kyrke tells me that his uncle, in cutting a road through Offa's Dyke at the Ffrith, found an inscribed Roman altar which has since somehow disappeared. Mr. R. V. Kyrke himself, when excavations were made close to the same spot in 1874, saw a hypocaust, flue-tiles, &c., and added he, "there are plenty yet *in situ* there if any one would excavate." There was evidently a Roman settlement at the Ffrith, and when Offa's Dyke was carried through it, the various objects found during the present century were either covered by the dyke, or thrown up with the earth which was used to make it.

[1] This supposes *Bruton* to be a corruption of the Welsh *Brython,* perhaps influenced by the English *Briton.*—E. P. Compare "Bryn Bruton," near Beaumaris.—A. N. P.

field-names,[1] and although *perhaps* containing the word *coed*, 'trees,' at the present time means nothing more than 'field.' *Bruton* is doubtless (if accurately spelled in the Survey) a loan-word from the English, and this shows that the name *Coitia Bruton*, in its present form, is comparatively modern and corrupt. Nevertheless, these field-names appear to me to embody a tradition, and to be worth recording. It is true that field-names into which the word *Saeson* ('The English') enters are not confined to the east of Wat's Dyke, but it is curious that nearly all the fields so named (*that are known to me*) lie a little west of *Offa's* Dyke, which was undoubtedly a national boundary, so that if such names should be found a little west of Wat's Dyke also, this fact will not invalidate the conclusion that Wat's Dyke was a national boundary as well. *Cae'r Saeson* in Treuddyn and *Gwerglodd y Saeson* in Brymbo were perhaps the sites of early struggles between the Welsh and the English.

I think it extremely probable that when these dykes were actually national boundaries they were defended on the western edge by strong palisades of wood, and also that along the top of each ran a broad, fairly level road,[2] so that thereby forces could easily be forwarded from the permanent stations or forts to any point which was threatened. Along these roads also messengers could run without any impediment. The tops of the dykes being flat and raised above the surrounding country, and also remaining for a long time comparatively bare of trees, we can understand why it is that so many ancient mansions and farmhouses were built either actually upon the *valla*, or a few yards to

---

[1] This name is, in fact, fairly common throughout the main body of the county of Flint.

[2] Between the Ffrith and Treuddyn the high road runs still for more than a mile along the top of Offa's Dyke.

the east of them, for it must be remembered that, on the
eastern side, the ground very gradually rises to the level of
the top of the dykes.

In the parish of Ruabon there are two townships called
Moreton, one on the west, and the other on the east of
Offa's Dyke. The former of these is indifferently called
Moreton Wallicorum ('Moreton of the Welsh'), and
Moreton uwch y Clawdd ('Moreton above the Dyke'), and
the latter *Moreton is y Clawdd* ('Moreton below the Dyke'),
of which a portion, east of *Wat's* Dyke, is called *Moreton
Anglicorum* ('Moreton of the English').[1] Here we seem
again to have Wat's, as well as Offa's Dyke, appearing as a
national boundary. Now these names are very old, and
when we remember that in 1620, and for centuries before,
nearly all the field-names of the townships in question were
Welsh, and most of the inhabitants Welsh-speaking, I
think we must conclude that the tradition was very ancient
which regarded Wat's Dyke, like Offa's, as a national
boundary. It must be borne in mind that the Mercians, as
I have shown in another paper, had conquered and settled,
about the time of King Offa, the country, or greater part
of the country, as far west as Offa's Dyke, and remained
there for some centuries, but that, about the eleventh
century, the Welsh drove them out, or assimilated them, so
that ever since the land directly east of the dykes has been
occupied by a population which still speaks Welsh, or (I
hope this reservation will not be forgotten) whose ancestors
spoke it until nearly two centuries ago.

[1] I cannot discover whether Moreton Anglicorum was a hamlet of
Moreton is y Clawdd, or a distinct township. The tithe survey of
Ruabon parish makes it a separate township, a result still more
favourable to the opinion above expressed, though it should be said
that while Moreton Anglicorum lies only a little east of Wat's Dyke,
the latter does not in any way form its boundary. They are mistaken who make *Moreton Anglicorum* and *Moreton is y Clawdd*
different names for the same township.

Of course no dependence can be placed on *The Book of Aberpergwm* or *Gwentian Brut* (not earlier in date than 1550), which states that after Offa had, in the year 765, constructed the dyke which is associated with his name, he afterwards, in the year 784, laid out another dyke, nearer to England. The writer, in speaking of the second dyke, has evidently Wat's Dyke in his mind, but, as he wrote so many centuries after the act he describes, is of little value as an authority. Nevertheless, I have little doubt as to Wat's Dyke being the work, if not of Offa himself, of one of the early Mercian kings, or of one of their warriors.

The name itself of the Dyke suggests for it an English origin. I will not put forth its English name as evidence of this origin, though that name is not to be disregarded, but will rather take its Welsh name. I am not sure that this latter has ever been recorded in any article dealing specifically with the dyke, and at the present time is no longer known even by the Welsh-speaking people who live along the line of it. But I have been fortunate enough to meet with three documents in which its old Welsh name occurs. In a deed of the year 1431 it is spelled *Clauwdd Wade*, in another of the year 1433 *Claud wode*, and in Norden's Survey of 1620 *Clawdd Wad*. I think it probable that *Wad* is an English personal name, and that it had originally in English some such form as *Wada* (a name well-attested), a name which got gradually degraded into *Wad* and *Wat*, and ultimately pronounced as *Wod* and *Wot*. That the form *Wad* existed we know, because we have such village-names as *Wadsley* ('Wad's lea'), *Wadsworth* ('Wad's holding'), and *Waddington*, which last, if it does not mean 'Town of the children of Wad,' must be a corruption of *Wadan tun*, that is, 'Wada's town,' *Wadan* being the genitive of *Wada* as *Wades* is of *Wad*. We have also Wadham. We see how *Wad* passed into *Wat* by considering *Wadetuna*, the form under which the name of Watton in Norfolk appears in Domesday Book, while two other Wattons are called in that book respectively *Wattune* and *Watane*. It thus looks as though in the Welsh and English names of Wat's Dyke we have preserved two forms, both current, of the same name, probably *Wada*, the name perhaps of the Mercian who, about the time of King Offa, constructed the dyke. Whether these conclusions be correct or not, I have given all the facts relating to the problem, as far as they are known to me. Perhaps it may be of interest to add that when, at the end of last century, Acton Park was laid out, a field in Wrexham Regis was enclosed within it which was called Cae Wad ('Wad's field'). I find this field so named in the year 1620. It was about a quarter of a mile east of Wat's Dyke.

Pennant is undoubtedly right in saying that Wat's Dyke has been often confounded with Offa's, but in the parishes of Hope and Mold, where they are both well known and recognized as distinct, it would be more correct to say that *each is called by the same name*. That is to say, the two dykes are not confounded but both are attributed to the same king. And this attribution is of no recent date. Now here we have revealed an important fact, and one which tends to confirm my impression that both dykes had their origin about the time of Offa. While south of the parishes of Hope and Mold, in fact, Wat's Dyke is called by a distinctive name, in the aforesaid parishes it is called by the same name as the dyke which runs nearly parallel with it. Thus in Hope Owen, township of Hope parish,[1] there is a farmhouse on Wat's Dyke which is called

---

[1] One group of townships in Hope parish is called *Hope Medachiad*. What is the origin of *Medachiad?*—E. P. In 1617, I find the name appearing under the form "Hope y Mudachid."—A. N. P.

Clawdd Offa—' Offa's Dyke.'   Also in Soughton, a township
in Mold parish, is another farmhouse on the same dyke
called *Bryn Offa*—' Offa's Hill,' and a little east of it one
known as *Llwyn Offa*—' Offa's Grove.'

I do not wish to lay greater stress upon this attribution
of both dykes to King Offa than the evidence will fairly
bear, but that evidence, it appears to me, is at least worthy
of consideration.

That the two dykes have, however, actually been confounded is not to be denied. Ralph Higden, for example,
does this in his *Polychronican* (fourteenth century), for he
says that Offa's Dyke " stretches to the mouth of the River
Dee, beyond Chester, close to Flint Castle, between Coleshill and Basingwork monastery." [1]   Now, it is quite certain
that it was Wat's Dyke, and not Offa's, which was visible
near Coleshill. Gutyn Owen, in his *Book of Basingwerk*
(fifteenth century), committed the same blunder, making
Offa's Dyke end between Mynydd y Glo (that is Coleshill)
and Basingwerk.[2] Pennant says that Wat's Dyke terminated
below the Abbey of Basingwerk, and the late Rev. H.
Longueville Jones in the 1856 volume of *Archæologia
Cambrensis* says that Wat's Dyke, taking here " the form
of a ditch rather than of a dyke," may be traced north-
wards " as far as the factory just above Basingwerk
Abbey."   But though the dyke points in the direction of
Basingwerk, I have during the last ten years, searched
again and again the immediate neighbourhood of the
abbey, without seeing any traces of it. Mr. Jones in the

---

[1] " . . . Usque ad ostium fluminis Deæ, ultra Cestriam, juxta
castrum de Flint, inter collem Carbonum et monasterium de
Basingwerk se protendit."

[2] " Ac ef [sef Clawdd Offa] sydd yn estynv or mor yr llall nid
amgen or dehev yn emyl Bristo tv ar gogledd gorvwch y Fflint y
rwng mynachlog ddinas Basing a mynydd y Glo." Rolls *Brut y
Tywysogion*, p. 8.

same article states that Wat's Dyke enters Wynnstay
Park from the north, and "passes straight through it
along the lawn a few feet in front of the house, and so by
Pen y Nant to Nant y belan tower, which is built just above
it to the eastward." But though Wynnstay House stands
on the line which Wat's Dyke would occupy, if it were
continued southward in a straight line, the truth is that
the dyke does not enter the park at all, but stops short a
few feet north of it, and is not found again to the south
until we pass altogether out of Ruabon parish. Even in
Chirk parish I could not find it, though perhaps a more
careful search might reveal traces of it.[1]

It will be remembered that "Watstay" is the older
name of the estate now known as "Wynnstay,"[2] and it is
generally understood that the name "Watstay" indicates
an interruption or *stay* of the dyke, where the house so
named stood. It is probable the gap in the dyke at Watstay has been very much enlarged since the house so called
got its name. When Sir John Wynn laid out Wynnstay
Park it is to be feared that if any portions of the dyke
remained within the limits of the park wall, they would be
speedily cleared away. Once, some years ago, being at
Ruabon, in view of Mr. Longueville Jones' statement quoted

---

[1] Mr. H. Longueville Jones in the article above quoted says that
from Nant y Belan tower "it may be supposed to follow the escarpment of the valley above the river Dee as far as the point where that
river turns to the northward, and then, crossing the river, to follow
the escarpment on the eastern side of the valley of the Ceiriog to
Pen y bank, where it is again found." If his supposition be correct
it is easy to understand how it came to pass that I saw no traces of
the dyke in Chirk parish, for I did not look in the right place.

[2] I have not had the opportunity of examining the Wynnstay
deeds, but my impression is that the name "Watstay" itself is not
much older than 1620, the year in which I first find it named. It
was Sir John Wynn (died January, 171$\frac{3}{9}$) who changed the name
from "Watstay" to "Wynnstay."

above, I asked an aged labourer whom I encountered,
whether he remembered any portions of the dyke within
Wynnstay Park, to which he replied that he never did, and
I ultimately extracted from him a bit of folk-lore and
popular etymology which it may be worth while to give.
First of all, he said that Wat's Dyke was really made by
the devil, in itself an interesting statement, inasmuch as
other great boundary dykes are attributed to the same
personage. He then went on to say that when the devil
in making the dyke came to the property afterwards belonging to the Williams-Wynns at Ruabon, some one, I suppose
the owner of the estate, held up his hands in horror, and
cried out, "What! Stay." The devil then, awed by the
importance of the family, did not resume his operations
until he had passed beyond the owner's property, and the
estate thenceforth became known as "Watstay"! And my
informant appeared really to believe the story he told me,
and to regard it as reasonable.[1]

I should now like to say something as to the northward
interruption of Offa's Dyke in the township of Treuddyn.
Pennant says that in his time the dyke stopped in its northward course at "*Cae Deon*, a farm near Treyddin chapel in
the parish of Mold." This is the name given in the edition
of 1778, but in later editions, or at any rate in the edition

---

[1] Since the above was written, I have seen in *Byegones* (August
12th 1874) a somewhat different version of the legend: "That two
devils were the makers of the dyke. That, by some reason or other,
the work was to have been completed from sea to sea before the sun
rose. Having worked hard and fast with that intention, they had
successfully carried out their operations until they came to Rhuabon,
when to their dismay the sun rose! Whereupon one devil said to
the other: 'We'n stay,' and the work has ever since remained in an
[sic! read *the*] unfinished state in which it was left by its beginners.
And the spot where they left [off] has ever since been called
'Wynnstay.'" The narrator of the story in this form was one David
Hughes, who in 1862 was in the eighty-first year of his age.

of 1810, *Caer deon* is changed to *Cae dwn*. There is no
farm bearing either of these names at the present time,
and immediately north of the present termination of Offa's
Dyke on the road between Llanfynydd and Treuddyn is
an extensive moor—Coed Talwrn—covered with the
remains of mining operations which have been carried on
during the last hundred years. It is therefore probable
that during the past century the dyke at Coed Talwrn has
suffered very much, and that the point at which it ended in
Pennant's time was more to the north than now it is, and I
found on referring to the tithe maps of Treuddyn, made in
1838, that rather more than a mile north of the present
termination of Offa's Dyke was a field called in the map-
schedule "Cae twnth ffordd." It is on the Leeswood
border, and a little west of Ty isaf, near Pont Bleiddyn.
Traversing the space between the present end of the
dyke and the field just named, it would pass another
field called *Maes y gareg wen* (' Field of the white stone').
It is quite possible that the field corruptly called [1]
"Cae twnth ffordd" in the tithe map schedule is a
reminiscence of the "Caer Deon," "Cae Dwn," or
"Cae twn" of Pennant.

It is evident that Offa's Dyke terminated formerly north-
wards near the coast west of Prestatyn, for in the sixth
year of Edward I., Robert Banastre petitioned the king;
and, after reciting that, in the time of King Richard, his
ancestor, also called Robert Banastre, was driven out of
Prestatyn Castle by the Welsh, goes on to say, "And
Robert le fiz Robert Banastre lost all his land in Wales at

---

[1] *Cae twnth ffordd* looks suspiciously like a corruption of *Cae tu
hwnt i'r ffordd,*—"the field beyond the road." It is difficult, however,
to assign limits to the alteration in Welsh place-names of which
Pennant (or his Welsh informants) were capable. See *Y Cymmrodor*,
xi. 59.—E. P.

that time, and led all his people (*tut sa gent*) from ' Pr ' statun *within the Dyke* into the county of Lancaster." [1]

For some distance south of the river Ceiriog, Offa's Dyke is treated even now as the boundary between Denbighshire and Shropshire, between Wales and England, but in the whole of the district above indicated, in which I have closely examined the dykes, they run through a tract which for centuries has been in Wales. It is therefore not surprising that these wonderful works should have appealed to the imagination of the Welsh, and should have been utilized by them, nor that they should have set stones and erected forts along them, and made them, *in some cases*, the boundaries between hamlets, townships, and parishes.

The name *Careg lwyd* occurs twice along Wat's Dyke in the district which I have especially examined. Thus in Hope Owen, on the west side of the dyke, is a field called *Erw'r gareg lwyd* (' Acre of the hoar stone '), and a farmhouse on the same dyke in the township of Bistre bears the name of *Y Gareg Lwyd.* The stone from which this farmhouse is named still stands a little west of the dyke and can be seen from Padeswood Station, while within a few feet of it is another stone, prostrate and partly embedded in the ground. South-west of Y Gareg lwyd and within a short distance of it, but on the other side of the railway line, is a mound covered with trees called *Bryn y castell* (' Hill of the castle '). I am tempted to describe another *Careg lwyd* though outside of my district. It is a few hundred yards to the south of the town of Oswestry on the western edge of the ditch of Wat's Dyke, about 7 feet high and from 16 to 20 feet circumference near the base. The house near it is also called *Careg lwyd*, and the stone is believed to have the peculiar property of turning round once in twenty-

[1] Translation from the original petition in Norman French in *Rolls of Parliament*, Anno sexto Edwardi I. See also *Archæologia Cambrensis*, vol. i. series i. pp. 334–346.

four hours at midnight! I have already mentioned *Maes y gareg wen* along the presumed course of Offa's Dyke. I have seen also a farmhouse called *Careg y big*, along the course of the same dyke, in the township of Upper Porkington and parish of Selattyn, so named, as I was informed, from a stone, bearing the same name, which formerly stood about ten yards west of the dyke. I do not know whether it is to be regarded as altogether accidental that these stones occur along the dykes; anyhow, I think that their existence in this connection should be chronicled. I should like also to call attention to the fact that the word *gorsedd* is often found as a place-name on or near the course of the dykes, a name which I think we must in these cases frequently have to translate *mound, tumulus,* or *judgment-seat*. *Yr Orsedd Wen* ('The white gorsedd') is the name of a farm-stead on the west side of Offa's Dyke in the township of Crogen Iddon in the old parish of Llangollen. Near it, but a little further from the dyke, is a large *carnedd*, opened about the year 1850, and described in *Archæologia Cambrensis* (Vol. II., 2nd series, pp. 9-19) by Mr. W. Wynne Foulkes.[1] On the other side of the dyke, on the top of Selattyn Hill, was another huge *carnedd*, on the site and out of the materials of which Mr. Gerald Carew of Pentre Pant built in 1847 a hunting lodge. During this operation two *cistfeini* and three or four burial urns were discovered.[2] Still nearer Yr Orsedd Wen, and on the west

---

[1] This is fancied to be the *carnedd* from which the house takes its name. A skeleton was found in it by Mr. Foulkes, who supposed it to be that of Gwên, one of the sons of Llywarch Hen. It is, however, called not *Gorsedd Gwên*, or even Gorsedd Wên, but *Gorsedd Wen*. Nor does it appear to have been ever known as *Gorsedd Gorwynion*, as suggested.

[2] On this tower was placed the following inscription:—

Gorsedd Orwynion
Oedd gwr vy mab oedd ddysgywen hawl [? haul]
Ar ryd Vorlas y llas Gwen.

side of the dyke are the remains of what was evidently another *carnedd*. It ought to be said that while Welsh people call this farmstead *Yr Orsedd Wen*, many English people call it *The Rossett*. And this leads me to say that on the western side of Offa's Dyke, in the township of Esclusham uwch y Clawdd, in front of Pentre Bychan Hall, is a meadow now called *Rossett Park*, but which I find from the Pentre Bychan deeds was always formerly known as *Yr Orsedd*.[1] If ever there was any mound in Rossett Park, it may well have been cleared away when, many years ago, the meadow was included in "the grounds" of Pentre Bychan Hall. However, not far from the Pentre Bychan

---

[1] I know two other places called *The Rossett* in the neighbourhood of Wrexham, formerly known as *Yr Orsedd*. One is a field in the township of Pickhill, and the other the well-known hamlet on the Great Western Railway between Gresford and Saltney. The older name for the latter was *Yr Orsedd Goch* ("The Red Gorsedd"). In Norden's Survey (A.D. 1620) it is in one passage called *Yr orseth goch*, and in another *Rosset goz*, so that it is evident, as I have elsewhere said (*Ancient Tenures of Land in the Marches of North Wales*, p. 64, note 1, and p. 65, note 2), "that *The Rossett* is the regular form into which, in this district, the name *Yr Orsedd* passes in being converted into an English word." Norden describes some of the lands at Yr Orsedd Goch as being of the nature of demesne, and there were at that place not merely "The Boardland [or Lord's] Chapel," still existing at the beginning of last century, but also the gallows for the rhaglotry of Marford, used until about a hundred years ago. Thus, in the case of Yr Orsedd Goch, at least, I think I am right in translating *gorsedd* as "judgment-seat." There is here now no mound, unless we regard the notable mound at Marford, now called simply *The Roft*, but formerly *Groft y castell*, as the original *gorsedd*. This mound was undoubtedly the head of the rhaglotry of Marford, and the lands at *Yr Orsedd Goch* were appurtenant to it as "Tir y bwrdd" or "boardland." Since the foregoing was written I have come across a note (dated 1814) of the names of all the fields in the Upper and Middle Berse estates in the township of Bersham. Among these names occur the following: "Bryn rosset (or 'r orsedd) mawr and Bryn rosset vechan, now in one." The equation of *Yr Orsedd* and *Rossett* is thus indubitably established.

Gorsedd, but on the east side of the dyke, adjoining Plas
Cadwgan, is a huge tumulus which rises directly from the
rampart. It may be worth while to say that close to it is
a field called *Cae'r Saeson*. This tumulus was opened in
the year 1797, when four suits of armour and the skeleton
of a horse [1] were discovered in it. The authority for this
statement is *The Monthly Magazine* published at Shrewsbury in the year named. The armour is said to have been
taken to Chirk Castle, where it cannot now be found, but
the description of it in *The Monthly Magazine* makes one
certain that it must have been late mediæval in its character.
" The armour was complete in helmets, gorgets or safe-
guards for the neck, an iron apron in front with a cuirass
for the back annexed to the aprons by hinges."

It is very difficult to decide as to whether the many
forts that lie along or close to the course of the dykes are
of Welsh origin, but I think the camp called *Hen Ddinas* [2]
near Owestry on Wat's Dyke, and the remarkable but unnamed camp in the township of Llai just above Gwersyllt
Mill on the same dyke must be contemporaneous with the
construction of the latter. I am not so sure as to the
origin of the big mount with a flat top called *Y Castell* a
few feet distant from Wat's Dyke in Erddig woods. Mr.
W. M. Myddelton has communicated to me the following
note from the Harleian MSS. relating to this mound by a
traveller from Chester in the year 1574 :—" By Wrexham

---

[1] Horses' bones have elsewhere been discovered in Offa's Dyke.
Thus according to Lewis' *Topographical Dictionary of Wales* (A.D.
1833) when the dyke was levelled near Brymbo Hall for the formation of railroads in connection with the railroads and collieries, " a
great quantity of the bones of horses in a state of excellent preservation, and horse shoes of rude workmanship were found."

[2] I cannot learn the authority on which this camp has ascribed
to it the names *Caer Ogyrfan* (or *Caer Ogyrfen*) and *Old
Oswestry*.

wthin a quarter of a myle toward Ruabon in park glyn [1]
standeth the ruyns of a Castell great which sometymes was
the chief house of the Prince of Bromfield." However we
may interpret this statement we may gather from it that the
people who lived in the sixteenth century near the Erddig
"Castell" regarded it as having been a place of considerable
importance.

The passages through the dykes were often so striking
and important as to acquire distinctive names. Thus *Adwy'r
clawdd* ('Gap of the Dyke') is a very ancient name for
the point at which Offa's Dyke is traversed in the township
of Bersham from Wrexham to Ruthin. If at Adwy'r
clawdd we walk along the dyke in a northerly direction
until we have passed the Wesleyan Chapel a few yards we
may pause. For here many years ago were dug up, immediately west of the dyke, a large number of very friable
urns containing burnt bones, all of which were broken and
scattered. I had this information from the grandson of
the man who disinterred the urns, and who often spoke of
his discovery. He said there was " quite a cemetery " there.
Oh, that some of these urns had been preserved, so as to
give us an opportunity of knowing to what period and to
what race they belonged! A little further northward, in
the same township, a road crosses Offa's Dyke at right
angles, at a place now called *Llidiart Ffanny* ('Fanny's
Gate'), but which, as I find from the old parish registers,
was always formerly called *Llidiart vani*, or *Llidiart vaney*.
What the second word of this place-name means, I cannot
be sure,[2] but it seems worth while to put it on record. An

---

[1] Parc Glyn Clywedoc (demesne land of the Lord of Bromfield)
included a great part of the present Erddig Park, as well as the
mound in question.

[2] Perhaps it is *fanè* for *fanau*. *Llidiart* in the hundred of Bromfield is always treated as feminine, so that it modifies the initial
letter of any word, treated adjectively, that follows it.

ancient farmhouse, having the same name, adjoins the gap.

Wat's Dyke divides Wrexham from Bersham, the township of Acton from that of Stansty, and the township of Bistre from that of Hartsheath. It divides, also, in part the hamlet of Hafod (formerly called *Hafod y gallor*) from the hamlet of Belan in the same township (of Ruabon). In most cases, however, it is not utilized in this way, but runs across hamlets, townships and parishes without reference to their boundaries. So, Offa's Dyke divides the township of Esclusham uwch y Clawdd from that of Esclusham is y Clawdd, and the township of Moreton uwch y Clawdd from that of Moreton is y Clawdd. Within the township of Ruabon also, it separates, in part, the hamlet of Rhuddallt from that of Bodylltyn (in which latter stands the British camp called *Y Gardden*), but here again the bounds of most townships and parishes along the dyke are determined without reference to the latter. It seems important to point out this fact, though it is difficult to say what precisely is the inference to be drawn from it.

And now I must apologize for the incompleteness and ill-arrangement of the materials I have presented to you to-night. The fact is that most of those materials were got together many years ago, and I have had but little leisure since to pursue my investigations into the history and condition of the dykes within the area dealt with. Moreover, since I undertook to write this paper, I have been so beset with ill-health and calls on my time, that I have felt myself incompetent to the work of arraying the facts I have to offer in their most seemly garments, or of arranging them in the best order. Let my statement of them therefore stand to lighten the labour of some one else who may hereafter address himself to the same task. In conclusion, I wish to express my obligations to Mr.

Egerton G. B. Phillimore, who has gone to the trouble of verifying my references, and made many suggestions of which I have availed myself. All the notes which are signed "E. P." were written by him.

Welsh Settlements, East of Offa's Dyke, during the Eleventh Century

WELSH SETTLEMENTS, EAST OF OFFA'S DYKE, DURING THE ELEVENTH CENTURY.[1]

By Alfred Neobard Palmer.

In the foregoing paper the forward movement of the Northern Welsh in the eleventh century has been incidentally mentioned. That forward movement, and the Welsh settlements in Cheshire and Shropshire which were the result of it, form the subject of the paper that follows.

Part I.—The Welsh Settlers in Cheshire.

Let us deal, first of all, with Cheshire. And here it will suffice to show that the hundred of Broxton in that county, which is the hundred adjoining the two Maelors, was, in its western and southern parts, for at least three centuries after the Norman Conquest, predominantly, I do not say exclusively, Welsh.

Perhaps it will be well to begin by asking how certain ancient and important families connected with the hundred of Broxton were represented during the epoch now under consideration—the three centuries or three centuries and a half following the Norman Conquest.

And here, at the very threshold of our inquiry, we come upon the fact that the chief family of the hundred, the holders of the barony of Malpas itself, themselves probably of Norman origin, became during the period under review, for two or three generations, partially Cymricized. Here

[1] Read before the Society, February 6th, 1889.

are the facts. Towards the end of the twelfth century a moiety of the barony was in the hands of David de Malpas, otherwise called "David the Clerk." There is much obscurity (which I do not profess to clear up) as to his marriage. Perhaps he married three times. Three ladies, at any rate, are mentioned in different pedigrees as wives to him—Constans, daughter of the Lord Owen Cyfeiliog; Catherine, daughter of Owain Fychan, of Maelor; and Margaret, daughter of Ralph ap Einion, an Anglo-Welshman.[2] It is said that this Ralph ap Einion had been in possession of the other moiety of the barony, and that, by marrying Ralph's daughter, David de Malpas became entitled to the whole barony. These statements can hardly be correct, as the other moiety of the barony belonged at that time to the Patric family, but it is probably true that Ralph ap Einion had considerable possessions in the barony, which his daughter carried to David de Malpas. This David was succeeded by his eldest son, Sir William de Malpas, Knight, who married Margaret, daughter of Cadwgan of Lynton, an Anglo-Welshman. Sir William had no legitimate issue, but his illegitimate son, "David the Bastard," or "David the Clerk" (the *second* so-called), managed to intrude himself into the half-barony. This second David the Clerk is said to have married Constans, daughter of Owen Cyfeiliog, but I think it probable, taking points of date into consideration, that if Constans married David the Clerk at all, it was the first of that name whose wife she was. That David the Bastard married Angharad, daughter of Madoc ap Maredydd, of Mechain, we know, and

---

[2] This Ralph ap Einion is more fully described as Ralph ap Einion ap Gruffydd, which last is said to have been the son of Owen ap Iago ap Idwal, Lord of Bromfield. I know no such Lord of Bromfield, but it is impossible not to wonder whether he was not a son of Iago ap Idwal ap Meurig, Prince of Gwynedd, who was slain in 1037.

that she had a daughter and heir who married, for her first husband, William Patric, the holder of the other moiety of the barony, and for her second husband a certain Roderic ap Griffin (Gruffydd) ap Llewelyn, an Anglo-Welshman who will be mentioned again. The true heir of Sir William de Malpas was his brother Philip. Now this brother was commonly called " Philip *Gôch*" (*Philip the Red*), an appellation which has no meaning except in Welsh. He married Catherine, otherwise Angharad, daughter of Jorveth (Iorwerth) of Hulton, another Anglo-Welshman, and had two sons, David, from whom descend the Egertons of Oulton, and Hwfa. I had almost forgotten to say that, according to the Welsh accounts, Beatrix, a daughter of the first David de Malpas, married Roderig ap Gruffydd, a younger brother of Madoc ap Gruffydd Maelor, the founder of Valle Crucis Abbey. But I think that this Roderig has been confused with the Roderig ap Gruffydd ap Llewelyn, who married the daughter of the *second* David de Malpas. I make no pretence of reconciling the various discrepancies, or correcting the several anachronisms which the pedigree of the earlier mediæval lords of Malpas presents. But I lay stress on a fact which stands out clearly, the fact, namely, that the members of the family represented by those lords, during the period now under consideration, intermarried with Welsh or Anglo-Welsh people, that they bore, as often as not, Welsh names, and that one of them—Philip Gôch— received an appellation which could only have been given by Welsh-speaking people.

Now let us look into the case of the well-known Cheshire family of the Dods of Edge and Broxton. The pedigree of the Dods begins with Cadwgan Dod, of Edge, whose son was Hwfa Dod, the son and successor of whom was Cenric Dod, who had two sons—Cadwgan, the ancestor of the Dods of Edge, and Stephen, the ancestor of the Dods of Broxton. Thus, if we grant that the Dods were a family of English origin, we see, from the fact of their adopting Welsh personal names, that they lived in a district in which such names were in common use.

The Stocktons of Stockton appear to have become for a time wholly Cymricized. William de Stockton, in the early part of the reign of Edward I., had by his wife Leuca (that is Lleucu), daughter of Ithel the Clerk, two sons—David de Stockton and Eynon (Einion) de Stockton. From David de Stockton, whose wife's name was Wenthlian (Gwenllian), the main stock proceeds. Einion, the second son of William de Stockton, was the father of Madoc de Stockton, Ithel de Stockton and Iorwerth de Stockton. The last-named appears to have been the father of Madoc ap Iorwerth of Coddington, whose son, Iorwerth ap Madoc of Coddington, was living in 1341.

The Hortons of Horton were probably originally wholly Welsh. Their pedigree starts with a certain Elia de Horton, who lived about the time of Edward the First. This Elia had two sons—Owen de Horton and Huva (that is, Hwfa), and a daughter Nest, who married Hwva ap Griffin (Hwfa ap Gruffydd). Owen de Horton, whose wife's name was Tangwystl, had three sons, William de Horton (mentioned in 1312), Wronow (that is Goronwy or Grono) de Horton, and Eynon Gogh (Einion Gôch). William de Horton had two sons, Philip and Owen. Grono de Horton had a son who was the father of David and Ithel.

And here I ought to say that the territorial names given in contemporary deeds to these freeholders of the hundred concealed in many cases their real nationality. Thus he whose name appears in the pedigree as David de Horton would doubtless have been known to his fellows as David ap Madoc.

Let us now look at the subject discussed in this paper

from another standpoint. In the recent edition (by Mr·
Thomas Helsby) of Ormerod's *Cheshire,* there are appended, in the case of many townships, valuable foot-
notes containing abstracts of ancient deeds and summaries
of other original documents relating to those townships.
I will now, taking four or five representative townships,
summarize these summaries, and see how far they confirm
the conclusions already expressed.

Let us begin with the two townships called respectively
Church Shocklach and *Church Oviat.* The following names
occur in the Plea and Recognizance Rolls : " John, son of
Llewelin, son of David of Schocklache," in the year 1340,
and " Ior (-werth) and Griffith, sons of David de Shocklach,"
in 1331 and 1356. Note also the following summaries :
In 1312 Rotheric, son of Griffin (Roderig, son of
Gruffydd) [3] and Catherine his wife, held lands in Church
Shocklach, between whom and Tegengle (elsewhere called
Tangwystl) de Horton, an action at law took place. In
1354, Margaret, who was the wife of David, son of Iorwerth
son of Gruffydd, sued John fitz Richard fitz Robert for
dower of a messuage and four acres of lands in Horton
next Shocklach, and sued also Richard fitz Robert for the
same, who vouched to warranty Griffith, son and heir of
David, son of Griffith. In 1310 Alice, who was the wife of
David Bolgragh (*Bolgrach* = " Scabby-belly ") sued Thomas
the son of William of Broxton for dower of two messuages
and ten acres of land in Shocklach Ovyat. In 1394 Ievan
ap David ap Ithel, of Shocklach, is mentioned as the lessor
of the lands in Shocklach of David de Shocklach. Again,
so late as 1428, " Gwervil," the daughter of David, the son

---

[3] Mr. Helsby thinks that this Roderig ap Gruffydd was the same
who had previously been the husband of Beatrice, the daughter of
David the Bastard, and who by his second wife became the ancestor
of the Schocklaches, of Shocklach.

of Iorwerth, of Shocklach, occurs. There is no mistaking the significance of names like these; they are the names of Welsh-speaking people (the nickname "Bolgrach," given to David, the husband of Alice, assures us of that), and they are the names, not of *villani*, but of freeholders and lords of manors.

But it will be said: Shocklach is so close to the admittedly Welsh district of Maelor, that all this is not so very surprising. Well, let us go further inland, and nearer Chester. Let us go to Coddington. But it is the same at Coddington. In 1288 we find "Yarward or Jorward (Iorwerth), the son of Madoc, the son of Eynon [Einion] of Cudynton," granting lands at Coddington, and fifty-four years later (in 1342) Iorwerth, the son of Madoc ap Iorwerth of Coddington, granting other lands there to William de Stockton and Robert his son, and in 1347 Iorwerth ap Madoc ap Einion of Coddington is also mentioned as a grantor of lands "in Pursalgh." The next year William de Stockton assigns to "John Caderig his brother" lands in Coddington, "lately held by" David ap Edenewey [Ednyfed], Kenard ap Cadogan, and Wladus [Gwladys] his widow. Finally, in 1362, it was attested on the oaths of twelve jurors that Gwenllian, daughter and one of the heirs of "Wylym ap Jon," of Coddington, was born there, and baptized in Malpas Church on the feast of the Purification of the Blessed Virgin in the 20th year of Edward III.

Let us now go further eastward—to Tushingham. In 1305 Leuca (Lleucu) daughter of Ithel the Clerk, granted lands in Tushingham to David de Stockton, her son. In the time of Edward III. " Kenwric [Cynwric] son of David," and " Kenwric, son of Hova," of Tushingham, are mentioned as having lands in the township, and in 1347 Roger, son of Ithel, son of Matthew of Tushingham, as granting other lands there. Finally, in the time of Richard II., the name of John, son of Roger, son of Hova of Tushingham, occurs as granting lands in Masefen.

Names such as the above could be repeated until my readers would be weary, and I must ask them to accept my statement that in the case of almost every other township in the western, southern, and midmost parts of the hundred, Welsh freeholders, or the descendants of Welsh freeholders, were, during the period now under review, quite common. In some townships the inhabitants appear to have been wholly Welsh. Yet the townships in which they lived bore English names. The inference is that, as in the case of the two Maelors, a district formerly English had been settled by Welshmen. When did this settlement take place? All the manors in which the aforesaid townships lay are said to have belonged, in the time of Edward the Confessor, to English lords, but that these were for the most part titular lords merely is plain from the further statement that their manors were in general "waste." This shows that the hundred had been harried, but gives no hint of any Welsh occupation of it. Nor was there, it would appear, any such occupation of it at the time when the Great Survey was taken, for there are no references to Welsh freeholders in the *Cheshire* Domesday Book, such as occur, for example, in the *Shropshire* Domesday Book. It looks, therefore, as if the Welsh migration into the hundred of Broxton[4] took place after the year 1086. If it was an armed and forcible migration, it probably happened at the time when the two Maelors passed wholly into the possession of the Prince of Powys ; but it may have been a

[4] Elsewhere in Cheshire, outside the hundred of Broxton, Anglo-Welsh proprietors of large estate might be found. Thus, in the year 1354, Urian de St. Pierre had seisin of a tenth part of the lordships of Ridley, Spurstow, and Halton, in the hundred of Edisbury, which were "held of Houa, son of Eygnon [Hwfa, son of Einion] in socage."

peaceable one, taking place under the direct encouragement
of the Norman lords, who wished to see their lands, then
waste, duly settled. In any case, the migration is an example of the eastward movement of the Welsh in the
eleventh century. So far as I know, attention has never
hitherto been called to the fact of this migration, nor to
the fact that the hundred of Broxton contained a Welsh-
speaking population for more than three centuries after
the Norman Conquest.

Part II.—The Welsh Settlers in Shropshire.

As to Shropshire, I shall only deal with that portion of
it—its north-west corner—which is best known to me.
This district, which includes the hundreds of Pimhill and
Oswestry, is very much larger than that bit of Cheshire of
which in Part I. we have been speaking, and the descendants of the Welsh who settled in it continued, in the
western part of the district, to speak Welsh down to our
own time. Much of what I wish to urge on this subject is
already very well known to those who live on the spot, or
who have given attention to its history. Still, as historians
in general seem either not to have recognized the pheno-
menon, or to have missed its true significance, and as many
important points in connection with it have never been
noticed at all, I have thought it best to set forth, formally
but briefly, the evidence for the statements made in my former paper as to the Cymricizing of this corner of Shropshire.
These statements are three :—1st, That this district was
once predominantly, and, except perhaps in a small portion
of it immediately east of Offa's Dyke, almost exclusively
English, or at least Anglicized ; 2ndly, That the greater
part of it was subsequently seized by the Welsh, and
settled by them, and that the western part became almost

exclusively Welsh; and 3rdly, That the people of this district, becoming soon after English, so far as their allegiance was concerned, continued nevertheless to speak Welsh for a very long time, and in the western portions of it to do so down to our own time. It is impossible, in a paper like this, fully to support or duly to qualify these statements, and all therefore that remains is to do the best I can under the circumstances.

Let us first take the old hundred of Baschurch, which roughly corresponds with the later hundred of Pimhill, and begin with the lordship of Ellesmere within that hundred. In 1177 Henry II. granted this lordship to Dafydd ap Owain Gwynedd, Prince of North Wales, who had married Emma, the king's sister, and in Dafydd's possession it remained until his death in 1204. After that event, King John took the lordship into his own hands, giving Owain ap Dafydd, the prince's son, lands elsewhere.[5] But six months afterwards the king re-granted the manor to the ruling Prince of North Wales, Llewelyn ap Iorwerth, who married Joan, the king's daughter, in whose tenure it remained for three or four years. Now we may be sure that two kings of England would not have given up to two successive Welsh princes such a district as the lordship of Ellesmere, if that district did not already contain a very large number of Welsh-speaking people. But we are not left to conjecture in this matter. In an "extent" of 1276, Madoc fitz Ralph and Ednyfed of Stocks are mentioned among the names of the free tenants, and we are also told that Meuric held one-third and Llewelyn Fychan two-thirds of the township of Greenhill; that Llewelyn Fychan and his brethren held the township of Estwick; and that Gwrgeneu fitz Madoc, Madoc fitz

---

[5] The lands were in Warwickshire, and it is from this Owain ap Dafydd that Hales Owen derives part of its name.

Iorwerth, Gwyn Fychan, and Llewelyn fitz Rouhard [Rhirid ?], and other Welshmen held four virgates of land in the township of Marton. In 1341 the greater part of the lordship of Ellesmere was exempted from the payment of ninths as being "*in Wales*," nor was it re-attached to Shropshire until the reign of Henry VIII.

In other parts of the hundred we meet with a state of things similar to that we have found in the lordship of Ellesmere. Thus we learn from Domesday Survey that in "Nessham" (= Great Ness) were six Welshmen who rendered twenty shillings, and at a later date we find various Welsh families planted in the more western townships of the hundred, and other evidences of a Welsh population. Now were these people the descendants of the Welsh whom the English found occupying the district when they first came into it? or were they later intruders into a district already Anglicized? I believe they were late intruders. All the evidence that supports this conclusion cannot be presented until we come to deal with the case of the hundred of Oswestry; but here is one point: If so many descendants of the original Welsh population of the hundred of Baschurch remained un-absorbed and un-Anglicized until late in the Middle Ages, would not some at least of the townships in which they lived have retained their ancient Welsh names? But at the time of Domesday, with one doubtful exception, all these names were thoroughly English.

We now come to speak of the hundred of Oswestry, or rather of that portion of it which lies east of Offa's Dyke, a district which is almost identical with the Domesday hundred of Merset. Except eight or nine townships near the dyke,[6]

---

[6] Llanforda, Tref ar Glawdd, Treflach, Trefonen, Llynclys, Bron y Garth, Treprenal, Llwyn Tidman, and Llan y Myneich.

and four [7] in the middle portion of the district, all
the townships which make up the latter bear English
names. Even in the western portion of the district the
townships that have English names far outnumber those
that have Welsh. And these names do not merely go back
as far as the Middle Ages, and up to and beyond the time
of the Domesday Survey, but township names of this class
appear to have been more numerous in the eleventh and
twelfth centuries than they are now. We read of Newton,
Caldicote, Hauston, Tibeton, Norslepe, and Ulpheresford—
names which have either been displaced by Welsh names
or which stand for townships that have since been added
to and absorbed by other townships. Such thoroughly
English names as Meresbury and Meresbrook have also
since been partially Welshified into Maesbury and Maes-
brook, and Porkington has been turned into Brogyntyn.
It is quite plain that the hundred of Merset was, in the
early part of the eleventh century, mainly, if not wholly,
English. In the time of King Æthelred the Unready, it
yielded a substantial revenue to the king's exchequer, and
Domesday Book gives us the names of the several lords of
manors there in the time of Edward the Confessor, and
these names are all English. Yet it is evident these lords
had become, in the Confessor's time, titular lords merely,
for it is recorded of nearly all of them that their manors
were then " waste," that is to say, yielded them no revenue.
From this it would appear that it was in Edward the Confessor's reign that the successive Welsh settlements took
place within the hundred, which in a few years converted it
into a district almost wholly Welsh. It is very possible, in
fact, that the hundred of Merset was at this time actually
re-organized, and made into a Welsh commote. The Rev.
R. W. Eyton, it is true, ridicules the statement made in

[7] Argoed, Tir y Coéd, Knockyn, and Henlle.

the most trustworthy texts that Croes Oswallt [8] was one of the three commotes composing a Welsh cantref; but the only defect in Mr. Eyton's otherwise admirable work is the lack of appreciation which it shows of the Welsh evidence. Now in the case of every Welsh commote the occupiers of land were liable to certain peculiar customs and services due to the lord of the commote. And the revenues of the lords marcher of Oswestry include items which represent many of these peculiar customs and services.[9] This seems to point

---

[8] *Croes Oswallt*, or 'Oswald's Cross,' is the Welsh form of the name "Oswald's tree," now Oswestry.

[9] Thus in the accounts of 1276 (given in full by Mr. Eyton), we find mentioned items called "Umbarge," elsewhere called "Treth-morkey"; "Kilh," elsewhere called "Treth canidion"; and "Mut"; and at another date we find one of the townships of the hundred (Aston) described as liable to a custom called "Keys." These words are much mangled by the transcriber, but not so far mangled as to be wholly unrecognizable. "Umbarge" stands evidently for *amobr*, a fee payable by all the men of the commote to the lord on the marriage of their daughters, and that this is the true interpretation is plain from the alternative name given to the custom—"trethmorkey," which is manifestly a transcriber's mistake for *treth merched*—'the daughters' tax.' "Kilh" stands for *cylch*, and "treth canidion" for *trêth cynyddion*. The *taeogion*, or bond-tenants of a commote, were liable for the entertainment of the lord's dogs and huntsmen, who were entitled to make a *cylch* or circuit among them, the tax payable in discharge of his obligation being called *treth cynyddion*—'the huntsmen's tax.' An officer of the lord of the commote called "Cais" (whose English title was "sergeant of the peace"), was also entitled to make a *cylch* among the bond-tenants, and it was the commutation for this custom which in the Oswestry accounts is called "keys," that is *trêth cais*. Finally, the payment called "mut" is evidently the same tax which in the adjoining commotes of the lordship of Chirk was called "treth muyt." I discussed this name in my *History of Ancient Tenures of Land in the Marches of North Wales* (p. 50, note 2), but could not explain it. It is described in the Oswestry accounts for 1276 as "a certain custom called *Mut*, paid by the men of Shotover in time of war for keeping their cattle at Oswestry in peace." Can any of my readers suggest the true form of the name? I fancy it should be *trêth*

to the conclusion that a part at least—what was called
" The Walcheria "—of Oswestry had actually been, though
but for a short time, a Welsh commote, and it conclusively
proves that the occupiers of land within that district had
become subject to the incidents of Welsh tenure.

The question, " Who were the Welsh chieftains who laid
violent hands upon the hundred of Merset ? " can only be
answered in part.   One of them, it is pretty certain, was
the Rhŷs Sais who has already been named.   He appears
to have seized a great part of Dudleston, and it was this
portion of his possessions which fell, after his death in 1073,
to his son Iddon, whose name is, *perhaps,* preserved to us
in Crogen Iddon in Glyn Ceiriog.   From Trahaiarn, the son
of this Iddon, at any rate, nearly all the notable families of
Dudleston are derived.   Cadifor ap Trahaiarn was the ancestor of the Edwardses of Cil Hendref.   Heilin ap Trahaiarn,
commemorated in " Pentre Heilin," was the ancestor of the
Holbeaches, and of the Kynastons of Pant y Bursley; and
Hwfa ap Trahaiarn was the ancestor of the Vaughans of
Plas Thomas.   Then, in the female line, Morgan ap Iddon
was the ancestor of the Wynnes of Pentre Morgan, and the
Eytons of Pentre Madoc were, in like manner, descended
from Tudor, another son of Rhys Sais.   Bleddyn ap Cynfyn,
afterwards the reigning Prince of Powys, may also be sur-
mised to have had a considerable share in driving the
English out of the hundred, and appropriating the land, for
it is pretty certain that his son, Madoc ap Bleddyn, was the
Madoc who at the time of the Domesday was in actual
possession of the manor of Burton (= Porkington), in which
manor he was ultimately succeeded by his great-nephew
Owain, whom the English called " Owen de Porkington,"

mwd, mwd or *bwd* being an enclosure within the precincts of the
lord's castle, to which the cattle would be driven from the common
pastures and woods when they were in danger there.

and who has since been known to the Welsh as "Owain Brogyntyn." Finally, Gwrgeneu ap Ednowein ap Ithel, who was living about the time of Edward the Confessor, is said to have been lord of Ruyton of the Eleven Towns, and, if so, was probably another leader in the forward movement of the Welsh which resulted in the temporary loss to the English of this part of Shropshire.

We shall probably not be far wrong in assigning the year 1055 as the date of the capture and settlement of the hundred of Merset by the Welsh; for it was in that year that Gruffydd ap Llewelyn ap Seisyllt, King of Wales, in conjunction with Ælfgar, the outlawed Earl of the East Angles, made his memorable harrying of Herefordshire and of the country which lay in his line of march.

Not only did Welshmen at this time occupy the hundred of Merset, but it became subject to Welsh law. That this was so has already in part been proved. Here is further proof. One of the townships, still recognized as such in 1302, became known as "Gwely Cadwgan," or "Cadwgan's Bed," the whole township being a *gwely* or tract of land belonging to a free family, the descendants of a certain Cadwgan, among whom it was parcelled according to the law of gavelkind. A *gwely*, called "Gwely Moelgoch," formed also a distinct portion of Weston Rhun, while another township was called "Rhandir Kneyris," or "Shareland of Geneurys," a name in which we have reference to the same method of partition by equal sharing.

No sooner, however, was Earl Roger of Shrewsbury firmly seated in his earldom than he hastened to establish his authority over the old hundred of Merset, so that at the time of Domesday every manor in the hundred, except Porkington, was held by Normans, the Welsh proprietors becoming free tenants, but preserving probably most of their privileges under the name of "customs of the manor."

These are the Welshmen who are evidently indicated in such Domesday entries as these :—" There six Welshmen render twenty shillings ; " or, " there two Welshmen have one carucate, and render thirty-two pence ; " or, " there one Welshman renders one hawk." [1]

The subjection of the people of the district to the allegiance, direct or indirect, of the English king did not for centuries make any serious inroad on their Welsh speech or characteristics. The lordships of Oswestry and Whittington were taken to be not in England, but in the Marches of Wales, and were not re-annexed to Shropshire until the time of Henry VIII. Every parish in the hundred of Oswestry, except that of West Felton, belonged not to the English see of Lichfield or Chester, but to the Welsh see of St. Asaph. The Anglicizing of the western part of the district did not really begin until about the time of Elizabeth, nor is the process, so long delayed, completed even now.

The general remarks that have been made as to the hundred of Oswestry apply also to that portion of the parish of Chirk, in Denbighshire, which lies east of Offa's Dyke. There was a " first English period " in Chirk also, but the

[1] It is quite likely, as Mr. Eyton has admitted, that, during the troublous times of King Stephen, the hundred of Oswestry may have fallen for a few years into the hands of Madoc ap Meredydd, Prince of Powys. This would explain the statement, made in the Welsh accounts, that this Madoc built Oswestry Castle, a statement which must then be taken as meaning that he *re*-built or repaired the castle. It would also explain the statement that Einion Efell, one of Prince Madoc's illegitimate sons, lived at Llwyn y Maen, near Oswestry, which was perhaps granted him by his father, and which he was afterwards allowed to retain. The immediate descendants of Einion Efell did actually live at Llwyn y Maen, and from him the Lloyds of Llwyn y Maen and Llanforda descended. It is very likely that it was from Einion's son, Rhûn, that Weston Rhun and Ifton Rhun got the distinctive part of their names.

That Whittington Castle was two or three times after the Norman Conquest in the hands of the Princes of North Wales we know.

district was so early and so thoroughly Cymricized, and remained Welsh for so long a time, that we ought not to wonder if no township-names dating from that first English period should have come down to us.   Yet there are two or three such names that have in fact come down.   "Chirk" itself is obviously an English corruption of the name of the river Ceiriog; it is true, Chirk had an alternative Welsh name, "Y Waun," but the name "Chirk" was also used at a very early date, certainly before the beginning of the fourteenth century.   "Halghton," or "Halton," is another of these township-names; and "Manatton," or "Maenattyn," the disused name of one of the old townships of Chirk parish, is also partly English.[2]   It was probably Rhŷs Sais, already named, or one of his immediate progenitors, who captured from the English that portion of Chirk parish which lies east of Offa's Dyke, for from Tudor ap Rhŷs Sais descend nearly all the ancient Welsh families of the district—the Lloyds of Bryn Cunallt, the Edwardses of Plas Newydd, and the Lloyds of Plas is y Clawdd.   This portion of Chirk is not mentioned in Domesday Survey, unless it be included in that "March of Welshland" (*Finis terræ Wallensis*) for which Tudor [ap Rhŷs Sais] is therein described as paying 4*l.* 5*s.* a year to Roger the Earl.

I have not dealt in the foregoing notes with the large tract of *Flintshire* lying east of Offa's Dyke, not having had time adequately to study the history of that district, but I believe the same general remarks which have been made as to the portions of Denbighshire and Shropshire some miles

---

[2] We may suppose that the original form of the name was *Acton* = 'Oak-town,' and that the syllable "man" or "maen" was added to distinguish it from other Actons.   Boreatton and Shottatton, in Shropshire, are known to have been at first called simply "Acton," and to have assumed the form "Atton" under the influence of the distinguishing first syllable, subsequently added.   "Sulatyn" is, in like manner, probably *Plough Acton*, and "Prestatyn" *Priest Acton*.

east of the Dyke will apply also to that portion of Flintshire which is similarly situated.

In reviewing the foregoing paper, we see that the large tract of country therein dealt with was (during, let us say, the ninth and tenth centuries) Anglicized quite up to Offa's Dyke; that subsequently (in the eleventh century) the Welsh swarmed across the Dyke in such numbers that the population, for something like fifteen miles east of it, became wholly or partially Cymricized; and that by the gradual Anglicizing of these intruders, a process which it has taken eight hundred years to effect, Offa's Dyke has now again become, roughly speaking, the border-line between those who speak English and those who speak Welsh.

Notes on
Ancient Welsh Measures
of Land

and

Ancient Welsh Measures
of Capacity

Archaeologia Cambrensis.

FIFTH SERIES.—VOL. XIII, NO. XLIX.

JANUARY 1896.

NOTES ON ANCIENT WELSH MEASURES OF LAND.

BY ALFRED NEOBARD PALMER.

THE study of ancient Welsh land-measures involves so many interesting questions that I should like to put on record the results of an investigation which I made into this subject above eight years ago.

The Venedotian Code explicitly declares that the Welsh *troedfedd,* or foot-measure, contained nine *modfeddi.* Now what was the length of the ancient *modfedd?* It may be conceded at once that the old measures of length were not calculated with the precision of modern times. But I maintain that the *modfedd* was *practically* identical with the English statute inch, and that the ancient Welsh foot contained nine such inches. This is how the inch and foot are defined in the Venedotian Code : " Three lengths of a barley-corn in the inch (strictly *thumb-measure*), three inches in a palm-breadth, three palm-breadths in the foot measure."[1]

The first time I tried the length of three barley-corns I found them measure exactly one statute inch ; but generally speaking, in the samples of barley I examined, three barley-corns set end to end measured rather more than an inch. Three barley-corns, however, repre-

[1] Ven. Code (*Dull Gwynedd*), book ii, ch. xvii, sec. 5.

sent too small a number to give satisfactory results ; I
therefore measured, three times, twenty-seven corns
taken without picking, the length of which, set carefully end to end, should equal the old Welsh foot
(*troedfedd*) of nine inches. The first twenty-seven corns
I tried measured 9.56 inches ; the second, 9.45 inches ;
and the third, again 9.45 inches. But here I may say
that a corn-merchant of great experience told me that
the corns in the sample I showed him were rather long,
and that if twenty-seven of them set on a line measured
about 9.5 inches, twenty-seven corns of the next
sample I got might very well measure about 8.5 inches.
However, we need not suppose that the Welsh *modfedd*
was absolutely identical with the English inch. It is
sufficient to imagine that the length of the two was
sufficiently near each other to warrant (when it became
necessary to equate the measures of Wales with those
of England), not merely the identification of the *modfedd* with the inch, but of the *troedfedd* with the half-
cubit of nine inches.

What makes it probable that this identification
really took place *in most cases*, is that the foot of nine
inches is actually contained in most of the customary
acres still, or formerly, in use in Wales.

Let us begin with the rod, or *llath*,[1] of eighteen feet,
which the Gwentian Code calls "the rod of Hywel
Dda"; eighteen such rods in length, and two in breadth,
forming the *erw*.[2] Now eighteen feet of nine inches
would equal thirteen and a half statute feet, or four and
a half yards ; and the rod of thirteen and a half statute
feet is still actually used in Montgomeryshire, Brecknockshire, Radnorshire, and elsewhere, although the

----

[1] I shall always use the word *llath* in the indefinite sense of a rod,
which is its right meaning, applying it to measuring poles of
various lengths. *Llath* must, of course, be distinguished from
llathen.

[2] Gwentian Code (*Dull Gwent*), book ii, ch. xxxiii, sec. ii. "A
deu naw troet ued yg gwialen Hywel da; adeunaw llath [auyd]
yn hyt yr erw, adwy lath o let."

erw of the Gwentian Code (729 statute square yards),[1]
so far as I know, nowhere survives. But if the *erw*
does not survive, "the rod of Hywel Dda" does ; and
if we set out a strip of land two of these rods in
breadth, and twenty of them in length, making the
strip thus ten times longer than broad, instead of nine
times, as the Code prescribes, we shall get what we
may call an *erw* (or, to use the local word, a *stangel*) of
810 square yards. Then three of these *erwau*, lying
side by side, will give the well known, so-called "customary acre" of 2,430 square yards, and four of these
will give the other well known, so-called "customary
acre" of 3,240 square yards ; which latter is called a
cyfar in Brecknockshire (*y cyfar Brycheiniog*), and an
ystang (colloquially a *stang*) in Montgomeryshire.

Thus : $(13.5 \times 2) \times (13.5 \times 20) = 7290$ sq. feet

And $\dfrac{7290}{9} = 810$ sq. yds.

Then $810 \times 3 = 2430$ sq. yds.

And $810 \times 4 = 3240$ sq. yds.

The first-named "customary acre" will then be twenty
rods long by six broad, and the second, twenty rods
long by eight broad.

That the Montgomeryshire *stang*, or "customary
acre", really had the form, and probably the origin,
postulated by the description thus given, will be made
clear by the following relation. Mr. Bennett of Glan
yr Afon, Llanidloes, at the instance of Mr. Evan Powell,
also of Llanidloes, was good enough to collect for me,
in the year 1887, some information as to the land-
measures of Montgomeryshire. In the prosecution of
his inquiries he called upon Richard Rees of Llawr y
Glyn, then eighty-two years of age, who many years
ago used to do all the *tori bettin*,[2] or sod-paring work,

---

[1] $\dfrac{(13.5 \times 2) \times (13.5 \times 18)}{9} = 729$ sq. yds.

[2] *Bettin*, also pronounced *betting*, and in South Wales, as Mr.
Phillimore tells me, *vieting*, in three syllables. *Bieting* is derived
from the English "beat", the early form of "peat".

in that neighbourhood. When he told Richard Rees on what business he was come, the old man, first of all, got out of his wain-house his measuring-stick, which he called "a quart rod", and then described its length : " Pedair llathen a haner yn exact" (*exactly four and a half yards*), said he. Well, there is " the rod of Hywel Dda", containing thirteen and a half square feet, or eighteen feet of nine inches. The old man finally took Mr. Bennett into the field, and measuring on the ground twenty times the length of the rod in one direction, and then, at right angles, eight times its length, said : " Dyna i chwi stang o dir" (*there's a stang of land for you*).

From this it is evident that the *stang*, or *cyfar*, of 3,240 square yards, has neither the form nor the contents of any of the *erwau* of the Welsh Codes ; is not, in short, an *erw* at all. Its form and its contents, however, become at once intelligible when we learn that it is composed of four *erwau* lying side by side, as the other customary acre, of 2,430 square yards, is composed of three such *erwau*, each *erw* being an acre in miniature (ten times longer than broad) built up out of the rod of Hywel Dda; the rod of Gwent (containing thirteen and a half statute feet) according exactly with the proportions indicated in the Venedotian Code, but not precisely with those given in the two other Welsh Codes.

The question now arises whether the word *erw*, in the comparatively modern sense in which it is made to mean an " acre" or " customary acre", be correct ; and the answer is,—Certainly not, if we are dealing with the *erwau* of the Welsh legal Codes. Even so late as A.D. 1620 the *erw* of Bromfield is carefully distinguished from the *acr*, or customary acre, which seems to have contained four *erwau*. There must have been once a Welsh name for " the customary acre"; in fact, in some districts we know that it was called a *cyfar*, and in others a *stang*,—if the latter be, indeed, a Welsh word ; but in other districts, especially in South Wales, where the customary acres are often large, we find that four *cyfeiriau*, or four *ystangau*, form a "customary acre", there distinctly called an *erw*; and the use of the name *erw* in this sense is in these districts very old. Still the word *erw* is never used with this meaning in any of the Welsh Codes.

And now two other questions are suggested. First, how are we to translate into English the word *erw*, as it occurs in the Codes, so as to convey an accurate idea of the form and contents of it, as these are there laid down? We cannot use the word "acre"; for though a Venedotian *erw*, like the English statute acre, is ten times longer than broad,[1] its contents are very much smaller. It might be called a "rood", to the area of which the *erw* roughly corresponds, if the rood were not *forty* times longer than broad. So that it appears as though there were no precise equivalent in English for the *erw* of the Welsh Codes.

Finally comes the last question, Is there any actually existing word *in Welsh* which we may employ to designate the *erwau* of the Welsh Codes, so as to avoid importing into our discussion of them the wholly different meaning which the existing use of the name *erw* connotes? Yes, I think so. There is the word *stangel*; and this, or the literary form *ystangel* (plural *ystangelau*), is the name which I shall often henceforth give to the *erw* of the Codes when I want to distinguish between it and the modern and larger *erw*.

I have said that the *shape* of the Montgomeryshire *stang* (twenty rods long by eight broad) differed from the shape of any of the *erwau* described in the Welsh Codes; but too much stress must not be laid upon this fact, for it is obvious that a piece of land whose dimen-

---

[1] The *erw* of the Gwentian Code was, as we have seen, nine times longer than broad; and the *erw* of the Demetian Code, as we shall hereafter see, eight times longer; and yet it is certain, from a study of the old "customary acres" of both Gwent and Dyfed, that even in those districts the *erw* (or *ystangel*) must have been altered in form so as to assume the *proportions*, in length to breadth, of ten to one.

sions are expressed by the multiples 20 × 8, contains precisely the same area as is expressed by the multiples 40 × 4 ; and a strip set out according to the dimensions last given would have exactly the form which the Venedotian Code at any rate requires.   George Owen, in his *Description of Pembrokeshire* (A.D. 1603), tells us, in fact, that " 8 poles in bredth, and xx in length, or 4 in bredth, and 40 in length, maketh a stange".[1]

It may well have been that in the arable areas of certain townships, the quality of the land, or the uneven character of its surface, was such as not to permit the full length of the furrow being obtained ; or other conditions may be imagined which rendered the one form for the stang more convenient than the other.

But the area of these stangs at once prevents them from being identified with the *erwau* (= *stangelau*) of the Codes.   And besides this, George Owen, after describing the composition of the Pembrokeshire stang, as above quoted, goes on to say, " 4 of these stangues make the Pembrokeshire acre"; that is, "the customary acre", or *erw* as it is now also called.

Now see what this involves.   Let us suppose that the stang is ten times longer than broad.   Here it is :—

40 rods

4 rods | a stang

Now place four of these together, side by side, so as to make the so-called *erw* or "customary acre":—

40 rods

16 rods {4 rods 4 rods 4 rods 4 rods}

a stang

a stang

a stang

a stang

16 to 40=8 to 20.

[1] 1892 edition, pp. 133 and 134.

Thus, not merely is the excess of contents increased fourfold, but no sooner have we recovered the correct form for the stang, but we lose it again straightway. It is plain that the modern *erw* is not the same as the ancient, and it is equally plain that the usual form of the modern *cyfar*, or *stang*, is due to three or four *stangelau* lying side by side, and that these *stangelau* correspond in form and approximate in area to the *erwau* of the Codes. The *stang* of Montgomeryshire would thus be plotted out :—

A stang.

How the word *erw* came to be applied to the "customary acre" I do not pretend to explain.

Richard Rees called his rod "a quart rod". In fact, a rod squared was called *a quart*, and contained $20\frac{1}{4}$ sq. yds. ($\frac{13.5 \times 13.5}{9} = 20.25$), and 160 *quarts* made a *stang*. But I dare say it would be known at Llawr y Glyn, as elsewhere, by the indefinite name *llath*. In South Wales I believe it was formerly called *pren naw* (= rod of nine), as containing nine *cyfelinau*, or cubits of one foot and a half each ($9 + 1\frac{1}{2} = 13\frac{1}{2}$ feet). In Carnarvonshire and other parts of Gwynedd the name *paladr*, or spear, is applied to it.

But in the Welsh Laws another rod is mentioned. The Venedotian and Demetian Codes both speak of " a rod equal in length to the long yoke".[1] This rod was

---

[1] "Gwyalen gyhyt a[r hyr yeu] honno." (Venedotian Code, *Dull Gwynedd*, book ii, ch. xvii, sec. 6 ; see also Demetian Code, *Dull Dyved*, book ii, ch. xx, sec. 8.)

used to set out the *erwau* of Gwynedd and Dyfed. It contained sixteen feet of nine inches, and was therefore exactly equivalent to a rod of twelve statute feet. It was in South Wales sometimes called *pren wyth* (= rod of eight), as containing eight *cyfelinau*, or cubits $(8 + 1\frac{1}{2} = 12)$.

Now this rod of twelve feet is still actually in use, and is the basis of at least two other "customary acres". If, following the directions of the Venedotian Code,[1] we set out with this rod a strip three rods broad and thirty long, we get an *ystangel* (for it is important to remember that the *erwau* of the Welsh Codes are *ystangelau*, and not acres), which contains 1,440 square yards ; and three of these *ystangelau*, lying side by side, will give "the customary acre" of 4,320 square yards, while four of them so lying will yield another "customary acre", that of 5,760 square yards, used in parts of Pembrokeshire and Glamorganshire, and found also in Cornwall.

$$(12 \times 3) \times (12 \times 30 = 12960 \text{ sq. feet}$$
$$\text{And } \frac{12960}{9} = 1440 \text{ sq. yds.}$$
$$\text{Then } 1440 \times 3 = 4320 \text{ sq. yds.}$$
$$\text{And } 1440 \times 4 = 5760 \text{ sq. yds.}$$

It is certain, however, that the last-named acre is, in many districts, derived from the rod of nine feet, and is built up after another pattern. (See p. 14.)

The Demetian Code also prescribes a rod of the same length :—"There are sixteen feet in the length of the long yoke, and there are sixteen yokes in the length of the *erw*, and two in its breadth."[2] The *erw*, or

---

[1] These directions are very vaguely expressed, and when I was writing my *History of Ancient Tenures in the Marches of North Wales* I had not yet caught their true meaning ; but that they were meant to have the signification above given to them is now, I believe, quite clear. I owe this explanation to the late Mr. O. C. Pell.

[2] Demetian Code (*Dull Dyved*), book ii, ch. xx, sec. 8. These sixteen feet are, of course, feet of nine inches, and are equivalent to twelve feet of twelve inches.

ystangel, of Dyfed would then contain 512 square yards, $\dfrac{(12 \times 2) \times (12 \times 16)}{9} = 510$; but I do not know of the existence of any such *ystangel*, or of any *ystang*, or "customary acre", derived from it. (See note on p. 5.)

This same rod is also actually used in setting out the *cyfar* of 2,560 square yards. This *cyfar* is called in Brecknockshire (to distinguish it from the *cyfar Brycheiniog* of 3,240 square yards) the *cyfar bach* (little cyfar) or *cyfar bieting*. (See note 2, p. 3.) But in that county it is treated as an *ystang*, being, as Mr. R. James of Llanwrtyd tells me, twenty rods long by eight broad. It may thus be composed of four *ystangelau* lying side by side, each *ystangel* being twenty rods long by two broad, and containing 640 square yards. Thus :

$$(12 \times 2) \times (12 \times 20) = 5760 \text{ sq. feet}$$
$$\text{And} \frac{5760}{9} = 640 \text{ sq. yds.}$$
$$\text{Then } 640 \times 4 = 2560 \text{ sq. yds.}$$

The *cyfar*[1] of Flintshire contained also, as I find, 2,560 square yards ; but since the Flintshire rod, as appears almost proved, was one of twenty-four feet, the *cyfar* derived therefrom must have been an *ystangel*, not an *ystang*, measuring twenty rods in its length, and two in its breadth. Thus :

$$\frac{(24 \times 2) \times (24 \times 20)}{9} = 2560 \text{ sq. yds.}$$

The length of the rod of Northern Powys, however, is known with absolute certainty. (See Norden's "Survey of the Lordship of Bromfield and Yale, A.D. 1620", Harleian MS., 3696.) It measured twenty-four feet, and there were one hundred and sixty square rods in the "customary acre". This acre was also composed of

---

[1] The English name for the Flintshire *cyfar* is "a yoking",—a name most significant, as indicating co-aration.

four " roods", equal in area to the *cyfeiriau* of Flintshire, and apparently called *erwau* in Welsh; each
" rood" being almost certainly twenty rods long by two
broad, so that the acre contained 10,240 square yards
(2,560 × 4).

The " customary acre" of Northern Powys was also
used throughout Staffordshire, Cheshire, and Southern
Lancashire (being there called " the Staffordshire" or
" Cheshire acre"), as well as in parts of Pembrokeshire,
Cardiganshire, Carmarthenshire, and Glamorganshire ;
where, however, it is differently derived.[1] In the last
named county it is called *erw Llangiwg*. I shall hereafter speak more fully of the class of names of which
this name is an example.

The " customary acre" of Northern Powys has been
displaced long since by the statute acre; but the 160th
part of it—the squared rod of 24 feet, or 64 yards
square ($\frac{24 \times 24}{9} = 64$) is still in use over a very large area.
The linear measure of twenty-four feet is also com-
monly used for hedging, ditching, walling, etc. In
Wales the measure of 64 yards *square* is called either
" the square rod", or *y rhwd sgwar*, while in neighbouring parts of England it is called " the Welsh rood",
" the square rood", or " the digging rood". It is chiefly
employed in connection with potato-growing or sod-
paring. I have found, or heard of, this measure as
being used throughout Montgomeryshire, Radnorshire,
Brecknockshire, Carnarvonshire, Anglesey, Eastern
Denbighshire, Hopedale, Moldsdale,[2] Cheshire, Shropshire, Northern Herefordshire, parts of Staffordshire,
and, if my memory serves me aright, throughout
Southern Lancashire also.

It will be observed that what I may call the central
and main portion of this large district is nearly conter-

---

[1] Derived there, not from the rod of twenty-four feet, but from
that of twelve, forty rods long by sixteen broad.

[2] Of course this " square rood" is the fortieth part of the Flintshire *cyfar*, as well as of the *cyfar bach* of Brecknockshire.

minous with the ancient, undivided, and unclipped
princedom of Powys before the advances of the Mercians and Northumbrians were made ; but I attribute
the wide use of "the square rood" to the diffusion
throughout North Wales of Cheshire methods of agriculture, and especially of the practice of sod-paring ;
for, whatever the local measures, all work of this kind
is done in Wales by the rood of sixty-four square yards.
The spread of this measure would be helped by the
fact of its identity with the fortieth part of the Flintshire *cyfar* and of the *erw* of Eastern Denbighshire. Its
very name, *y rhwd sgwar*,[1] shows that it is an immi-
grant from England. Its course was evidently from
Cheshire, through Denbighshire and Flintshire to Carnarvonshire and Anglesey, whence it probably spread
through Merionethshire, Montgomeryshire, and Radnorshire, to Southern Shropshire and Herefordshire.
On this supposition we understand how it is sometimes, in the two counties last named, known as "the
Welsh rood".

In South Wales, the rod or *llath* is often called a
bat (Breton, *baz* = a stick ; Irish, *bat*, *bata* = a stick or
staff; Middle English, *batte;* Modern English, *bat*, as
in cricket-*bat*). It varies in length in almost every
hundred, sometimes in every parish. It is either nine,
eleven, eleven and a half, or twelve feet,[2] while in some
parts of Glamorganshire the double bat is used as a
rod or pole. It is a mistake to suppose that the name
bat was confined to the rod of eleven feet. George
Owen of Henllys calls all the poles used in Pembrokeshire "land battes". The rod of eleven feet, however,

[1] Its commonest name in Wales is *rhwd o dir*, a rood of land.
[2] "In Pembrokeshire the pole differreth allmost in every hundred
of the sheere from other, for in some place the pole is but ix foote,
and in some place xii foote, and so differinge betweene both, as
shall appeare ; and this seemeth to be first so devised according to
the goodnes of the ground, for in the best soyle is vsed the least
measure, and so of the contrarie, the pole being knowne, they dif-
ferre altogether in somming of the acre."—Owen's *Description of
Pembrokeshire*, p. 133, ed. 1892.

is worthy of especial notice, if only because in one part
of Glamorganshire it was known as *llath Eglwys Silin*
(the rod of Eglwys Silin, or of Silin's Church),[1] a name
which suggests that the rod generally used in a particular district was kept in the parish church of that
district.   In the *Appendix to the Report of the Commissioners of Weights and Measures*, printed in 1820,
this rod is called that of " Eglwys haw",[2] a name which
suggests a similar conclusion.   So the "customary
acre' derived from the rod of eleven and a half feet was
known as *Erw Ferthyr Tudfyl* (= the acre of Merthyr
Tudfyl), and *Erw Llanfabon* (= the acre of Llanfabon).
And I have already called attention to another "customary acre" called *Erw Llangiwg.*

Of the rods or *bats* of nine and of twelve feet I have
already spoken.   The *bats* of ten, of eleven, and of
eleven and a half feet, are peculiar in this respect, that
they do not make up an even number of feet of nine
inches.   The first makes thirteen feet of nine inches
plus one-third of a foot ; the second, fourteen such feet
plus two-thirds of a foot ; and the third, fifteen such
feet *plus* one-third of a foot.   Now these several frac-
tions represent exactly, the first and third, one palm-
breadth ; and the second, two palm-breadths.   So that
the fact of the continuance of these *bats* is no way fatal
to the assumption of the former existence of the foot
of nine inches, each foot divided into three palm-
breadths, but is confirmatory of that assumption.   The
bats of ten, of eleven, and of eleven and a half feet, are
plainly intractable survivals of traditional *llathau.*   It
is also to be said that the "customary acres" derived
from these *bats* do not contain an even number of
square yards.

---

[1] Mr. Thos. Thomas of Pontypridd, tells me that the rod of
Eglwys Silin is really twenty-two feet long; that is to say, it is a
double bat of eleven feet.   Of the "customary acres" derived from
double *bats* I shall speak hereafter.

[2] "Eglwys haw" is plainly a mistake, standing either for Eglwys
Silin or for Eglwys Wrw.

In looking at the "customary acres" of South Wales, built up from the *bats* already named, it would appear that they should be arranged in two great groups, each group comprising two corresponding classes. There is, first, the group of "acres", each of which is derived from a *single bat*, and is composed of four *ystangau*, containing 640 or 768 square *bats*. There is, secondly, the group of "acres", each of which is derived from a *double bat*, and consists of a single *ystang*, containing 160 or 192 square *bats*.

FIRST GROUP. *First Class.*—Beginning with the first class of the first group, each *ystang* is forty rods long by four broad, and four such *ystangau* lying side by side, as shown on p. 6, form the so-called *erw* or "customary acre". That is to say, the *erw* is forty rods long by sixteen broad; and instead of, as in English statute measure, multiplying the square of the rod by $40 \times 4 = 160$, we have to multiply by $40 \times 4 \times 4 = 640$, to get the area of the "acre". This explains the fact that, spite of the shortness of the rods, the contents of the acres are larger than the contents of the English acre.

Second Class.—In a few cases, however, as with the acres of the second class of the first group, the *ystang* is not ten times longer than broad. In these exceptional cases its length is twelve times greater than its breadth. That is to say, the *ystang*, while four rods broad, is forty-eight (not forty) rods long; so that instead of multiplying the square of the rod by $40 \times 4 \times 4 = 640$, we have, if we want to get the area of the acre, to multiply by $48 \times 4 \times 4 = 768$; and the "acre is thus 48 rods long by 16 broad, and its length is in proportion to its breadth as three to one. This seems to have been the form assumed by the "acres" known as *Erw Eglwys Silin, Erw Ferthyr Tudfyl*, and *Erw Llanfabon*, in all which cases the four *ystangau* forming the *erw* were called *cyfeiriau*.

SECOND GROUP. *First Class.*—Now we come to the

first class of the "customary acres", or *erwau* of the second group. Each of these *erwau* was forty *double* rods long by four broad, and was composed of four *ystangelau* lying side by side, the *ystangel* in this case being a true rod, forty times longer than broad.

Second Class.—In the second class of this group, the length of the *ystangelau* is forty-eight times greater than the breadth; and as there are four of these *ystangelau* in the *erw*, the latter is twelve times longer than broad. A simple calculation will show that in the first class there are 160 square *bats* of double length, and in the second class 192 such square *bats*.

I do not desire to burden this paper with formulas specifically intended to prove these several points; but if the reader care to examine the formulas given further on in this paper, to illustrate other points, he will find all these statements proved.

I have shown on p. 8 how the "customary acre" of 5,760 square yards *might* be produced from the rod of twelve feet; but in South Wales it appears, in fact, to have been produced from the rod of nine feet, and to have differed somewhat in form from the " acre" which the rod of twelve feet would have yielded; that is, instead of being thirty rods long by twelve broad, it was forty long by sixteen broad. Thus:

$$(9 \times 4) \times (9 \times 40) = 1440 \text{ sq. yds.}$$
$$\text{And } 1443 \times 4 \qquad = 5760 \text{ sq. yds.}$$

Similarly I have shown on p. 9 how the *cyfar* of Brecknockshire, containing 2,560 square yards, was derived from the rod of twelve feet; and on the same page how the Flintshire *cyfar* and the old Denbighshire *erw*, both having the same contents, were derived from the rod of twenty-four feet; but the *ystangel* of 2,560 square yards, contained in *Erw Llangiwg*, though derived from the same rod as the first-named *cyfar*, had different form, and although similar in form to the last-named *cyfar*, was derived from a different rod. It was obtained thus :

$$(12 \times 4) \times (12 \times 40) = 2560 \text{ sq. yds.}$$

And four of these *ystangelau* (so actually called) made the *erw*, or "customary acre" of 10,240 square yards $(2560 \times 4 = 10240)$ formerly used throughout parts of Pembrokeshire, Cardiganshire, Carmarthenshire, and Glamorganshire. Thus we see that acres having the same area in different parts of the country may have a quite different origin.

Now I must speak of the "customary acre" of 7,840 square yards, called *Mesur Meisgyn*, because used in the Vale of Miskin as well as in Pembrokeshire and other parts of Glamorganshire. According to the *Report of the Commissioners of Weights and Measures* (1820) it is derived from the rod of ten and a half feet, already mentioned, and is built up thus :

$$\frac{(10.5 \times 4) \times (10.5 \times 40)}{9} = cyfar \text{ of 1960 sq. yds.}$$

Then 1960×4 = acre or *erw* of 7840 sq. yds.

Mr. Thomas of Pontypridd, however, tells me that the rod actually used is the *double bat* of twenty-one feet. In that case the "acre" would be a true *erw* in form, though not in area, and would be obtained thus :

$$\frac{(21 \times 4) \times (21 \times 40)}{9} = 7840 \text{ sq. yds.}$$

Now this rod of twenty-one feet suggests some interesting conclusions. First of all it is the double *bat* of ten and a half feet mentioned in an earlier paragraph of this paper. It is the triple *bat* of seven feet, of the existence of which I have evidence in Breconshire ;[1] and it is the half *bat* of forty-two feet which appears

---

[1] Near Llanwrtyd. My authority for this statement is Mr. R. James of that place. Mr. James also tells me that a " perch of turf-balk" in the neighbourhood of Llanwrtyd is "eleven feet in length, and a yard and one peat in breadth."

to have been formerly used in several districts of South Wales. Thus this twenty-one feet rod, or its double, or one or other of its component parts, was evidently very widely diffused.

And here must be stated a very curious fact. The rod of twenty-one feet was also the rod of Ireland, or of a great part of Ireland. Was the Irish rod, then, introduced into South Wales by Erse invaders? Or have it and the rods derived from it been bequeathed to us by the pre-Brythonic people of this country who in many districts long remained unabsorbed by their Cymric conquerors? These are questions easy to put, but difficult, if not impossible, to answer.

Now let me sweep up the leavings of the feast. There are only two rods remaining of which I need say anything. There is, first, the *gwrhyd* (= a man's height). I have heard of it, but do not know enough about it to touch on it to any purpose. I may point out, however, that in the Acts of the Apostles (Welsh Bible) it translates the Greek word ὀργυιά, which in the English Bible is rendered "fathom" (= six feet ?). If this be its true length, the *gwrhyd* would be the half *bat* of twelve feet. But perhaps, like other rods, its length varied in different districts.

I have now only to speak of "the rod of Anglesey". Mr. Thomas Prichard of Llanerch y Medd, has one of these rods in his house, and has seen another, both measuring exactly forty inches. Of forty inches also was the Anglesey rod, which documentary evidence attests, although in a manuscript printed in the 1881 volume of *Archæologia Cambrensis* (p. 64), the length of it is given as thirty-nine and a half, or thirty-nine and five-eighths inches, "or much thereabouts". But this rod of forty inches, which, like the rod of thirteen and a half feet, was also called a *paladr*, was in use in Carnarvonshire as well as in Anglesey. Mr. Thomas Roberts, C.E., Portmadoc, tells me that he once saw an old map and terrier, dated 1755, at the beginning of which was the following note :

" Parish of Llangybi, Hundred of Eifionydd :

> 5 Welch yards and a quarter (40 inches to the yard)
>   each way   .   .   .   = 1 pole or paladr
> 30 poles   .   .   .   = 1 yard land
> 5 yard lands and 8 poles   .   = 1 statute acre."

We may disregard the last item, and assume that if the " yardland", or true *erw*, had thirty *pelydr* in its length, it had three in its breadth. Then this is what we get as the contents of that *erw* :

$$\frac{(5.25 \times 40) \times (5.25 \times 40)}{144 \times 9} = 34 \text{ sq. yds.} = 1 \text{ sq. } paladr$$

And $34 \times 30 \times 3 = 3060$ sq. yds. $= 1$ *erw* or " yardland".

On the other hand, the *Report of the Commissioners of Weights and Measures* (1820) declares that five *llatheni* (= yards) and a third " make an acre of 3,240 square yards, each containing thirty perches of thirteen and a half feet square" (p. 22). But it is quite plain that the Commissioners have here made a muddle, confounding two distinct rods and two distinct "customary acres"; and it is possible to put one's fingers on the point where they have gone astray. Their mistake is due to a misunderstanding of the word *yardland*. They have translated it by the word *llathen*, which means a yard-measure. Dr. Owen Pugh has made a similar blunder. *Llathen o dir* is " a yard of land". The Anglesey and Carnarvonshire " yardland", on the other hand, is not the English " yardland", which is a group of scattered strips of ploughed land. It is simply an incorrect English name for a Welsh *erw*. I believe the " customary acre" derived from the rod of forty inches was, as above shown, 3,060 square yards ; but, as already has been said, the more common " customary acre" of Carnarvonshire and Anglesey was that of 3,240 square yards ; and this, as the Commissioners admit, was derived from the rod of thirteen and a half feet, "the rod of Hywel Dda"; and in Anglesey and Carnarvonshire, the acre of 3,240 square yards was in

later times, at least, it appears, not built up as shown
on p. 3, but thus :

$$\frac{(13.5 \times 3) \times (13.5 \times 30)}{9} = 607.5 \text{ sq. yds.} = \text{the real } erw \text{ or `` yardland''.}$$

Then $607.5 \times 5\frac{1}{3} = 3240$ sq. yds.

This, however, seems a strange method of laying out
an acre, and I cannot help thinking that it was plotted
at first as I have shown on p. 3, and that its later
form was due to some confusion arising out of the fact
of *two* prevailing measures in Anglesey and Carnarvonshire.

I ought to say that very few of the aforenamed
measures are now used, although most of them still
lingered in some districts less than a hundred years
ago. They are nearly all now superseded by the
measures known as "imperial" or "statute".

And now let me resume. I have not asserted the
absolute identity of the primitive Welsh *troedfedd* with
the measure of nine English inches, but only their
practical identity. What I have stated is that the
length of the two was so nearly equal as to have led,
in most cases, to their identification, when it became
necessary to equate the measures of Wales with those
of England. Spite of the existence of several rods
which I have described as being probably "intractable
survivals" of old Welsh *llathau*, I believe such an equation to have actually taken place, and I have shown
that nearly all the "customary acres" of Wales can be
explained on the assumption of that identification.
What was the exact length of the early *modfedd* and
troedfedd, I do not know. I leave the settlement of
this question to those who have minutely studied, not
merely the land-measures of a single corner of Britain,
but those of other parts of the same country and of the
Continent, and have compared them with each other.
I have but put on record the results of my researches
into those land-measures of Wales, the existence of
which can be proved, and have indicated the conclu-

sions which seem to follow. I do not pretend that all
the deductions I have announced are valid; but since
the problems bound up in a consideration of the subject
herein treated have occupied my attention for years, I
have ventured to think it might be well to put my
conclusions on record, so that other students may
supplement and correct them.

I hope hereafter to write a paper, supplementary to
the present one, in which "Ancient Welsh Measures of
Capacity" will be dealt with.

Archaeologia Cambrensis

SIXTH SERIES.—VOL. XIII, PART III

JULY, 1913

ANCIENT WELSH MEASURES OF CAPACITY

By ALFRED NEOBARD PALMER

THIS paper is supplementary to, and fulfils a promise contained in a paper on "Ancient Welsh Measures of Land," printed in *Archæologia Cambrensis* for January, 1896 (pp. 1-19). The delay of over seventeen years has been inevitable, but though during that interval, especially in 1909, some fresh material has accumulated, I have had leisure to reflect on the facts gathered, and to discern a certain harmony and relation in the confusion which once confronted me. It is unlikely that I shall learn much more on this subject than is already known to me. So, at last, this little paper comes to be written. One fact has been impressed on my mind, that in some cases, even when the name of a Welsh measure has been preserved, and is still in use, it does not quite represent the ancient capacity denoted by that name. Measures of adjoining districts have not merely during the last two hundred years been equated with English measures, but have also been equated with each other. The great English corn-markets have in fact exercised a levelling influence in the respect indicated. In other cases, where the measures in vogue were not near enough in capacity to be equated, the names denoting them are gone, or are going out of use.

The attempt, however, to recover as far as possible

the old names of measures of capacity and ascertain what they signified, say from three to six hundred years ago, is worth the pains involved if only to help scholars who have to search Welsh records and meet therein with strange names of measures, the explanations of which in the dictionaries are not to be found.

Let me begin with the district with which I am best acquainted—the Lordship of Bromfield,[1] in the northeastern part of the county of Denbigh.

Mr. John Brunt, a corn chandler in Wrexham, showed me, in November 1909, a circular, wooden, iron-bound, eared vessel, which he inherited from his father, but had never himself used, marked half-a-bushel, which was found to contain four Imperial gallons and $22\frac{1}{2}$ lbs. of oats unheaped.

Afterwards, in March 1910, I visited Erddig Hall, where the measures formerly used in Wrexham market are preserved. One of these was a cylindrical brass vessel, with two ears or handles, issued from the Exchequer in 1716. This contained exactly eight gallons—namely, one bushel. I further saw there a dish-like measure, having two ears and sloping sides, marked 1663, of exactly the same capacity. Thus it is evident that, since 1663 at least, the standard measures used in Wrexham market have been Imperial. Still, we know that in the area now being discussed one other measure was contemporaneously employed, and that other names were formerly given to Bromfield measures of capacity.

It may be desirable in considering these measures to go back as far as we can actually trace them—that is to say, to the Great Survey or "Extent" of Bromfield and Yale in the 15th year of Richard II, 1391 (Add. MS., Brit. Mus., 10,013), and here, as in later times, occasionally, we must distinguish between the measures used for wheat and those for oats. In 1391, then, corn

---

[1] Bromfield contains the ancient parishes of Wrexham, Gresford (including Holt and Isycoed), Ruabon, Erbistock, and part of Bangor Isycoed.

(that is wheat) was sold throughout Bromfield by the "melliet," at that time worth 1s. 8d., each melliet containing two "hoops," or "hopes" (Latinized into "hopæ"), each hope containing 16 normal "parts" (half-gallons, let us say). And there were 8 melliets in a quarter. The English word "bushel" was then used for the Welsh "melliet" of wheat corn.

In the Survey of Bromfield and Yale, 23rd year of Henry VII ("Land Revenue Miscellaneous Books," No. 251, Public Record Office), exactly the same measures, with the identical divisions or multiples, were employed, but we now find the word "melliet" of 1391 spelled "malett," or "melett," showing that the *ll* of "melliett" was pronounced as *l*. Contrary to expectation, the value of wheat had then depreciated slightly here.

In marginal and other notes to the later "Extent," called "Tidderley's Survey" of Bromfield and Yale ("Land Revenue Miscellaneous Books," No. 249, Public Record Office), made, it is to be inferred, between 1543 and 1546, the price of a melied, or malett, of corn (wheat) varied from 1s. to 1s. 4d. After a little past the middle of the sixteenth century I have not hitherto found the name "melied" mentioned, but it may be convenient to state once more that it was the eighth part of the "quarter," and so corresponded with the modern bushel.[1]

Oats were formerly always sold in Bromfield by the "hoop," or "hope," so that when two hoops were mentioned, they were described as such, and not treated as one melied or malet, as would have been the case with wheat. This was so in 1391, and again in 1508.

---

[1] As a matter of fact, the word "bushel" was used in 1391 in a very vague sense. Thus, in one passage of the "Extent" of that year, a bushel of wheat was said to be worth 1s. 8d. (f. 137b)—that is, it was a malet, and in another passage (f. 68b) there were said to be two bushels (hopes) in a malet. In other words, whenever the term "bushel" was used in any important sense, it had to be strictly defined; but it always carried with it the idea, I imagine, of containing four parts or pecks.

About 1543-6 the value of the hoop of oats varied here from $2\frac{1}{2}d$. to $3d$., where again we notice a depreciation, a hoop of oats being worth, in 1391, $4d$. The hoop being the sole customary measure for oats, this was also in 1391 *once* called a bushel, but it was necessary to say "a bushel of oats," because a bushel of wheat denoted then a melied. In spite of this, it is probable that in capacity a hoop of oats and a hoop of wheat were equal.

In Shirburn MS. D. 30 (now Llanstephan MS. 117 at the Welsh National Library, Aberystwyth) is a note relating to the parish of Ruabon, in Bromfield, apparently written by Ieuan ap William ap David ap Einws, who records:—" O. K. 1551 pan vv y drvdanieth mawr ar yr yd pris y velied wenith xiii*s*. iiii*d*. ; pris y rryc xii*d*., pris yr haidd x*s*., pris yr hobed keirch iii*s*. y vlwyddyn honn" (J. Gwenogvryn Evans' Catalogue Welsh MSS., Vol. II, Part II, p. 570). This passage, rendered into English, would run thus :—" In the year of our Lord, 1551, when there was the great scarcity of corn, the price of the melied of wheat was 13*s*. 4*d*., of rye 12*d*. (doubtless a mistake for 12*s*.), of barley 10*s*. (and) the price of a hobed of oats 3*s*., this year."

It will be noticed that the melied was still in common use in Bromfield as late as the year.1551 for wheat, rye, and barley, while oats were sold by the hobed, or hobaid (a hoopful). That oats were still alone vended by the hobed tends rather to confirm the identity of this hobed with the old hoop or half-melied.

But we must add a caution. We know that about 250 or 300 years ago a measure came into use in and almost throughout Denbighshire, called the " hobet," which was essentially different from the old hoop, hope, or hobaid. This latter was the 16th part of a quarter ; the new hobet which was introduced was the third part of a quarter. As this hobet was not a statutory measure, and since, for a hundred years or more, its contents have been expressed solely in terms of weight,

an actual hobet measure has never been seen or heard
of by me.   The hobet of wheat had to conform to the
weight of 168 lbs., the hobet of barley to that of
147 lbs., while the hobet of oats weighs 105 lbs.   And
wherever it arose, this hobet has spread through a
great part of North Wales, so that great care is necessary to avoid identifying it with the old hoop, or
hobaid, which is not now used, because of the inevitable confusion which the use of the two names would
involve.

Putting this recent hobet out of view, we see that
the standard melied of Bromfield corresponded to the
Winchester bushel of 8 gallons, although its subdivisions were different, and this correspondence lasted
from at least as far back as 1391 to the present time.

We may express the old measures of Bromfield in
the following table :—

Quarts.	Gallon.	Hoop.	Melied.	Quarter.
16	4	1	—	—
32	8	2	1	—
256[1]	64	16	8	1

And for comparison, the Winchester measures are
also given :—

Quarts.	Gallon.	Peck.	Bushel.	Quarter.
4	1	—	—	—
8	2	1	—	—
32	8	4	1	—
256	64	32	8	—

When the word "bushel" superseded the word
"melied," the statute peck, or fourth part of a bushel,
came into vogue in Bromfield—this peck should therefore contain 8 quarts or 2 gallons.   But, in addition,
the "hobet peck," or quarter of a hobet, is well known,
and contains about 20 quarts.

[1] But how much did these quarts hold?   Were they Imperial
quarts of 40 fluid ounces, or quarts of 32 fluid ounces?   The answer
to this question, if it could be found, would probably explain many
of the diversities and discrepancies encountered in these comparisons.
And the gallon is also involved.   Was it an Imperial gallon of 160
fluid ounces, or a local gallon of 132 fluid ounces or less?

Here is an endless source of confusion, unless one is
first acquainted with the different connotations of the
same word.

A measure was formerly used in parts of Yale, the
twin lordship with Bromfield, called the "gogret"
("gograid"—sieveful), while in other parts of that district the Bromfield melied and hoop prevailed.   In
1391 a gogret of oaten flour was worth 1s., but I cannot ascertain at what a melied of oaten flour was valued
in the same time of the same year. Perhaps it was only
a question of nomenclature, or the gogret may have
denoted a measure slightly smaller than the melied.
Mr. John Brunt kindly inquired for me of Mr. William
Jones of the Felin, Llandegla yn Yale, who said
that he had never heard of hoops or gogrets, but that
many years ago the Llandegla and Llanarmon peck
was smaller than the Wrexham peck, which contained
18 quarts, how much smaller he could not distinctly
remember, less by three or four quarts, he thought.
When Mr. Jones spoke of a peck, he must have meant
an obsolete peck, for the present peck (or "pecked") of
Yale is simply the quarter of the Denbighshire hobet.
Both the "phiol" and the "cibyn" were employed in
Yale, there being 36 phiols in a "pêg," or quarter of
504 lbs., and 15 cibyns in the same quarter *of wheat*.
Mr. Jones supplied a table of Yale measures.   This
table shows that the introduction of the Denbighshire
hobet and peck has destroyed the coherence of the Yale
measures and accounts for the complete disappearance
of the old gogret and hoop.   Here is the table :—

	Wheat. lbs.	Barley. lbs.	Oats. lbs.
Quart	8	7	5
Phiol	14	13	9
Cibyn	32	27	20
Peck	42	37	27
Hobet	168	147	105
Pêg, or Quarter ...	504	420	315

The gogret of Yale is only defined once in the "Survey of Bromfield and Yale" 1391, and then only by its value, the gogret of oaten flour being then worth 12d. We shall recur to the discussion of it hereafter (see p. 232).

We now pass on to a consideration of the ancient measures of capacity in that part of the ancient princedom of Gwynedd, which contained the present counties of Carnarvon and Anglesey.

In the "Extent of Anglesey" A.D. 1294 (printed in Appendix Aa of the late Dr. Frederic Seebohm's "Tribal History of Wales"), corn and meal of every kind are represented as reckoned by the "crannoc," called "y crynog" in modern Welsh, a crannoc of corn (wheat) being then worth 2s. 6d. and a crannoc of oats 8d.[1] The crannoc was also divided into four parts called "bushels," "bushel" being an English name for some Welsh word, which we may assume provisionally to be "storad." Indeed, the "istor" of grain is once mentioned in the same Extent, but not explained or its price given. The "crannoc of Llewelyn" is also many times mentioned, although nowhere therein defined. But we learn from the "Valor" of the Priory of Priestholme (Penmon), taken in the year 1374 ("Record of Carnarvon," p. 249), that in all 13½ crannocs of corn were due from the "gavellæ" enumerated: the sum of "hopes" of corn of the measure of the Lord Llewelyn, late Prince of Wales, from the same gavellæ is 106, and should probably be 108, so that each crannoc apparently contained 8 hopes or hoops of that measure.

Whether the crannoc of Llewelyn differed from the customary crannoc of the country, it is impossible now to say. I think it likely that there was no essential difference between the two, but that when the "crannoc of Llewelyn" was named, all that was meant was the crannoc used in his time—that is, the crannoc employed within the memory of many persons then living; that

[1] A crannoc of oaten flour was at the same time 2s., and a crannoc of barley flour 1s. 4d.

measure would, on this supposition, contain 4 bushels (storads) and 8 hopes (2 hopes to the bushel), and correspond to the Carnarvon peget (crynog) or quarter now in use.

In Michaelmas 1348 (*anno principatus E. princ̄ sexto*), a hope of dry oats was reckoned, within certain lands of the Bishop of Bangor (see "Record of Carnarvon," p. 93), to be worth $\frac{3}{4}d.$, so that on the basis of 8 hopes to a crannoc, a crannoc of oats would be worth 6$d.$, whereas in 1294 it was valued, as we have seen, at 8$d.$ This may point simply to a depreciation, but the difference is not great. The hope of oats of Gwynedd, worth $\frac{3}{4}d.$ in 1348 and 1$d.$ in 1294, must have been smaller than the measure bearing the same name in Bromfield and Yale, where in 1391 the hope of oats was worth 4$d.$ Judging by value alone, the former would be about a fourth in size less than the latter. The equation of the hobets of the two districts took place at a later date.

A measure called the "gogor," or "gogret" (gograid), was also used in the Bishop of Bangor's land within the area now under discussion in 1348 ("Record of Carnarvon," pp. 100-103), when a "gogor" of corn (wheat) was reckoned to be worth 13$d.$, a gogor of oats 2$\frac{3}{4}d.$, a gogor of barley 4$d.$, and a gogor of malt 4$\frac{3}{4}d.$, and the identical values obtained in the same district (Tyndaethwy, Anglesey) on 24th June, 1399 (see "Record of Carnarvon," p. 234). The essential discrepancies of these values with those of the crannoc forbid us to postulate with confidence any relation between them. We can only guess that a gogor was something like half-a-crannoc. We have met with this word gogor or gogret before, in Yale, but the gogret of Yale and the gogret of Anglesey and other parts of Gwynedd were apparently not identical. The word in both areas has for centuries gone out of use, and all attempts to clear up its capacity with absolute certainty have hitherto proved fruitless.

In an agreement made between the abbot and con-

vent of Enlly (Bardsey Island) on the one hand, and
the canons secular of Aberdaron and the men of the
"Abadaeth" on the other, made in 1252 ("Record of
Carnarvon," p. 252), other measures are mentioned,
namely, "cribrates" of corn and meal, and "gwyelyns"
of barley, but they are not defined in any sense, and it
is useless to discuss them. We shall meet with the
word "cribrate" again (see p. 242).

Something should be said here as to the effect on
Welsh measures of capacity produced by the "Compli-
cio Monete et Mensurarum" printed on p. 242 of the
"Record of Carnarvon." Intended to effect uniformity,
its immediate result was to create confusion, for the
old measures continued in use and slightly varied in
every district, although called by the same name.
Next the effect, ultimately at least, of the above-
named and similar statutes, was to equate the name of
one of the old measures with the Winchester,[1] or
London bushel, making 8 bushels to the quarter, and
to express the smaller measures in terms of it, their
older names being often retained. The surveyor of
1294 made 4 bushels in a quarter, as did other sur-
veyors, as we shall see; however, his bushel was in
reality a "storad" (four storads making a crynog), but
the term was now made by the "Explicio" twice the
size, or two storads, and a new measure apparently
made.

So late as the beginning of the seventeenth century
there was still great diversity and uncertainty of measures both in Anglesey and Carnarvonshire. An unknown Anglesey man, writing at that time (see *Arch.
Camb.*, 1881, pp. 60-62), says that there were then,
and had been before, "two sorts of usual measure of
corn" in the island—namely, the Carnarvon bushel and
the Beaumaris bushel, the former being "wont to be

[1] The term Winchester, as applied to the standard quarter and
bushel, refers, of course, to that city having been the old capital of
England, and to its measures as fixing the standards for the whole
kingdom. A "Winchester bottle" contains an Imperial half-gallon.

the bigger than the Bewmares bushel by the one-eighth part or thereabouts," and neither being "Winchester measure" truly.   And "these measures were not permanent or settled," but rather almost yearly altered and changed, according to the will and pleasure of the officers and clerks of those markets," and "in some houses, especially among the malt women, there were two severall bushells, the one bigger to buy barley, and the other lesser to sell malt," and that, after the pains taken by the justices to establish the Winchester bushel, the number of diverse measures rather increased, so that in Beaumaris there were then two measures, one called "the Town measure" (the bigger), and the other the "water measure," while at Carnarvon three were used, called "the greater, lesser, and the middle measure, and so many subdivisions of these also."

I do not doubt there was a slight difference in the bushels of the two towns, but believe that there was no such complete anarchy in respect to measures as indicated in the account just given.   Perhaps the matter of "scorage" might in part account for that apparent anarchy.   "Scorage" is a slight over-measure given to the purchaser to enable the latter to make a profit. There is also the question of whether in one case the bushel was "stricken" and in the other "heaped"— a distinction noted in Latin mediæval accounts and expressed by the terms "sine cumulo" and "cum cumulo."

In the "Goleuad" for 1820, under the heading "Marchnadoedd" (markets), occurs the following sentence :—"Y trefydd isod (Llundain, Amwythig, Trefaldwyn, Dinbych, Carnarfon, Mon.) yn ol y Peg, neu Y Grynog, sef, 8 Winchester bushels"—that is : "The towns named below (London, Shrewsbury, Montgomery, Denbigh, and (in) Anglesey, according to the Peg or the Crynog, namely, eight Winchester bushels".   Also in the "Goleuad" for 1827-8 the average selling price of various sorts of grain is quoted : wheat, 70s. the

crynog (quarter), etc.[1] These citations are enough to
establish the fact that the word "crynog" still survived
in the first quarter of the nineteenth century, and
denoted, or was supposed to denote the quarter containing 8 Winchester bushels; that it represented, in
name at least, the old crannoc of Carnarvon and Anglesey is quite clear.

In the Rev. Walter Davies' "General View of the
Agriculture and Domestic Economy of North Wales"
(published in 1810), the Carnarvonshire and Anglesey
"peget" (he does not employ the word "crynog," but
peget and crynog are but two names for the same
thing), is the Winchester quarter of 8 standard bushels,
and is said to contain 2 hobeds, 4 storads, 8 bushels,
16 kibins (cibyn), 64 gallons, and 256 quarts, according to the following table on p. 465 of his work :—

Quarts.	Gallon.					
4	1	Kibin.				
16	4	1	Bushel.			
32	8	2	1	Storad.		
64	16	4	2	1	Hobed.	
128	32	8	4	2	1	Peget or Quarter.
256	64	16	8	4	2	1

Here we see a general adaptation of local measures
to English standards, and the probability is that very
little alteration was required in equating them with
such standards.   That Mr. Davies' description was
correct, if not complete, I satisfied myself by personal
inquiries, made in July, 1896, when I consulted old
Carnarvonshire farmers and corn dealers.   The cibyn
was still occasionally used, although falling into desue-
tude.   A cibyn which I saw at Carnarvon was a
circular wooden vessel, one diameter of which inter-
nally (10 in.) being less than at the other end (12 in.),
the depth 12 in., containing therefore exactly 4 gallons

---

[1] Also in the same part of the "Goleuad" the Chester prices are
given, which may be worth while to translate : Wheat, 9s. 3d. the
measure of 75 lbs. ; barley, 5s. 2d. the customary measure ; oats,
3s. 4d. the measure of 46 lbs.

or half-a-bushel. I was informed that 480 lbs. of wheat, 420 lbs. of barley and 315 lbs. of oats went to a Carnarvon quarter or "peged." The Carnarvon "hobed," which is half-a-peged and corresponded with the old Bromfield hobed, contained then 240 lbs. of wheat and 210 lbs. of barley, while the Denbighshire hobet contains 168 lbs. of wheat and 147 lbs. of barley, the former being larger than the latter in the proportion of 10 to 7. The Carnarvon hobed of oats ($57\frac{1}{2}$ lbs.) is also larger than the Denbighshire hobed of the same grain, but does not exceed it in the same proportion. I could not hear anything of the Carnarvon hoop or hope, which I believe to have been a quite different measure from the hobed and much smaller than it. The slight discrepancy in weight between the London and local quarter will not escape attention.

The Carnarvon measures were used until comparatively recent years throughout nearly all Anglesey, as well as in the districts of Arfon (wherein is Carnarvon town) and Eifionydd, but not in those of Lleyn or Arllechwedd, if Conway town be taken as typical of Arllechwedd. I know nothing of the old measures of Nant Conwy.

Before dealing with these exceptional districts, let me quote two entries from the " Valor Ecclesiasticus," Hen. VIII, 1535, wherein the food renders to Cymmer of two townships in Lleyn are given in terms of the crannoc and hope or hoop, or of the hope only. In that record (vol. iv, p. 426) the rents of the "villata of Newgole" are given thus :—" Redd xxiiii -kyrnocks ix^{li} xii^{s} ac ii hopis xvi^{d} frument p̄cii cujusl't le kyrnock viii^{s} de redd' tenenc' ville ix^{li} xiii^{s} iiii^{d}." Here we see that the price of a kyrnock—that is, of a crannoc of wheat in 1535 was in "Newgole" 8s. and of two hopes 1s. 4d. ; in other words, there were 12 hopes in a crannoc and the price of each hope was 8d. So also the food rents of the township of " Ugh Selle " belonging to Bardsey Abbey are estimated in the same volume (p. 418) " p annū," thus—

" ccviii hobbetts frument' p tenent' villar' ann$^{ti'}$. solvend' et quil't hobett appciat' ad vi$d$.   .   ciiij$s$.
lx hobetts ordei p pdict tenent . sup^a . dict . vill'
solvend' ann$^{ti'}$ & quil't hobbett appciat^r . ad iiii$d$.
xx$s$.

Te$^{rr'}$ D'nical (Ugh Selle)
ccxiiii hopes fr'i p tenent' ten' p'dict an$^{ti'}$. solut' &
quil't hope appciatr ad viii$d$.   .   . lxxvi$s$."

There seems to be no substantial difference here
between hobets and hopes, except perhaps that the
former were stricken and the latter heaped, or that the
demesne land was of higher quality.   However, if we
multiply the value of a hope of wheat from the demesne
(8d.) by 12, we get 8s. the crannoc, which was the
price of wheat that year.   We note also that when a
hobet of wheat was 6d., a hobet of barley was 4d.
The hope or hoop of Carnarvon was exactly intermediate in capacity between the cibyn and bushel as
there understood and therefore contained 24 quarts.

We now investigate the country of Arllechwedd and
Creuddyn of which Conway or Aberconwy formed the
market town.   In the accounts of the trustees of the
mills of Conway from the Feast of St. Edward the
Confessor, in the 22nd year of Henry VIII to the same
feast in the year following (printed in Canon Robert
Williams' " History of Aberconwy," pp. 193-195), it
can be proved that the measures used in Conway in the
reign of Henry VIII were the cibyn, the peck, the
half-peck, the hoop, the strike and the quarter, the
average price there of a hoop of wheat being then 16d.
and a hoop of oatmeal 1s.   Of these the strike and the
quarter are mentioned in connection with Creuddyn in
1352, when the lord paid for a strike (" estrik ") of
wheat 8d. (" Record of Carnarvon," p. 2).   But the
exact relation of these measures one to another is
somewhat difficult to define, although it is clear that
the hoop of Conway was larger and the cibyn smaller
than the measures bearing the same name in Carnarvon.
Canon Robert Williams' explanation given in 1835,

of the old Conway customary measures, is that "two cibyns make one peck, four pecks one hoop, two hoops one strike, and four strikes one quarter" and I am bound to say this explanation best fits the prices given and the other facts available.   In other words, the Conway hoop has been made, by increasing its capacity, into the English bushel, while the cibyn was made one-fourth the size of the Carnarvon cibyn.   And this straightening out and adaptation occurred before the time of Henry VIII.   We thus get the following table of the old Conway measures :—

Quarts	Cibyn.			
8	2	Peck.		
32	4	1	Strike.	
64	8	2	1	Quarter.
256	64	8	4	1

We now turn to Lleyn, the chief market town of which is Pwllheli. The old local measures here are the phiol or phiolaid, the cibyn, the storad or bushel, the têl or telaid, and the quarter. Many personal enquiries made in 1896 failed to elicit clearly the exact relations of these to one another, with entire satis-faction to myself. But Mr. J. G. Jones of Rhiwlas, near Oswestry, who is a native of the neighbourhood of Barmouth, afterwards gave me explanations which enable me to compile the following table :—

Quarts.	Phiol.			
$10\frac{2}{3}$	1	Storad.		
32	3	1	Telaid.	
64	6	2	1	Quarter or Pĕget.
256	24	8	4	1

A Lleyn cibyn, Mr. J. G. Jones tells me; is a phio-laid and a-half, and a phiol contained 12 quarts, and a cibyn 18 quarts : if so, the Lleyn cibyn was identical with the measure so called at Carnarvon, and the peget would contain 288 quarts, but it (the Lleyn cibyn) was apparently somewhat smaller ($15\frac{7}{8}$ quarts), as shown above.   The Lleyn storad is, it will be noticed, half the size of the Carnarvon storad. The table shows signs of compromise and adaptation. Rev. Walter Davies ("General View of Agriculture and Domestic Economy in North Wales," p. 466) said in 1810 that "in Lleyn, Pwllheli market, the subdivisions of the peget are the same in quantity and differ only in names." But this statement is, strictly speaking, not correct, if the information given me be trustworthy.

Parenthetically, it may be observed that Mr. Roger Mostyn, on p. 19 of his "Cyfrifydd Parod" (published at Amlwch in 1870), mentions a phiol or phiolaid containing 14 lbs. of wheat, 13 lbs. of barley, and 9 lbs. of oats : three such phiolaids made a peck, and 4 pecks went to a "hobaid" of 168 lbs. of wheat, 147 lbs. of barley, and 105 lbs. of oats, three of these hobaids making a Winchester quarter of 504 lbs. of wheat, 420 lbs. of barley, and 315 lbs. of oats. Mr. Mostyn does not say where these measures prevailed, most unfortunately for my object, which has long been to trace the origin of the Denbighshire hobet, here appearing as a component part of an interdependent system of measures.

Let me now turn to Merionethshire and first to Dyffryn Ardudwy. The local measures here formerly in use were the cibyn, têl or telaid, bushel, and occasionally the phiolaid. Mr. J. G. Jones told me that the cibyn of Ardudwy "was a small round measure made of straw, of the shape of a beehive," and that the storad was unknown, but whether the cibyn, têl, and quarter of Ardudwy had the same relation to each other as the measures of the same name in Lleyn, of which I have just treated, it has been impossible for me hitherto to determine with certainty. The impression I formed is that there was some difference between the two systems.

In *Arch. Camb.*, 1867, pp. 183-192, is printed an "Extent of Merioneth," taken either in the latter part of the reign of Edward I or during the time of

Edward II. This "Extent" shows that the crannoc was then in use throughout the county including Ardudwy, and under the commot of "Estymaner" 26 crannocs $1\frac{1}{2}$ bushels of corn (wheat) are said to be worth 66s. $6\frac{3}{4}d$. at 2s. 6d. a crannoc : if this be carried out, it will be found that a crannoc contained 4 bushels, also 53 crannocs $1\frac{1}{2}$ bushel of oaten flour are said to be worth 106s. 9d. at 2s. a crannoc : this again shows that there were 4 bushels in a crannoc, and we see that a crannoc of Merioneth was equal to the crannoc of Carnarvon in 1294 (see p. 16), contained 4 bushels or storads and was of the same value in money. A crannoc of oaten flour was worth at the same time 2s.

Mr. J. G. Jones told me that about Bala "phiolaid" is the name given to the fourth part of a peck, that is to two quarts, and that a hobed there means two "mesurs"; the "mesur," however, belongs to the system of measures of the adjoining county of Montgomery, while the "hobed" is "the Denbighshire hobet" already spoken of, and the relation between the two systems above indicated is roughly right.

Mr. Jones also said that in Dyffryn Ardudwy a *batch* of oats, taken to a mill to be ground into meal, is called a "clwydad" and denotes ten sacks of oats, each sack containing 5 bushels.

I take the Flintshire measures next in order. I am inclined to believe that in the east portion of the main division of the county (Tegeingl or Englefield) the Chester measures[1] largely prevailed. But in the central and western portions of the county the "hoop" was the customary measure for all sorts of grain and meal. It was so in 1612, 1627, 1638, and 1642 (see Pennant's "History of Whiteford and Holywell," 1796, pp. 38-40, and Peter Roberts' "Cwtta Cyfarwydd," pp. 172 and 178). But its contents varied from 20 to

---

[1] At West Kirby in 1535, wheat measured by the Chester bushel was 1s. 8d. a bushel ("Valor Ecclesiasticus," vol. iv, p. 437). In 1827 the Chester "measure" contained 75 lbs. of wheat, 46 lbs. of oats, and 38 quarts of barley.

nearly 22 quarts. Pennant, "Hist. Whiteford," etc., p.
38, *n.*), writing of the hoop, says that it was "answerable
to the present peck," and was quite right, and he was
also correct when he said (p. 162) that the later Flintshire peck or hoop was half a "measure," and a measure
half-a-hobet.   But this last is the Denbighshire hobet,
and it is of this that Pennant spoke (p. 27), when, in
1761, he bought a "stock of wheat at 8*s.* the hobbett,
consisting of two measures of 41 quarts each."   In
another part of the same book (p. 163, *n.*), he says :
"A hobbet consists of 84 quarts—that is to say, of
two 'measures' of 42 quarts each, showing the slight
variability of the hoop, but when, as on p. 28, he or
the Rev. Henry Parry whom he quotes identified the
hoop with the hobet, a sad blunder is made, for he has
elsewhere shown that there are 4 hoops or pecks in
a hobet.   Of course, a "hobaid" should be practically
the same as a " hob " or hoop but where it is not equivalent we know that a new measure has been fitted in
to the old system, with a probable variation and
adaptation of the unit of that system.

The table of Flintshire measures about the middle
of the eighteenth century therefore may be presented
thus, taking the hoop at $21\frac{1}{2}$ quarts :—

Quarts.	Hoop or Peck.			
$21\frac{1}{2}$	1	Measure.		
43	2	1	Hobet.	
86	4	2	1	Quarter.
258	12	6	3	1

The number of quarts here in a quarter is rather
excessive ; but, on the other hand, I once saw a document, dated April, 1756, which stated that a *Mold*
quart was smaller than a Winchester quart. The peck
also is not a true peck and there is no proper bushel.
The "measure" had been introduced from Chester : the
hoop only was comparatively old, and had been
originally smaller, perhaps not larger than 20 true
quarts.

We next turn our attention to Denbighshire, and first to the northern part of the Vale of Clwyd, the Lordship of Denbighland (Rhufoniog and the greater part of Rhos).

In the "Extent of Denbighland," A.D. 1334 (Harl. MS. 3632, Brit. Mus.), the "crannoc" is but twice mentioned, and then only in respect of oats, which were worth then 8*d*. a crannoc, the exact price of the same measure of oats in Merioneth about A.D. 1300 (see p. 240). We also find the "cribrate," or "cribran," again mentioned as in Aberdaron (see p. 233): in Isdulas (Denbighland) in the before-mentioned year, 26 cribrates of oats at Whitsuntide were worth 3*s*.— that is to say, a trifle over five farthings a cribrate, so that there were, on the basis of price at the same time, 6 cribrates in a crannoc.[1] I have also noted "4*d*. p. fiolet" at Denbigh in 1742 for mixed corn; this "fiolet" is the same as the phiolaid of Yale and of Lleyn, but as to its exact capacity I can say nothing. "Hoops" were also apparently used, but all tradition of these measures of corn has long vanished in the district named, and the "Denbighshire hobet," as it is called, a convenient measure, the third of a Winchester quarter, containing 168 lbs. of wheat, 147 lbs. of barley, and 105 lbs. of oats, has replaced all other old measures. In 1742 (*Arch. Camb.*, 1853, p. 154) the price of oats at Denbigh was 2*s*. 6*d*. a hobet, of barley 5*s*. 7*d*. a hobet, and of wheat 5*s*. a measure (probably the Chester measure of 75 lbs.). The hobets here mentioned were Denbighshire hobets, already established, whether originating in the Vale of Clwyd or introduced from one of the English border counties, remains quite undetermined, so far as I can discover.

---

[1] In 1535 the "cronnock" was employed in measuring salt at Northwich, a cronnock of salt being then worth 4*s*. ("Valor Ecclesiasticus," vol. iv, p. 437). In the charter of 27 Ed. III, granted to Chester for the repair of its walls, various tolls are permitted to be levied from each crannoc of corn, beans and peas, etc., for sale, ½*d*.; from each crannoc of salt for sale, ¼*d*., etc.

In the Lordship of Ruthinland or Dyffryn Clwyd,
occupying the southern part of the Vale of Clwyd, I
can only say that in the middle of the fourteenth century the commonest measure for all sorts of grain, as
well as for meal, was the "hoop," but the quarter and
the bushel had been introduced, and, according to the
rates of prices, there were 12 hoops in a quarter, as in
Flintshire. A quarter of oats, about 1349 or 1350,
was worth from 2s. 4d. to 3s., and a hoop of oats 3d.

Chirkland, when it first comes within my view, from
the standpoint of this paper, in the "Chirk Castle
Accounts, 1605-1664," partakes of the character of a
border district, in which the old hobets of Bromfield
and the "strikes," bushels, or measures of Montgomeryshire were both used. Of Montgomeryshire we shall
presently speak.

As to the country of Cynlleth Is Rhaiadr (Co. Denbigh) I have no clear information, but Mr. J. G. Jones
tells me that in Llanrhaiadr yn Mochnant a quarter of
a peck is called a "cernyn."

Passing now to the districts forming collectively the
County of Montgomery, I shall first of all refer to an
inventory of the castle of "Doluoryn" (now called
"Dolforwyn"), February 7th, 132½ (printed in *Arch.
Camb.*, 1901, p. 308), wherein the following sentence
occurs "Also in the Garner near the Square Tower, 100
quarters 6 bushels of corn, value of a quarter 6s. 8d."
This sum will only come true if we assume that there
were 8 bushels in a quarter, each bushel being priced
at 10d. On p. 314 of the same volume, an *Inquisitio
post mortem* (January 9th, 138½), after the death of
Edmund de Mortimer III, from which the following
entries are taken :—"And there is there a certain rent
of corn—namely, cix quarters 1 bushel, to be paid at
the Feast of St. Michael, and it is worth by the year
xxli. xvis. vid., the worth of a bushel 6d.   And there
is there a certain rent of oats to be paid at the same
Feast—namely, xxi quarters, which are worth by the
year xviiis., the worth of a bushel ijd."   Commenting

upon these entries, if 109 quarters and 1 bushel were worth £21 16s. 6d., each quarter would be worth 4s., and as a bushel was worth 8d., there were 8 bushels in a quarter : as to the oats, if a bushel was worth 2d., a quarter would be worth, on the basis of 8 bushels to a quarter, 1s. 4d., and 21 quarters of oats would be worth 28s., not 18s. : it is probable that an "x" has been omitted before xviiis. In the *Inquisitio post mortem*, September 1398, of Roger de Mortimer, touching his rents and possessions in the neighbourhood of the same castle, quarters, bushels, and pecks are also mentioned.

What does this prove ? That the English bushel and quarter were introduced : doubtless they were set up in the market towns of Montgomeryshire, but there was no local measure which could at first be equated with this *ascertained* bushel, although nearly 12 hoops were understood to be roughly equivalent to the quarter, and the local measures survived side by side with the statutory measures.

In Montgomeryshire wills, hoops, strikes, measures, and bushels of corn are mentioned. A "mesur," "strik," or "stric," were identical, and contained 2 hoops, and to this mesur, or "strike," the name "bushel" was often applied though inaccurately, and generally speaking, by the end of the eighteenth century in common speech, we have to treat the Montgomeryshire strike as identical with the bushel. As we shall see, Walter Davies made an attempt to distinguish between the two, but his bushel is not the statute bushel. Even the "mesurs" and "hoops" slightly varied in different parts of the country. The Llanfyllin "mesur" was the same as those of Welshpool—namely, 40 quarts, that is to say, one Imperial gallon, plus 8 quarts, and was known as "Mesur mawr," but in the eastern part of the country the Oswestry "bushel" (or "mesur") largely prevailed, and is *said* to have contained 36 quarts—that is, one Imperial gallon, plus 4 quarts, and to have been called "Mesur bach" ("Bye-gones,"

October 12th, 1892, p. 417).   But in Miss Jackson's "Shropshire Word Book," 1879, the Oswestry bushel of wheat is represented as weighing 75 lbs. of barley and as containing 38 quarts, and this is confirmed, so far as barley is concerned, by the testimony of William Rogers of Kynaston, farmer, who, in 1820, deposed that the Oswestry bushel *or* strike contained "about 38 quarts" of barley (" Bye-gones," November 27th, 1889, p. 260).   Here a letter over the initials of E. E. (printed in " Bye-gones," March 13th, 1912, p. 209) will come in aptly : — " Forty years ago the weight by which wheat was sold was 3 strikes of 38 quarts (each), of 75 lbs. as now ; barley, 4 strikes of 265 lbs. nett ; oats, 200 lbs., of 4 strikes of 38 lbs. to the bag, or 50 lbs. to the strike . . . . The weight of barley was *altered* about thirty years ago, at the instance of Mr. John Thomas, who called a meeting of farmers and maltsters, and, after a good deal of grumbling, it (*i.e.*, the alteration) was adopted all over the district.   Barley and oats were sometimes sold by the measure, one heaped half-strike and seven stricken ones to insure good measure."

This letter confirms me in the opinion to which I have come—an opinion which may be thus expressed : The " mesur " or strike was always stricken ; the statutory bushel was smaller, but might, in some cases, be made equal to a strike of low capacity by being heaped : the apparent identification of the bushel with the strike is thus explained.   Seven instead of eight strikes were larger than a Winchester quarter, so six strikes with a heaped half-strike or hoop were considered as constituting that quarter : this explains the association of 3 strikes of wheat in the letter just given to make with scorage a half-quarter.   Further, as the hoop varied from 19 to 20 quarts, so the strikes varied in the different market towns of the county ; but when, during the last century, grain began to be sold by weight only, the strike was fixed as containing 38 quarts (that is, two hoops of 19 lbs. each) and as weighing for wheat 75 lbs., for barley 66¼ lbs., and for oats 50 lbs.

Along with the statutory bushel, the peck was introduced in the late thirteenth century. This was roughly equivalent to a heaped hoop, as is indicated by the word "peccaid," which denotes in Montgomeryshire the contents of a hoop (heaped). Other names for those contents are "cernynaid" (see p. 243) and "pedwerydd" (fourth part).

It is necessary to note here the evidence of the Rev. Walter Davies on p. 466 of his book, already referred to, where he says that "in Montgomeryshire, a cylindrical vessel containing 20 quarts is called a hoop, two of such hoops make a strike or measure, and two strikes or measures make a bushel of 80 quarts, equal to a Denbighshire hobed." The former part of this statement was correct when Mr. Davies wrote, but I deny that "two strikes or measures make a bushel." A statutory bushel weighs 63 lbs., and two strikes of 45 lbs. each would weigh 90 lbs.; a bushel of 80 quarts, according to Mr. Davies' definition, would weigh nearly 160 lbs., but this is nearly the weight of a Denbighshire hobet of wheat, and the truth is, the learned author, when he spoke of bushels, meant hobets, or hobeds, in which case the statement becomes intelligible and accurate. We will now allow Mr. Davies to proceed :—" A bushel (hobed) of oats at Welshpool is 7 hoops or half-strikes heaped. A bushel (hobed) of malt is nine-tenths of the corn measure. In different markets the hobeds vary from 80 to 84 quarts, and some innkeepers, it is said, have different measures in the same market town, wishing at one time to please the buyer, and at another time the seller. Some strikes are only seven-eighths of the 40 quarts."

The hoop in Montgomeryshire varied from 19 to 22 quarts, and the whole system of measures in the county is very like that formerly prevailing in Flintshire (see p. 241), thus taking the hoop at 21½ quarts :—

Quarts.	Hoop.			
21½	1			
43	2	Strike or Mesur.	Hobet.	
86	4	2	1	Quarter.
258	12	6	3	1

Walter Davies adds that "it appears there are but two kinds of corn measure in the six counties of North Wales, although disguised by different denominations and subdivisions." In view of the facts above given, it will be seen that this statement can be considered as only approximately accurate.

Such terms as "dyrnaid" (fistful) and "mawaid," colloquially pronounced "mawet" (both hands full), define themselves, and can hardly be regarded as measures of capacity, yet they were used as such, especially by millers, who the broader their hands the more flour or corn they took. The miller of Wrexham, for example, is mentioned in 1391 as taking of each horseload of corn ground into flour one full handful of flour, namely, a mawet. But the mawet was in the same year one of the tolls of Wrexham market, and is more accurately and fully described in the document just quoted (Add. MSS. 10,013, ff. 150b and 151b), as "one mawet, namely, two joined, broad, full handfuls of corn, oaten flour or salt."

I shall conclude this paper with a reference to the measures used for coal, iron-stone, and lime in Bromfield.

In a deed, dated June 9th, 1757, relating to ironstone thereby leased under certain lands in Esclusham for use in Bersham furnace, the "farme" or royalty provided to be paid was two shillings "for every dozen strike or measure of ironstone" that should be raised out of the said lands. The capacity of the "strike" is not defined, but it was undoubtedly the Montgomeryshire strike or "mesur" introduced by Mr. Charles Lloyd of Dolobran who first worked Bersham furnace.

In another lease of almost the same date (April 21st,

1757), also seen by me, whereby a coal-pit in the old parish of Ruabon was let, the lessees agreed to pay the lessor 1s. 4d. for every single " scare of big and small coal, and 2s. 8d. for every ' double scare,' the Dimensions of which several scares are hereinafter particularly mentioned—that is to say, the Height of every Single Scare of Big Coal to be two yards, the Breadth three-quarters of a yard, and the Depth half-a-yard, the Height of every Double Scare of Big Coal to be one yard and a-quarter, the Breadth one yard and a-quarter In the Bottom, In the Top three-quarters of a-yard, and the Dimensions of every Scare of Small Coal to be one yard." It is seldom that a measure of capacity is defined so precisely as here, and therefore the passage has been quoted in full ; but it might well have been made more precise still : was the scare, for example, rectangular or circular in section ? The balance of probability seems to lie in its being rectangular and therefore to contain about 130 gallons in a single scare.

An inspection of "The New Bersham Company's" first ledger, which began to be kept in 1762, reveals the fact that a " scare" then contained four " piches,"[1] the word " piche"[1] still survives at Brymbo, but has a somewhat different signification, denoting a truck load used down the pit, carrying 10 cwts. of coal.

In 1829 the " ton" at Brymbo was reckoned as containing 2400 lbs., that is to say, 20 Cheshire hundredweights, and containing 120 lbs. And in the same year I find the ton of 21 hundredweights mentioned as in use there on some occasions, for weighing coal and ironstone, probably as " scorage" to dealers. Here we are dealing with weights, not measures, but the information given in passing may be acceptable.

In a lease of the year 1814 relating to three lime-kilns on Hope Mountain, Flintshire (but near Brymbo, which is in Denbighshire), the customary barrel of *burnt lime* therein mentioned is declared to be " of the

---

[1] The *i* in "piche" has the sound of *i* in wine, and the *ch*, that of *ch* in " church."

common and usual kind — namely, 2 ft. 5 in. in
diameter inside, and 2 ft. 1 in. deep inside, and containing 58 gallons, or thereabout." If the barrel were
circular, the dimensions given would indicate a vessel
having a capacity of almost exactly 58 gallons.

I very much regret that it is not possible for me to
deal on the same lines with the measures of capacity of
South Wales, but my knowledge of those measures is
too piece-meal to enable me to discuss them with any
thoroughness or authority.

I should like to make the following correction in my
paper in *Arch. Camb.*, 1896, on " Ancient Welsh
Measures of Land":—

Page 4, 7th line from top, for "square" read
          "statute."
Page 7, 6th line from bottom, for the symbol +,
          read ×.
Page 8, 6th line from top, make a like correction.
Page 9, 2nd line from top, for "510" read "512."
Page 13, 15th line from bottom, for "ystang" read
          "erw."

I may also be allowed to refer to the Haverfordwest
acre of 1577, mentioned in *Arch. Camb.*, 1903, p. 43,
where we read that the "poll ats the quarter, wher-
with thei measure contayneth in length xi foote : iiii
of those quarters in length, and one in bredth doe
make a yarde termed ' virgaṫ terr . Tenne (should be
four) of these yardes in length iiii tymes accounted
(wch by a quadrant accompt is xl yardes) make a
Roode or Slange : iiii of these Slanges make an aker :
So as everie aker is xl polles long and xvi brode. Also
viii of these akers make a Bovate or Oxeland, and viii
bovates make a Carucate ats a plough Lande. So as
everie carucate conteynes lxiiii akers," etc.

First let it be noted, touching this acre so described,
that its shape is such as to be 40 poles long by 16
broad, which corresponds with the shape of many other
Welsh acres, but differs from that of an English acre,

which is 40 poles long by 4 broad. This, however, is due to the fact that the Haverfordwest acre contains four slangs (? stangs), or roods, lying side by side, each rood a miniature acre (erw) 40 poles long by 4 broad. It would be plotted, therefore, thus :—

HAVERFORDWEST ACRE, 1577.

Each slang is made up of 4, not 10, virgates of land, where a virgate is $(11 \times 40) \times (11 \times 1) = 4840$ sq. ft.

Each slang is $(11 \times 40) \times (11 \times 4) = 19,360$ sq. ft.

Each acre is $(11 \times 40) \times (11 \times 16) = 77,440$ sq. ft.

But do these "feet" involve a lineal foot of 12 in. or one of 9 in. ?

In neither case, it will be observed, do the sums of square feet yield an even number of square yards (see my paper in *Arch. Camb.*, 1896, p. 12). The Haverfordwest measure denominated a "quarter," is elsewhere called "a quart rod" (see the same paper p. 4).

Referring to the Flintshire, or rather Englefield *erw* or *cyfar* of 2560 yards square, based upon a perch of 24 ft. (see the same paper, p. 9), it seems desirable to say that I have since found in Exchequer Depositions, Flintshire, Michs., 21 Jas. I, No. 32, a statement which has led me to modify my views. Thomas Haughton, of "Carnethwen" (Carneddwen), Flintshire, gent., aged

74, deposed on September 23rd, 1623, "That this deponent did and doeth use to survey lands in Englefield and in other places where he usually measureth, there goeth eight score square p'ches to an acre, and that in Englefield he useth to measure one and twenty foote upon the pole for a p'che, excepte in the townshippes of Fflint, Caerwys, and Rutland in wch. places he useth statute measures and in the Com of Chester he useth to measure xxiiii foote upon the pole to the p'che, but this deponent doeth not knowe that the p'che conteyneth xxv foote in any place."[1]

On this I have to say that in the middle of the seventeenth century down to the middle of the nineteenth century, the erw or cyfar containing 2560 square yards was firmly established throughout Flintshire. It now appears, however, that it was introduced from Cheshire, and that there was an older acre of Englefield based upon the rod of 21 ft., which was remembered, made up of 120 squared rods of that length. This acre therefore contained 5880 square yards composed of four erws of 1470 square yards each. Thus—

$$\frac{21 \times 21 \times 120}{9} = 5880 \text{ square yards.}$$

In the parish of Hawarden in the county of Flint but outside Englefield, other deponents stated at the same time that no perch was there known, but the area of land was estimated by the "lowndes" it contained, each lownde being in turn extended by its seedness, so to say, in barley. One witness (Thomas Mayors, of Ewloe, aged 70) said that "they have eu^r (ever) accompted there land thereabouts by the lowndes and to ev'y lownde there three Wynchester measures and a pecke of barley or thereabouts"; and Edward Griffith,

---

[1] The perch of 25 ft. was used for the Great Extent of Bromfield and Yale in 1391, but I do not believe that it "caught on": certainly, by the end of the seventeenth century, the perch of 24 ft. was well established, as is elsewhere shown (Palmer and Owen's "Ancient Tenures of Land," etc., 1910 edition, p. 8).

of Hawarden, yeoman, aged 76, had heard "by report of ancient men that an acre in the parish of Hawarden was three lowndes, and there went an old bushel of barley of Chester measure for sowing every lownde, and that a bushel of Chester measures is three measures and a peck." The so-called acre of Hawarden was of the most indeterminate sort.

Similarly in Montgomeryshire a like system of estimating land was common in the seventeenth and eighteenth centuries, such phrases as "two hoopes seedness," "Three measures seedness of land," abounding in "terriers," and other documents.

So also in Denbighshire, at "The Rosset Gogh Greene" (Yr orsedd goch) two tenements, at the beginning of the seventeenth century, containing in all 7 acres, were described (Harl. MSS. 2039, fo. 78), as holding respectively "the seed of Fortie and four new measures," and "the seed of Ten new measures and Two peckes." The "new measures" referred probably to the recent introduction of the "Denbighshire hobet." The "acres" were also in all probability not statute acres but Cheshire acres. And here a useful formula may be given : to convert Cheshire acres (of 10,240 square yards) into statute acres (of 4840 square yards) divide by 2.115 : to convert statute acres into Cheshire acres, multiply by 2.115.

The Major Printed Books and Articles
of A. N. Palmer

1883   The Town, Fields, and Folk of Wrexham in the Time of James the First.*

1884   Mediaeval Seal found at Little Vownog, Bersham, co. Denbigh. (*Montgomeryshire Historical & Archaeological Collections*)

1885   The History of Ancient Tenures of Land in the Marches of North Wales.

1886   The Portionary Churches of Mediaeval North Wales. (*Arch. Camb.*)

1886   The History of the Parish Church of Wrexham.*

1887   Modern Welsh Surnames. (*Antiquary*)

1888   History of the Older Nonconformity of Wrexham and Its Neighbourhood.*

1888   John Lloyd's Notebooks, 1637-1651 (*Arch. Camb.*)

1888   Notes from the Registers of Erbistock, Denbigh and Flintshire. (*Arch. Camb.*)

1889   Notice of the Discovery of Sepulchral Slabs at Vale Crucis Abbey (*Arch. Camb.*)

1889   Notes on the Early History of Bangor Is y Coed.* (*Y Cymmrodor*)

1890   The Later History of the Parish of Bangor Is y Coed.* (*Y Cymmrodor*)

1890   Welsh Settlements, East of Offa's Dyke, during the Eleventh Century.* (*Y Cymmrodor*)

1891   Offa's and Wat's Dyke.* (*Y Cymmrodor*)

1892   Supplementary Notes to the Later History of Bangor Is y Coed.* (*Y Cymmrodor*)

1892   Some Welsh Place Names. (*Transactions of the Liverpool Welsh National Society*)

1893   History of the Town of Wrexham.*

1896   Notes on Ancient Welsh Measures of Land.* (*Arch. Camb.* and *Y Llenor*)

1897   Owen Tanat, a story of Welsh life.

1899	John Wilkinson and the Old Bersham Ironworks.* (*Y Cymmrodor*)
1900	The Broughtons of Marchwiel.* (*Y Cymmrodor*)
1900	Morgan Lloyd (Morgan Llwyd) O Wynedd. [Published address given at Wrexham]
1901	A Destroyed Tudor Building in Wrexham. [The Hand Inn] (*Arch. Camb.*)
1902	The Adventures of a Denbighshire Gentleman of the Seventeenth Century in the East Indies. [Captain Roger Myddelton of Bodlith] (*Arch. Camb.*)
1902	Lloyd of Bryn Goleu.
1903	The History of the Thirteen Country Townships of the Old Parish of Wrexham.*
1905	The History of the Townships of the Old Parish of Gresford.* (Reprinted from *Arch. Camb.*)
1910	The Town of Holt in County Denbigh, together with the Parish of Isycoed.* (Reprinted from *Arch. Camb.*)
1910	A History of Ancient Tenures of Land in North Wales and the Marches. [Expanded edition of the 1885 publication written in collaboration with Edward Owen, F.S.A.]
1913	Ancient Welsh Measures of Capacity.* (*Arch. Camb.*)
1992	A History of the Parish of Ruabon.*

Relics of the Ancient Field System of North Wales. (anon.)

Notes on Certain Powysian Poets. (*Y Cymmrodor*)

The Crofter System of the Western Isles of Scotland and the Callernish Stones of Lewis. (*Y Cymmrodor*)

Sunant Hall. (*Arch. Camb.*)

New Minster and Hyde Abbey, Winchester. (*Arch. Camb.*)

Two Charters of Henry VII, Bromfield and Yale and Chirk. (*Y Cymmrodor*)

Palmer also published a number of historical articles in the magazines *Wales* and *Byegones* as well as scientific articles in *The Leather Trades Review*.

N.B. The items marked * have been either published or republished by Bridge Books of Wrexham.